Parenting today can be deeply challeng[...] provides wise guidance and strategies t[...] too loud and too much for our kids. Th[...] parents, caregivers, and anyone else who[...] shaping the next generation.
    AUNDI KOLBER, MA, LPC
        Therapist and author of *Try Softer* and *Strong like Water*

As a licensed counselor who has worked with children and families for years, I can confidently say that *Turn Down the Noise* is a game changer for parents navigating our overstimulating world. The book's strength lies in its comprehensive approach, addressing the impact of technology, the importance of rest, and the need for play. *Turn Down the Noise* is a resource for parents seeking to create a balanced, emotionally healthy family life in the face of modern pressures. It's a compassionate guide that will resonate with many parents and caregivers.
    AMY WINE, MA, LPC-S, LMFT-S
        Counselor, marriage therapist, and performance coach

What does it look like to "be still and know that [he is] God" in the midst of today's overstimulating world? In *Turn Down the Noise*, Sarah Boyd blends deeply relatable stories with evidence-based research, offering not just a diagnosis of the noise around us but hope and clear steps for being still, allowing us to cultivate spiritual, emotional, and mental resilience in our families. With compassion and insight, she equips parents to create an environment in which they and their children can embrace the slow, gentle path of flourishing. It is a must-read for anyone seeking to slow down and create meaningful connections with their family.
    AMANDA ERICKSON
        Coauthor of *The Flourishing Family: A Jesus-Centered Guide to Parenting with Peace and Purpose*

Raising kids? You need this thoughtful, practical book. Sarah's deeply researched work and caring words of wisdom will help you feel seen, validated, and supported in all the stages of the parenting journey. As someone in the thick of parenting, I highlighted my way through—and I'll be sharing copies with friends too.

    KAYLA CRAIG
    Author of *Every Season Sacred* and *To Light Their Way*; creator of Liturgies for Parents

Turn Down the Noise spoke to my heart as a woman and a mother like no other book has. Sarah's ability to recognize the overstimulation in today's world and illuminate a hopeful path forward is balm to the soul and offers practical guidance for the daily tasks of parenting. Beautifully written, full of encouragement, and incredibly insightful, this is a book you will reread many times and want to share with every parent you know.

    ROBIN LONG
    Founder of Lindywell and author of *Well to the Core*

Sarah Boyd is a leading voice in the conversation around the chronic stress and overstimulation plaguing today's families. As we work to empower the next generation, *Turn Down the Noise* is an integral resource for equipping parents and children with what they need to slow down, embody new rhythms, and advocate for what they need to truly thrive.

    KATHRYN GORDON
    CEO of the Jon Gordon Companies; wife; mother; and bestselling author of *Relationship GRIT*

Sarah Boyd is one of the sanest women I know. And I trust her. Which is why I'm so grateful for this book. In *Turn Down the Noise*, Sarah gathers her training in psychology to help us think about building wise families in an insane world. Buy this book. Read this book. Let this book change you.

    DANIEL GROTHE
    Pastor and author of *The Power of Place*

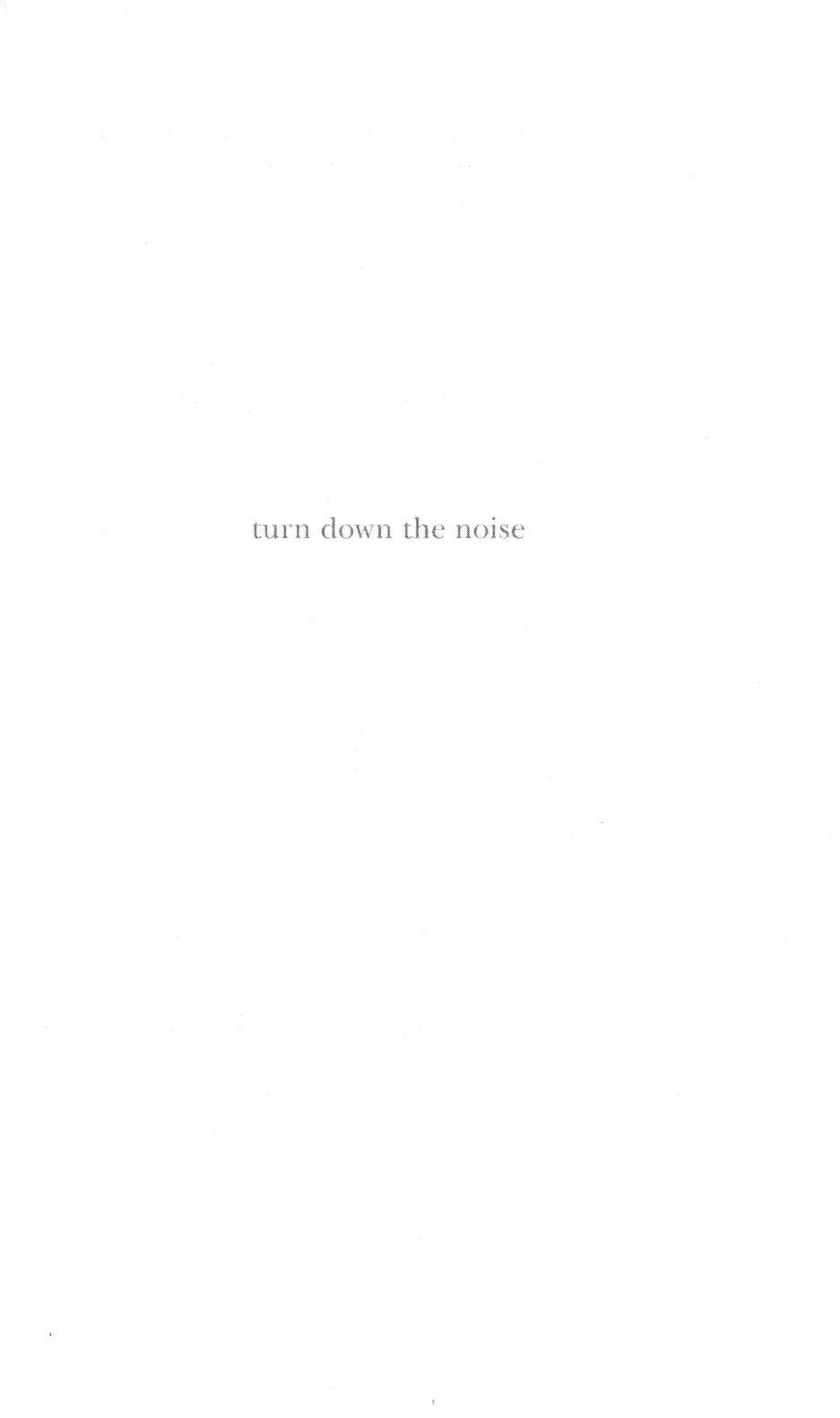

turn down the noise

TURN DOWN THE NOISE

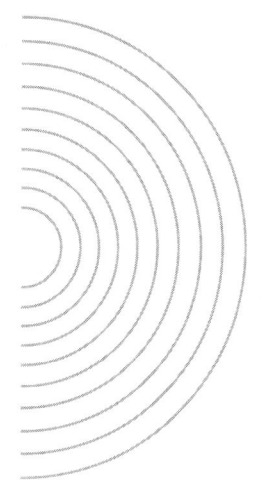

a practical guide to building
an emotionally healthy family in
a chronically overstimulated world

SARAH BOYD

M.Ed. Psych.

TYNDALE
REFRESH®

Think Well. Live Well. Be Well.

Visit Tyndale online at tyndale.com.

Visit Tyndale Refresh online at tyndalerefresh.com.

Tyndale, Tyndale's quill logo, *Tyndale Refresh*, and the Tyndale Refresh logo are registered trademarks of Tyndale House Ministries. Tyndale Refresh is a nonfiction imprint of Tyndale House Publishers, Carol Stream, Illinois.

Turn Down the Noise: A Practical Guide to Building an Emotionally Healthy Family in a Chronically Overstimulated World

Copyright © 2025 by Sarah Boyd. All rights reserved.

Author photo by Scott Surplice, copyright © 2017. All rights reserved.

Designed by Julie Chen

Edited by Stephanie Rische

Scripture quotations are taken from the Amplified® Bible (AMPC), copyright © 1954, 1958, 1962, 1964, 1965, 1987 by The Lockman Foundation. Used by permission. www.lockman.org.

The URLs in this book were verified prior to publication. The publisher is not responsible for content in the links, links that have expired, or websites that have changed ownership after that time.

For information about special discounts for bulk purchases, please contact Tyndale House Publishers at csresponse@tyndale.com, or call 1-855-277-9400.

Library of Congress Cataloging-in-Publication Data

A catalog record for this book is available from the Library of Congress.

ISBN 979-8-4005-0039-8

Printed in the United States of America

31	30	29	28	27	26	25
7	6	5	4	3	2	1

To Colin,
for being my calm
amid the chaos of noise.

And to Jonah and Georgia,
the loves of our lives.

CONTENTS

Introduction 1

PART ONE **Finding Freedom from Overstimulation and Chronic Stress**
CHAPTER 1   How Loud Is Your World? 11
CHAPTER 2   The Individual's World 29
CHAPTER 3   The Child's World 49
CHAPTER 4   The Parent's World 65
CHAPTER 5   The State of the World 85

PART TWO **Raising Emotionally Healthy Children**
CHAPTER 6   Self-Regulation: Cultivating Emotional Maturity 105
CHAPTER 7   Co-Regulation: Being Your Child's Safe Place 123
CHAPTER 8   Connection: Building Healthy Attachment 135
CHAPTER 9   Coping Skills: Giving Children Emotional Tools 149

PART THREE **Developing Practices to Turn Down the Noise**
CHAPTER 10   Space: Making Room for Creative Play 169
CHAPTER 11   Slowing: Reducing the Pace of Family Life 183
CHAPTER 12   Simplifying: De-Stimulating Your Home 197
CHAPTER 13   Shepherding: Navigating Media and the Online World 207
CHAPTER 14   Sabbath: Cultivating Rest and Life-Giving Routines 225
EPILOGUE   Conducting Your Family's Symphony 243

Acknowledgments 249
Notes 251
About the Author 261

INTRODUCTION

Sitting in the passenger seat, I quickly turned the air-conditioning to full power and aimed it toward my face. The air blew my hair back, as if I were some famous singer with an onstage wind fan, but even the cool air wasn't enough to calm my flushed face.

My agitation was building. Everything was annoying me. My family was annoying me. The cars on the road were annoying me. Even the smiles of people walking their dogs outside were annoying me. Although there were golden skies and palm trees swaying outside the window, inside the car a storm was brewing.

It had been two weeks since we'd moved our young family from Australia to California. My children, then two and four, had endured a fourteen-hour plane flight, followed by a week of jet lag, while my husband, Colin, and I were running a million miles an hour trying to set up life in a new country. Everything felt hard.

The bank wouldn't let us open an account without a document from the government. The government wouldn't issue the document without a bank account.

The rental properties wanted a strong credit rating, but because we were coming from another country, our credit rating was nonexistent.

We were temporarily living in a vacation home while we tried to secure a long-term lease. We were living out of eight suitcases while the rest of our belongings would be arriving by ship in the coming weeks.

And my children were exhausted and hungry, refusing to eat the food in this new country because it tasted "weird," upset that their toys hadn't arrived yet, and overwhelmed by all the change over the past few weeks.

After a long day of frustrating phone calls and appointments, when the kids were clingy, we decided to put everyone in the car and go to a local playground by the beach. We hoped the break and fresh air would do everyone good. But the car ride wasn't doing anyone any good.

The kids were whining, asking why I didn't buy the "proper" food and if I could go back to the store right now to get the bread they liked (which was only available in Australia). Colin, who was also frustrated by the resistance we were facing about getting life set up, was playing music loudly. Then one of the kids requested a specific song, and when Colin put it on, the other child screamed, "That's unfair!" and a fight broke out.

That's when I lost it. I yelled, "Everyone be quiet! I am sick and tired of the complaining!" Then I went on a long, emotional rant about how much was going on, how I was doing my best, and how it was all too much.

The kids were crying now—not because of their fight, but because I'd raised my voice.

Then I started crying because of the overwhelm, exhaustion, and guilt that comes from reacting to the people you love in ways you don't love.

Overstimulation is an invisible epidemic in our world. It's a problem for children, parents, families, grandparents, teachers, and anyone who works with children. Yet we often don't notice how prevalent the problem has become and how it is impacting our daily lives.

We see glimpses . . .

We notice how screen time is affecting our children.

We have a nagging sense that the busyness we experience on a regular basis is not ideal.

We are overwhelmed when dealing with our children's big emotions, and we feel guilty about our own emotional reactions toward our children.

We worry that our exhaustion is negatively affecting our ability to parent and lead the children in our lives.

But all too often, these glimpses are overshadowed. Life keeps moving, and we're using all our energy to keep up. It's inescapable: overstimulation is the cultural air we breathe. Yet the problem of overstimulation and chronic stress is much broader and deeper than the glimpses we notice throughout our days.

In the last couple of decades, we've seen significantly increased rates of mental illness in children and adolescents (in particular, anxiety and depression). This trajectory was already on the rise before the spring of 2020, and in 2021 it was found that one in four youths under the age of eighteen are experiencing symptoms of clinical anxiety or depression.[1] There has also been a significant increase in attentional struggles and behavioral problems among children.

There are, of course, many driving factors behind these statistics. Yet even though we are more educated about resilience and emotional health than ever—we have more access to individualized professional support, and there is less of a stigma about going to therapy—the statistics are still heading in the wrong direction.

So what's going on?

An Environment of Overstimulation

For many years, I believed that I had a "black thumb." This is a nice way of saying that despite all my best intentions, I seemed to kill most of the plants I tried to grow.

I had dreams of a thriving garden. I would visit nurseries or other people's gardens and marvel at how they were able to cultivate such healthy plants. But whether they were herbs on our apartment balcony or a pot of flowers at our front door, my plants would last only a short time before they died. I became too scared to buy more plants. Then, a few years ago, I finally made up my mind that I was going to work this thing out.

My husband, Colin, and I bought two raised gardening beds for our backyard and filled them with soil. I researched the easiest flowers to grow and read about zinnias. My two children and I planted the seeds straight into the soil and, in just a few months, reaped a bed of bright, colorful, thriving flowers.

After this experience, my confidence in gardening soared. I became overly zealous and, without looking much into different types of flowers, bought every seed I liked and planted them all in my garden. To my dismay, while some of the flowers grew, most of them didn't even sprout.

I returned to my faithful zinnias, confused about why my gardening efforts were failing again. It wasn't until I researched the seeds and gardening zones that my mistake became clear.

A major lesson in Gardening 101 is being aware of what zone you're in. These zones define the environmental conditions of your garden. Not all plants thrive in every environment. The reason the zinnias had bloomed so beautifully was because they grow well in most zones.

If a plant isn't growing, experienced gardeners know to look first for what is (or isn't) happening in the environment rather than blaming the plant.

As Alexander den Heijer says, "When a flower doesn't bloom, you fix the environment in which it grows, not the flower."[2]

This is as true in raising children as it is in cultivating a garden. What if the increasing rates of burnout, emotional and behavioral challenges, and mental illness are not the problem? What if, instead, they are *symptoms* of the problem?

What if the problem of overstimulation in our world is a problem with our *environment*, not a problem with us or our children?

The world has changed. Our children are growing up in a very different world from the one we grew up in. We are parenting in a different world from the one we grew up in. There is more choice, complexity, and pressure than ever before.

Yet this change of environment has happened so slowly that it can be easy to miss it.

The increased pressure at school and work.

The increased pace of life.

The decreased free time.

The way technology has fundamentally changed the way we interact with one another.

When you look at any one of these changes individually, they don't necessarily explain why the chronic stress of children and adolescents has skyrocketed. But like most parts of life, it isn't just about one thing; the problem is the compounding of *all* the things, the way a snowball rolling down a mountain gradually gains momentum and size. If you've felt bowled over by the exhaustion of daily life—flattened by the sheer amount of noise in your home, your schedule, your brain—you aren't alone. And it's not your fault.

The underlying assumption in our culture is that strong individuals should thrive no matter their environmental conditions, no matter the pace or demands of their life, no matter the circumstances of their grief, no matter their endless exposure to troubling world events and information. If the individual breaks under the pressure, society is quick to label them as weak or less resilient, without pausing to question the environment they're living in. We don't necessarily need to "fix" our children or ourselves; it's the environment we're living in that's making us sick.

How I Came to This Work

I began my career studying psychology because I was (and still am) deeply interested in how we *become*—how we grow, develop, and transform into healthier versions of ourselves. I worked in church and community organizations with youths before my husband and I began a consulting business teaching resilience principles to corporations going through major transitions.

I felt prompted into further study in my late twenties and started a program to get my master's in educational psychology, with a focus on child and adolescent development. I planned to complete my degree in one year while also working part-time with our business. Toward the end of that year, Colin and I decided we wanted to start a family. We were excited about what the next season might hold for us.

Then one Friday morning in November, I was sitting on our

apartment balcony in the early morning sun, having a cup of tea. I was exhausted after completing my final thesis the night before. I would be handing it in for the completion of my master's that day.

Then my phone rang.

It was my doctor, whom I'd seen at a routine appointment a few weeks earlier, saying they'd found some inconsistencies in testing a lump on my neck. He was clearing his schedule and wanted me to come in immediately. My mind went blank. I couldn't quite understand what this was or why it required immediate attention, and then came the word that turned my world upside down: *cancer*.

In the movies when someone gets devastating news, the world slows down and starts spinning. This happens in life too—people's voices get muffled and time moves in slow motion as everything you once knew no longer feels real.

During the next eighteen months, I was treated for an aggressive form of thyroid cancer, with multiple surgeries, radiation sessions, and other treatments that left me so fatigued I had to take leave from work. I went from feeling hopeful and certain about the future to questioning everything about who I was and what my future might look like.

I'd been studying and teaching resilience for years, but I didn't feel resilient during this experience. I felt sad, fearful about what my future might look like, shaken in my identity and my faith, and confronted with my mortality. I felt as if my life were on pause while everyone else was just moving along as usual.

After a year and a half of treatment, I was declared in remission, and we were given the all clear to start a family. I quickly became pregnant, and we were blessed with our wonderful son.

I'll never forget the moment when he was placed on my chest. My world changed forever with the weight of unconditional love and the responsibility of shepherding a little heart in the world.

Just over two years later, we were blessed again to welcome our beautiful daughter, and my heart expanded all over again.

The transformational experience of becoming a mother, so close to the life-altering experience of cancer, made me realize how important it is to cultivate resilience and emotional health for the next generation. I can't control the circumstances my children will have to walk through, but I can provide a loving foundation and the skills to equip them to handle hard things.

When my son was five years old, I founded Resilient Little Hearts, an educational company that resources parents, educators, and professionals to support resilience and emotional health in children. We do this through educational content, online courses, and children's books. Our passion is to equip the next generation with the skills they need to thrive in an ever-changing world.

Hope for the Next Generation

We can't change the world our children are living in. Despite our desire to make the world safe and beautiful for them, this isn't always within our ability to do.

What we *can* influence is the environment they experience during their childhood and adolescent years. We can also help them cultivate the skills they need to navigate the world in healthy ways as they mature.

That is what this book is about.

In part 1 of this book, we look at how overstimulation and chronic stress impact our children and practical ways we can reduce these inputs. The goal is to bring the problem out of the shadows so we can see it for what it is and be empowered to do something about it.

In part 2, we look at the keys to raising emotionally healthy children, including cultivating strong, healthy relationships, teaching emotional regulation and coping tools, and growing in our own emotional maturity along the way. This is important because the healthier and better equipped we become, the more we'll be able to create a healthy environment for our children to thrive.

In part 3, we look at five practices to use when we become aware that we or our children are struggling with overstimulation or chronic stress. These aren't more things to add to your to-do list but rather a toolbox of options to use when you need them. As we implement these practices, they increase our capacity to recover and build resilience.

The purpose of this book is to equip you in your everyday life. Not your perfectly curated, I'm-on-top-of-everything, winning-at-life life, but your real life—made up of endless sleepless nights, the juggling of work and children's schedules, a messy home (no matter how much you try to clean it), and lots of ugly crying (from you as well as your children!). Maybe you feel alone in building your family, maybe you feel completely frustrated with a certain child, maybe you're overwhelmed by the demands of just keeping up, or maybe you're struggling with pangs of guilt before falling asleep at night as you run through the list of things you wish you'd done better that day.

Raising children is beautiful and challenging. Building a home is raw, tender, hard work. It's my hope that the strategies shared in this book will positively impact your *real* life.

I'm not promising that after you read this book you'll never feel overstimulated or stressed again. I'm not promising that your children will never be overstimulated or that family life will become effortless and easy. (Wouldn't that be nice?)

That is not realistic.

My hope is that after reading this book, you'll be able to recognize the signs of overstimulation and chronic stress more quickly and feel confident to respond with a toolbox of options for navigating it so you can build recovery and resilience for yourself and your family.

> This is how we cultivate emotionally healthy children: one family, one classroom, one relationship at a time.

This is how we cultivate emotionally healthy children: one family, one classroom, one relationship at a time.

It's my belief that generations should grow from strength to strength. It's my hope and prayer that we can change the current trajectory of mental health statistics in this country so our children—and the next generation—can thrive.

It's time to turn down the noise.

PART ONE

Finding Freedom from Overstimulation and Chronic Stress

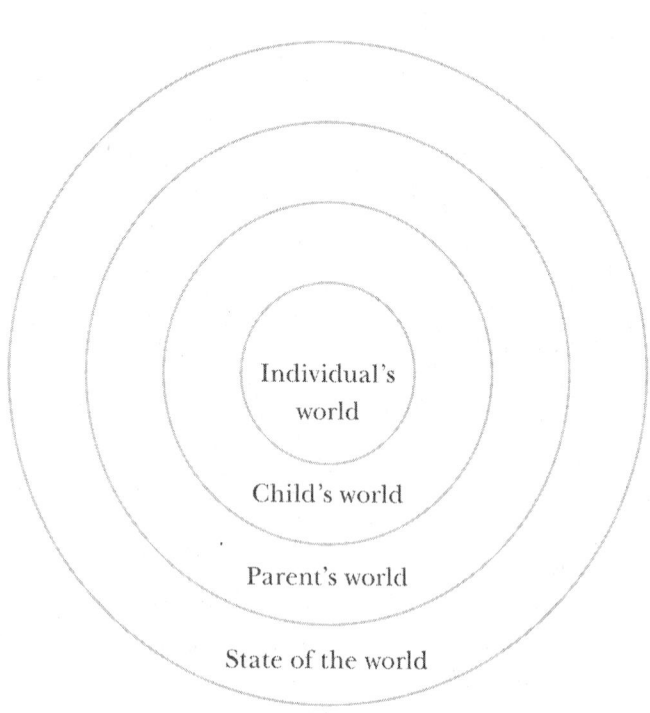

CHAPTER 1

HOW LOUD IS YOUR WORLD?

> We will make the whole universe a noise
> in the end.... The melodies and silences
> of Heaven will be shouted down.
> C. S. LEWIS

Local residents often enjoyed the lakefront shores of the harbor in Milwaukee, Wisconsin, in the 1970s, having picnics and eating ice cream. The gentle breeze and the pink hues of the setting sun painted a picturesque scene of summer in the Midwest.

A few miles into the harbor stood the Milwaukee Breakwater Lighthouse. With two-story art deco–style lighthouse keeper's quarters, it was a structure of safety and beauty on the water.

Attached to this lighthouse was a foghorn that regularly sounded a loud, low drone. It had to be loud enough for ships to hear over two nautical miles away. The foghorn sounded whenever ships came into the harbor or when weather conditions changed. Sometimes it blared every fifteen seconds.

Many local residents grew used to the sound of the foghorn. Some even associated it with nostalgic memories of spending time along the lakefront. Even though the noise was constant, it wasn't something many people paid much attention to.

Yet there was one individual who noticed the consistent volume of the foghorn—and he was fed up with it.

Kenneth Schermerhorn was the conductor of the Milwaukee Symphony Orchestra. As an expert on sound, with a sensitive ear, he issued a formal complaint to the US Coast Guard (which was also printed in the local newspaper). Kenneth stated that the intensity of the foghorn, along with its frequency, was a "flagrant form of noise pollution" that not only negatively impacted the study of music and performance but also inhibited one's ability to properly tune a piano.[1] Although he was aware that the sound was needed for the safety of the ships in the harbor, he was concerned about how far the noise was carrying inland and interrupting life there.

Kenneth, who had a deep understanding of sound, was the first to notice the problem with the noise.

The Increase of Noise

Our world has become increasingly filled with noise. It's estimated that noise pollution doubles or triples every thirty years.[2] Much of this change is the result of urbanization, which dramatically increases land and air traffic, as well as neighborhood and city development. Car alarms, lawn mowers, and sirens are the background noise to our homes—homes that are also louder inside with technological developments such as televisions, speakers, and music in our headphones.

The World Health Organization reports that noise pollution is the second most dangerous environmental toxin, after air pollution.[3] Noise pollution disrupts sleep and heart health, and can even lead to long-term hearing loss.

Noise pollution is so harmful because our brains interpret loud noise as a threat. Even when we logically understand that the noise we're hearing isn't dangerous, it still unconsciously inundates our nervous system with low-grade stress.

Gordon Hempton, an acoustic ecologist, says that "silence is an endangered species on the verge of extinction."[4] This belief has motivated him to advocate for and protect the last "quiet places"—areas across the United States that are currently untouched by human sound or noise pollution. For an area to qualify as a quiet place, it has to have multiple fifteen-minute intervals with no human sound interruptions (such as air traffic or construction). Gordon has named the Hoh Rain Forest in Olympic National Park, Washington, as possibly the quietest place in the United States. He calls it "One Square Inch of Silence."[5]

For many of us, it wasn't until the pandemic prompted worldwide lockdowns that we noticed the noise. It was only once the traffic on the roads and in the air ceased that we began to notice the birdsong. The cheerful whistles and peeps from these tiny creatures provided a glimmer of hope during a challenging time, and somehow the birds' singing seemed clearer and louder than usual.

Yet it wasn't just the lack of background noise or our increased focus that made the birdsong seem louder. Scientists explained that during the lockdown, the birds were recovering an acoustic strength and range of song they had lost decades before as a result of high levels of noise. The background noise in the environment had changed the way the birds were singing and communicating.[6]

Noise changes the way we interact in the world.

When we think about the increase of noise in our world, it's not just physical noise that we should be concerned about. Another kind of noise that's becoming louder is the foghorn of chronic stress—the constant drone of increased pressure, pace, complexity, and choice.

We are living in an environment where the volume—literal and figurative—is turned up too high. And when things get too loud, we become overstimulated.

Family Life Is Overstimulating

It was 9:30 on a Saturday morning, and I had just gotten dressed for the day. I was in my bedroom doing my makeup in front of our wardrobe mirror. Within seconds, my daughter came into my bedroom and started talking to me about an art project she wanted to try, asking if I could organize her supplies. Before I could answer, my son walked into my room and began to talk to me (over the voice of his sister) about a new trading card he'd acquired and why it was a great card. Then, before I could answer either of them, my husband walked in, and without noticing that I currently had two children talking to me about different things at the same time, started talking to me about a business idea he just had.

I was standing there with my mascara in my hand, looking straight ahead into the mirror, wondering how long it would take anyone in my family to realize that they were all talking to me at the same time. And the problem was, I wasn't hearing any of them.

Neuroscientists call overstimulation a state of "frazzle," or cognitive overwhelm that occurs when you're overcome by too much sensory input—sight, sound, smell, taste, or touch, as well as internal sensations such as pain or discomfort—causing you to struggle with processing your environment.

It doesn't matter whether you're an introvert or extrovert—if you're the life of the party or if you like things quiet—family life is filled to the brim with sensory input. Home is often a place filled with crying, tantrums, fights between siblings, and all the noise that results from joy, play, and discovery.

For parents, it's overstimulating because children are loud and have no filter, and because being a parent is demanding and stressful, and often requires that we multitask to get anything done. Even though neuroscience studies show that individuals who multitask experience frazzle and overwhelm more often than those who don't multitask,[7] it's often an unavoidable reality for a parent. This season of life involves tending to the constant needs of your children and providing financially for them, while also navigating your own health, relationships, and commitments.

Children are easily overstimulated. As they grow and their brains develop, they are slowly increasing their capacity to handle more sensory input. Yet because of the stimulation of our world and their stage of development, children can become overstimulated regularly. Many times what looks like a tantrum from our child is actually overstimulation. This is particularly true when our child isn't fighting us over a specific request.

This was Rachel's experience. It was only two weeks before Christmas, and Rachel still hadn't finished her holiday shopping. Pregnant with her second child, she placed her two-year-old son, Jack, into the stroller, determined to finish shopping for gifts.

The stores were decorated for the holidays, with bright flashing lights, decorations in every window, and holiday music playing loudly overhead. Although Rachel had arrived early, the shops were already crowded with people who were stressed and rushing about to find what they needed.

The first thirty minutes made Rachel think she would get her to-do list completed that day. Jack sat in the stroller, taking in the scene around him, and besides wanting snacks, he seemed mostly calm. She had purchased three presents from one store and now needed to go to two more shops before she was done.

The problem was, Jack was already done. He begged to get out of the stroller, so Rachel let him walk while she packed the stroller full of her purchases. It was difficult to chase after him, especially since she was pregnant. Then a crowd of shoppers went by, almost knocking Jack over before Rachel managed to get to him. Within seconds, Jack had spread his body across the wall, screaming so loudly that everyone in the store was looking, while he hit the wall harder and harder. Rachel scooped him up and tried to reason with him. Jack was screaming and trying to wrestle out of her arms, accidentally hitting her in the face so hard that she realized it was time to go home.

More often than not, overstimulation results in a heightened emotional reaction. Maybe for you, overstimulation manifests as irritability, emotional upset, aggressive outbursts, fatigue, brain fog, loss of focus, or a "spaced out" feeling. Maybe for your child it looks like endless crying, emotional meltdowns, aggressive outbursts, or being "out of it" (as if they aren't listening to you). When we look at this story through the lens of overstimulation, we can compassionately realize that Jack wasn't having a meltdown because he wanted Rachel to buy him a toy or ice cream. He was just tired and overwhelmed by the environment he was in.

There isn't anything wrong with you if you or your child have times of feeling overstimulated. This is a normal response to the experience of living in our overstimulating world!

Looking at the Whole Picture

Along with sensory input, overstimulation is also caused by a buildup of other noise underneath the surface. Imagine it's 5 p.m. and you're attempting to make dinner while simultaneously managing your children's needs (a sensory input nightmare), and *then* you add any variety of additional circumstances—you didn't sleep the night before, you're stressed about a financial situation, or you just had a conversation with someone who made you really angry. On the other hand, how would you feel in this same situation if you had a good night of sleep, felt steady about your finances, and just spent some time with one of your closest friends?

Overstimulation isn't just about the sensory input in a particular situation; it's also influenced by what's going on under the surface.

Each of us has a threshold for sensory input and stress. This refers to the amount of noise we can tolerate before we hit our limit and experience overstimulation.

Consider a balloon. You can blow air into the balloon over and over again, but at a certain point, if you keep blowing air into it, it's going to pop.

Some people have a higher threshold for stimulation than others; some have a lower threshold. But we all have a threshold.

You have a certain threshold for sensory input and stress.

Your child has a certain threshold for sensory input and stress.

If our life circumstances push beyond our threshold, we experience overstimulation and all the emotions that come with it.

There's no shame in wherever our threshold lies. Some individuals are more vulnerable to overstimulation than others, meaning they experience overstimulation more often and more quickly than others. This may include (but isn't limited to) individuals with:

- a genetic or underlying physical health condition
- attention deficit hyperactivity disorder (ADHD)
- autism spectrum disorder (ASD)
- sensory processing disorder (SPD)
- differences in learning, such as dyslexia, dysgraphia, dyscalculia, or dyspraxia
- a highly sensitive personality
- a mental health condition, such as obsessive-compulsive disorder (OCD) or generalized anxiety
- a history of trauma

Children or parents with these differences experience overstimulation more frequently than others and often require additional strategies and support to navigate overstimulation.

There is nothing innately wrong when you or your children experience overstimulation; it's simply a signal from our bodies that requires listening to. The problem comes when overstimulation leads to ongoing chronic stress, which impacts the nervous system.

How the Body Responds to Stress

I was doing laundry when I heard a scream from my daughter's bedroom. My heart immediately started pumping more quickly as I rushed toward her, worried about what I would encounter. As I entered her bedroom, she screamed, "There's a spider!" When I turned to look at the wall where she was pointing, I saw a tiny spider, the size of a speck of dust. My body immediately relaxed. I took a deep breath and removed the spider from her bedroom.

This is the healthy dance of our nervous system. The nervous system is a complex network of nerves and cells that send signals to and from different parts of the body, controlling much of what our body thinks, feels, and does. We become stressed and our bodies are filled with energy so we can deal with the stressor, and then once the situation is resolved, we move back into a state of rest and repair.

Our nervous system includes two main parts:

The **sympathetic nervous system** (SNS) is activated automatically when our bodies encounter a stressor (for example, a screaming child in another room). It mobilizes our fight, flight, or freeze response to deal with the stressor. It pumps our bodies with adrenaline, releases glucose for energy, increases our heart rate and breathing rate, raises our blood pressure, and slows down all "non-important" functions (such as digestion and reproduction). This reaction causes our sight, hearing, and other senses to become sharper and our bodies to become tense and more alert.

The **parasympathetic nervous system** (PNS) is activated when our bodies enter a state of rest and repair. Our heart rate decreases, our breathing slows down, our blood pressure lowers, our muscles relax, our immune system is strengthened, our mood lifts. This is a physiological state of relaxation and recovery. It is the feeling you experience after a really good meal or a full-body massage or when you finally get your children to sleep at night.

The sympathetic nervous system and the parasympathetic nervous system are designed to work in a flow, back and forth. When we become stressed or overstimulated, our SNS activates, and then once the stressor is resolved, we relax into our PNS state. This back-and-forth dance between stress and recovery is the body's incredible way of keeping healthy and building resilience.

Sympathetic Nervous System
Stress response: fight, flight, or freeze

Increases heart rate

Increases breathing

Raises blood pressure

Sharpens senses

Releases glucose
for energy

Pumps body
with adrenaline

Parasympathetic Nervous System
Relaxation response: rest and repair

Decreases heart rate

Slows breathing

Lowers blood pressure

Relaxes muscles

Strengthens
immune system

Lifts mood

As much as we might wish that life consisted only of relaxing by the pool, we all know this is not reality. In fact, such a life would not actually move us toward health. Stress is good for us in many ways! It motivates us to get out of bed in the morning and helps us reach our peak performance when completing tasks. You can have a healthy, regulated nervous system even if you experience times of stress or negative emotions.

The problem occurs when the dance back toward recovery stops and we get stuck in a chronically stressed state. In psychology, this is referred to as a dysregulated nervous system, meaning the nervous system is not in the flow between activation and restoration. This means that we're not experiencing times of rest, relaxation, or repair.

This can happen to any of us. You know those days when everyone and everything feels annoying. You may be exhausted but also full of energy, wanting to sleep but not able to. You may feel that everything is urgent and important but you're failing at accomplishing any of it. You may start questioning yourself or your decisions or your whole life. You may feel agitated at the people you love and overly frustrated at minor inconveniences that arise.

If stress continues over a longer period of time, it can be significantly detrimental to our mental and emotional health. Studies show that chronic stress leads to burnout, physical health problems, and emotional disturbances, and it also contributes significantly to mental illness.[8]

When we think about individuals who experience chronic stress, we often think of people who have faced significant trauma or someone with an extremely demanding job. We usually don't think about ourselves. But the reality is, the day-to-day expectations and commitments of raising children in our world can lead to chronic stress. Parental burnout is becoming more common. Studies show that 66 percent of working parents report being burned out.[9] These statistics increase when their child has attentional differences or mental health challenges, or if they are solo parenting. Studies also show that many stay-at-home parents struggle with burnout and depression.[10]

Burnout begins with feelings of overwhelming exhaustion, which over a longer period of time cause us to distance ourselves from our family (or anything we love), eventually resulting in feelings of numbness or a lack of fulfillment in parenting or life.

What's more, in the conversation about chronic stress, we almost never think about our children. They're children—what do they have to worry about? They don't face the financial demands or relational complexities that adults do. They aren't exposed to all the issues of the world the way we are. Could our children *really* be chronically stressed? The rising rates of mental illness and attentional challenges indicate they are.

Contributing Factors

There are multiple contributors to overstimulation and chronic stress. Being aware of them and being able to identify them for yourself and your child is a huge step toward reducing them. Over the next few chapters, we will unpack these contributors with the goal of bringing awareness about them and finding simple, practical ways to reduce them.

This begins with the individual's world, looking at each person's threshold for stimulation and stress. Some people are more vulnerable to overstimulation and chronic stress because of their temperament, neurodiversity, or past trauma. Being aware of each individual's threshold gives us a helpful starting point to help our family thrive.

Next, we look at the child's world. Children have a significantly lower threshold for stimulation and stress than adults do. In addition, the landscape of childhood has changed over the years, with small changes compounding to create a more stressful environment. As we unpack these developmental differences and changes in culture and education, we will be able to reduce the overstimulation and chronic stress for our children.

Then we dive deep into the parent's world—your world. So many adults, especially parents, report feeling overwhelmed, yet we desperately don't want our stress to negatively impact our children. We also don't know how to change this for ourselves (in real life, it doesn't work to just "stress less" or go to a spa). We look at the key influences in parents' stress, along with practical ways to reduce them.

Finally, we look at the state of the world, with the cultural messages and beliefs that add pressure to our already overstimulated environment. As we unpack these messages, we can craft a more truthful and empowering belief system to give us confidence to live in a countercultural way.

So What Can We Do?

So are we just supposed to wrap ourselves and our children up in cotton wool and pretend that life isn't hard or challenging?

Such an approach is not only unrealistic but also unhelpful. Life has many challenges, and our role as parents is to prepare our children for the world. Instead, we need to increase our awareness of chronic stress and turn down the noise when it becomes too loud.

Tips for Navigating the Moment of Overstimulation

It was 4:13 on a Tuesday afternoon, and I was already *done* for the week. You know the feeling you're supposed to have at the end of the week? Yet it was only Tuesday. The past two days had included full days of work, with back-to-back meetings, new projects, and a lot of problems to solve. I needed to make decisions about future travel arrangements and summer schedules for my children, plus I had meetings after school with my kids' teachers. Then when I returned home, I needed to be available for all the emotions of kids who were exhausted after a long day of school, in addition to cooking dinner and doing our evening routine.

I was standing in front of my fridge, which was full of food, yet I couldn't think of anything to make for dinner. Truthfully, I didn't want to make dinner at all (I secretly wish some magical person would come and make dinner for me). Then one of my children called out, "Mom!" for the hundredth time since school pickup, with that whining tone that sounds like nails on a chalkboard. I took a deep breath. I was aware of how I was feeling, and I didn't want to take it out on them. I answered their questions and requests as patiently as I could, reminding them for the seventh time to start their homework.

Back in the kitchen, I got a message on my phone about a dress-up day at school that had just been announced (and it was in two days). My mind started racing about how I could organize a costume that quickly, feeling frustrated about another thing added to my list of obligations. I was still standing in front of the fridge. My heart started beating faster.

Then my other child called, "Mom!" and started asking about the new clothes I'd told them I'd buy, as they'd just had another growth spurt and no longer fit in most of their clothes. I explained that I hadn't had time to buy them yet. They expressed their frustration with me, and I reminded them again that it was time to start their homework.

I went back to the kitchen, trying to work out when I would have time to buy new clothes while at the same time wondering where time was going and how they were growing up so fast. I was still standing in front of the fridge. My heart was beating faster . . .

Then I heard screaming from the living room. I raced out to find both my kids fighting, one of them in tears and the other yelling. My mind was spinning, trying to figure out how to navigate the situation, while also frustrated that they still hadn't started their homework. I was overwhelmed by my exhaustion and my to-do list, and I still had no idea what to make for dinner.

I couldn't tell if my head was about to explode or if I was going to burst into tears.

When we experience overstimulation in our everyday lives, it can feel as if we are stuck with no way to get out. Sometimes when it's repetitive, happening day after day, we can begin to feel hopeless that these feelings could change. The truth is there are some practical steps you can take to ensure that you can confidently navigate this emotional experience.

Here is a process to help you navigate the moments of overstimulation for yourself or your child.

1. TEMPORARILY REMOVE YOURSELF FROM THE ENVIRONMENT

It's difficult to calm your stress while you are still in the scenario that's causing you stress. The first step in navigating overstimulation is to temporarily remove yourself from the situation.

If you're overstimulated, this might mean walking outside in the fresh air for a few minutes or locking yourself in your bedroom or bathroom to catch your breath (of course, after making sure your children are safe).

If your young child is overstimulated, you might scoop them up into your arms and take them to a quieter place in your home, away from other children, or leave the playground to sit in the shade for a while.

If your older child or teenager is overstimulated, you might create a space for them at home that's theirs to escape to (such as their own room or a specific place in the house), or you might allow them to listen to music or an audiobook with headphones on. You might also give them verbal permission to leave the group or activity if they need to and go to an agreed-upon place.

2. DO SOMETHING THAT HELPS YOU RETURN TO CALM OR CHANGES YOUR EMOTIONAL STATE

What helps someone return to calm varies for each individual. It also varies depending on how much time or freedom you have to employ calming techniques.

This could include anything that's quiet and calming, something that prompts laughter, or an activity that distracts you from the current situation. You could pray or meditate, listen to an audiobook, walk barefoot on the grass, water the garden, or go for a short walk or run (if someone can stay with your child). This might also include any activity that changes your emotional state, such as getting everyone outside or having a dance party or announcing you're having pancakes for dinner.

Warm and cold therapies also help regulate our nervous system. Cold therapies have been shown to reduce cortisol levels; reduce stress, anxiety, and depression; and improve mood.[11] Heat therapies have been found to induce relaxation, increase blood flow, and relieve pain.[12] To use these therapies, you could take a drink of cold water, chew ice, run your wrists under cold water, or stand in front of a fan, air conditioner, or freezer. Alternatively, you could make a cup of hot tea or coffee, lie on a heat mat, or take a hot bath.

For a younger child, you could give them a hug or provide quieter activities for them to do, such as drawing, playing with Legos, looking at books, listening to calming music or an audiobook, playing with water outside, or taking a warm bath.

For an older child or teenager, you could sit with them if they need to talk or allow them space to themselves, go on a walk with them, have them swim in cold water (if you have a pool or are close to the ocean), have them listen to an audiobook or music, or have them take a warm shower or bath.

You know your child or teenager best, so pay attention to what causes them to feel calm, and support them to do more of that.

It's important to mention that scrolling your phone (which most of us naturally do when we're feeling overstimulated because we're looking for relief and distraction) tends to make the overstimulation worse. This is because although you may find some funny memes or videos (which can be distracting and hilarious), you will also be shown information that is upsetting, scary, or anger-inducing. If you're looking to reduce your overstimulation in the moment (and if the other strategies aren't working for you), you'd be better off watching a few minutes of your favorite show or comedian on Netflix than accessing a social media platform.

3. REPAIR, IF YOU NEED TO

In the moment of overstimulation, we may say or do things we later regret. The same is true for children. It's important that we don't ignore this break. Once everyone has returned to calm, we need to do the emotional work of repairing the relational connection.

Relationships aren't perfect. We all make mistakes. We might lose our temper, yell, or say critical words. Healthy relationships aren't those that never have problems but those in which each party takes ownership of their mistakes and works to repair them. (This refers to the everyday mistakes of parenting and isn't addressing or condoning neglect or abuse.)

Even if there was a reason behind your hurtful words or actions (overstimulation or your child doing the wrong thing), your actions still hurt your child and created a rupture in the relationship. When you take responsibility for your actions and apologize, you are repairing this emotional connection, maintaining the fabric of trust for a healthy relationship. You are also modeling "best practices," holding yourself to the same standards that you're trying to teach them. As children become older and move into adolescence, they become very attuned to hypocritical behavior—instances when you set boundaries on their behavior while not following these expectations yourself.

If your child has overstepped boundaries in your home, it's important to talk with them about it once they've returned to calm. First, normalize their emotions. There shouldn't be punishment for thoughts or feelings; our role is to guide them toward appropriate behaviors. This may involve having a conversation with them about how we behave in our home or asking them to clean up the mess they made during their meltdown. This isn't about shaming them for their behavior but about guiding them toward more appropriate behaviors in the future.

Repairing our relationship allows us to begin again.

While my kids were still screaming and I was attempting to comfort both of them, my husband entered the room, announcing he'd finished work early and was wondering if we wanted to go to the beach.

Having him finish work early was a rare occurrence, and even though we're lucky enough to live only ten minutes from the beach, we almost never go on a school night. My mind was running through all the things not yet done, but when both the kids stopped crying and yelled, "Yes!" I knew it was the right thing to do.

As we walked onto the beach, my son ran ahead and jumped into the waves, closely followed by my husband. My daughter took my hand, and we walked toward the shallow water together. Her pure joy was apparent from her giggles and squeals as the cold water enveloped her legs. As I stood there with my feet in the water, I felt my whole body relax. The waves began to wash away my overwhelm. Underneath it all was a woman feeling the weight of the world and all these little hearts and big people relying on her.

But for that moment, the waves of the sea were able to wash it all away.

Turn Down the Noise Today

It might seem daunting to think about turning down the noise in such a loud world, but you can start with small steps (which add up to a big difference!). Here are some suggestions for turning down the volume that you can try this week.

1. Pre-organize one or two calming activities for yourself or your child that you can quickly grab for moments that begin to feel overstimulating. You might load an audiobook on your phone or pack a small bag of Legos and drawing supplies for your child.
2. Begin to notice if there are consistent times or days that are overstimulating, and make a plan for them. For example, if you are repeatedly overstimulated during the preparation and cooking of dinner, you might consider making dinner earlier in the day (or finding that magical person I'm still looking for to prepare it for you!). If your teenager is repeatedly overstimulated in the car after school, you might consider bringing snacks and headphones for them in the car. When you notice the repeated moments, you can plan ahead for them.
3. Try one new calming technique for yourself this week, and pay attention to how it feels. This could be quietness, distraction, humor, cold therapy, or heat therapy. Remember, everyone is different, so don't be discouraged if some of these strategies don't work for you—just keep trying until you find one that does.

CHAPTER 2

THE INDIVIDUAL'S WORLD

You have been criticizing yourself for years, and it hasn't worked. Try approving of yourself and see what happens.
LOUISE HAY

Individual's world

My feet were throbbing in a pair of shoes that were too tight, and by now I was uncomfortable in the dress I'd chosen for the occasion. It had felt fine at the beginning of the night, but after long hours of sitting and dancing and listening to speeches, the straps were feeling heavier and the material more annoying.

I was at a birthday party for a good friend. There was a large crowd of people, half of whom I didn't know well. The music was so loud at times that I had to yell to hold a conversation. The lights on the dance floor were flashing. It was getting late, and I was exhausted after getting swept into conversations with acquaintances who wanted to have deep, meaningful chats about their lives.

I was done. Overstimulated. Exhausted. I found myself

annoyed by all the tiny things that hadn't annoyed me a few hours earlier. It was time to exit and say goodbye for the night. I turned around to find my ride and saw my husband, Colin, in the middle of the dance floor, high-fiving everyone and living his best life.

I breathed deeply, trying to compose myself. This was the same situation we encounter at every party we attend. My extroverted husband loves parties and thinks he's running for mayor when he enters a group full of new people. If you ever get the chance to meet him in person, you'll feel like he's your best friend within a few hours. Everyone loves him. *I* deeply love him.

Yet this situation repeatedly causes heated marital "conversations" because I'm always ready to leave the party early and he's always ready to get the party started.

One of the reasons for this is because my husband has a greater threshold for sensory input than I do. As we become aware of these differences and learn to accept them, it increases our connection with one another and empowers us to make wise decisions toward a more peaceful life—at home, at school, at church, in our community, and in our friendships. These individual differences aren't "good" or "bad"; they're just different. If you have a different threshold than others, it doesn't make you better or worse than them; these are just differences in how we navigate and process the world.

There are three main reasons why some people have a lower capacity for stimulation and stress than others do: high sensitivity, neurodiversity, and mental illness or trauma.

High Sensitivity

One of the main individual differences that determines your personal threshold for overstimulation (or your child's threshold) is the trait of high sensitivity.

Having a highly sensitive personality (also called sensory processing sensitivity) is a temperament or a trait, not a medical diagnosis. About 20 percent of the population identifies with this personality trait.[1]

Of these, approximately 70 percent are introverts and 30 percent are extroverts, so it is a separate trait from introversion/extroversion.[2] These individuals have a more sensitive nervous system than those without the trait. This trait doesn't just refer to individuals who are "sensitive" or "emotional"; rather, what determines the trait is the depth at which they notice and process information or stimuli.

Individuals with this trait are highly empathetic, closely connected to their emotions, intelligent, creative, and tenderhearted. They are deep thinkers and naturally desire to assimilate information in the world around them. Highly sensitive individuals have a gift. They are often innovators, artists, creators, and those who wrestle deeply with the problems of this world in order to help others.

But they also have a particular kryptonite. Just as Superman has superhuman powers but can be zapped of all his powers with a glowing green rock, the kryptonite for highly sensitive individuals is overstimulation.

As someone who has the trait of high sensitivity, I can personally relate to this experience. In my work as a creative entrepreneur and writer, I think deeply about the topics I'm sharing about. As a parent and a friend, I'm deeply empathetic toward others, noticing and encouraging them through life's joys and challenges. Yet I also become overstimulated more easily than others (my family jokes that my favorite phrase is "Alexa, turn off the music!").

Highly sensitive people experience overstimulation more easily and more often than those without the trait. Without healthy boundaries, they are also more vulnerable to mental health challenges such as anxiety or depression. These two vulnerabilities—overstimulation in the short term and mental health challenges long term—are closely connected.[3] If you are repeatedly overstimulated, you might experience chronic stress. If this chronic stress is left unmanaged, over time it can lead to a higher vulnerability to mental health challenges.

The Neuroscience of High Sensitivity

Understanding high sensitivity is key to understanding how we can come alongside those who may be experiencing higher levels of overstimulation. There is sometimes a misunderstanding about this trait and whether it's actually a trauma response. This can be triggering for parents who have noticed that their child is highly sensitive and worry that the child might have experienced trauma the parent doesn't know about.

In truth, high sensitivity is considered to be a genetic trait.[4] Like other personality traits, it's something people are born with. While it's true that those who have experienced trauma can develop a more sensitive nervous system from that experience, it's also true that some people are simply born with the trait of high sensitivity. Some parents report that their newborn was more sensitive than other babies from birth—they noticed something different right from the beginning.

And there *is* something different, even at a neurological level. Individuals with high sensitivity have been shown to have different brain patterns and area activation than those without the trait.[5]

- **Highly sensitive individuals have more active mirror neurons (brain cells that are closely associated with empathy).** They don't have more mirror neurons than others, but the ones they do have are more active for social and emotional processing.[6]
- **Highly sensitive individuals have a stronger neurological response when shown "emotional" images.** MRI results reveal a stronger activation of more areas in their brain than those without the trait.[7]
- **When at rest, highly sensitive individuals' brains are working harder.** This is because of a stronger activation in the cingulate and premotor area of the brain, and it accounts for why highly sensitive individuals are deep thinkers and processors.[8]
- **Neurologically, highly sensitive people notice more subtleties in their environment than others do.** When shown images of landscapes with slight differences, these individuals have "significantly greater activation in brain areas involved in high-order visual processing."[9]

Individuals with high sensitivity aren't "too sensitive" to stimulation; they are actually noticing and absorbing more stimuli from the environment than those without the trait. They then process and integrate this new information. In a way, individuals with a highly sensitive temperament are so tuned in to the noise in their environment that they are hearing things other people don't hear.

THE HIGHLY SENSITIVE CHILD

Evelyn was a tenderhearted five-year-old. She was always asking her parents deep philosophical questions about God and the world. She was artistically gifted, painting and drawing beautiful pictures that her parents proudly displayed all over the house. When the neighbor's cat got sick, Evelyn made a special box with blankets and food, going over to check on it daily because she wanted to make sure it was okay.

Yet Evelyn also struggled with overwhelm. When her family had plans to go out with friends for the day, Evelyn resisted even changing out of her pajamas because she didn't want to be gone so long. When she watched *Sesame Street* on TV, the Count character scared her so much that she started having bad dreams. And anytime she lost her temper with her younger brother, she felt so guilty that before her parents even spoke to her about her behavior, she would run to her room, condemning herself for being a horrible person.

Evelyn's behavior often required a lot of extra work for her parents. In their exhaustion, they wondered what was going on, because Evelyn's younger brother didn't exhibit these same behaviors. He didn't show resistance about leaving the house, and he could watch anything age appropriate on TV and not get upset. The truth was, there wasn't anything wrong with Evelyn; she just had a highly sensitive temperament.

Highly sensitive children are a gift. They are tenderhearted, asking deep philosophical questions well beyond their age, noticing when others are upset or hurt, and seeing the beauty in the world.

Highly sensitive children are deep thinkers—creative, intelligent, and empathetic. They are the heart-centered leaders we need for our future. But highly sensitive children can also present unique challenges for those raising and teaching them. They may struggle with the daily transitions of life, be more prone to emotional meltdowns, and seem overly fearful and overwhelmed. As parents and teachers of these kids, we often worry about their future.

Parents who are raising highly sensitive children often feel like they are at their wit's end while navigating challenging behavior, because all the typical advice just isn't working. What we see on the surface are emotional outbursts or resistant behaviors that make daily life exhausting. But underneath it all is a child who is overwhelmed.

> Highly sensitive children are deep thinkers—creative, intelligent, and empathetic. They are the heart-centered leaders we need for our future.

Highly sensitive children often have a critical inner voice. This inner critic causes them to experience deep guilt and shame about anything they've done "wrong." As you navigate the journey of teaching your highly sensitive child appropriate behaviors, it's important to remember that they're likely to be way harder on themselves than you would be, and their inner voice is more critical than anything that you might say to them. Helping them navigate this harsh inner voice is a crucial part of the journey of raising a highly sensitive child.

Because of their sensitivity, children with this trait are more significantly impacted than others (for good or for bad) by their early relationships and experiences. Although this may feel like a lot of pressure for parents and educators, it's empowering to know that as you create an emotionally healthy environment, you're providing a strong foundation for them to flourish now and in the future.

If you're blessed with a highly sensitive child, it's crucial to remember that they're not trying to make our lives hard; they are struggling—and they're communicating that in the only way they know. When we understand the inner world of our highly sensitive child and find ways to reduce daily stimulation, we will start to notice positive differences in them.

This was what happened for Evelyn's parents. Once they understood that Evelyn had a highly sensitive temperament and learned strategies to support her, much of the tension in their family life was reduced. When they made plans to go out with friends, they would go out for half the day and give Evelyn the afternoon to be at home. They started paying more attention to what Evelyn was watching on TV—even when it was age appropriate—so she wasn't watching things that would scare her. They also started an open dialogue with Evelyn about her inner critic in an attempt to normalize the imperfections of being human.

Although these changes didn't change Evelyn (the trait of high sensitivity is not something we can change), they reduced the number and intensity of meltdowns and resistance points they were experiencing. Even more than that, they became advocates and safe spaces for their tenderhearted little girl who was learning to navigate the world.

THE HIGHLY SENSITIVE PARENT

Sometimes, in our efforts to understand our children, we discover that we, too, have the trait of high sensitivity. Since it's a trait, it tends to run in families. This was the case for Jane. When she was dealing with challenging behavior from her nine-year-old son, she began searching for answers about what was going on. As she read books and found research on the trait of high sensitivity, she realized it described her son exactly. She was relieved to finally understand what was going on with her son so she could support him. Yet as she learned more, she began to realize that she herself likely had a highly sensitive temperament.

If you're like Jane (and me!), you're not alone.

There are many benefits of being a parent with high sensitivity. You are more likely to think deeply about the process of raising your child and what they need to thrive (it may even be why you picked up this book!). You are empathetic toward your child and tuned in to what they need from you. You are effective at facilitating creative and interesting activities for the family and creating rhythms that give your child a deep sense of certainty. If you're raising a child who is also highly sensitive, you are better able to understand how they experience the world and therefore more able to meet their needs.

The challenge of being a parent with high sensitivity is that you're far more likely to experience overstimulation yourself. As a result, you may lose your temper more often or desperately crave time away from home life. You may also experience a more critical inner voice, and you may feel guilty about your parenting or your reactions to your children. You are more vulnerable to experiencing burnout from the constant, stressful demands of life. This is why it's especially important to prioritize looking after yourself by taking breaks from the noise and stress when you can. Self-care is particularly important for the highly sensitive parent, because without it, the loud and overstimulating job of raising children will cause your sensitive nervous system to become stressed on a regular basis. If you're able to take care of yourself along the way, you will be far more likely to experience joy and fulfillment in your work and life, as well as show up as a more present and engaged parent, spouse, and friend.

THE NON-HIGHLY SENSITIVE PARENT

Just as there are benefits to being a highly sensitive parent, there are also advantages to being a parent who doesn't have this trait. The noise of family life doesn't seem to affect you as much—you're able to handle far more noise and intensity before experiencing overstimulation. You're also far less likely to worry or feel guilty about your parenting, and you're often able to bring joy and lightheartedness into family life.

If you're a parent who doesn't have the trait of high sensitivity and you're raising a child who does have the trait, the primary challenge is that you may struggle to understand them. Because it's not your own experience, you may become more easily frustrated at them. You might even feel that you don't like who they are (although you would never admit that out loud) because they are so hard to handle and you don't know why.

When you take some time to deeply understand the trait of high sensitivity and respect that your child has a lower threshold for stimulation and stress, it will increase your empathy, patience, and connection with your child.

David was an extroverted, lighthearted father of a twelve-year-old son and two daughters, ages nine and six. He loved being a dad and enjoyed playing rough-and-tumble games, riding bikes with the kids for long hours, and laughing together. But he was having trouble connecting with his son, Will.

It began when Will was younger. Instead of laughing at his dad's well-meaning teasing, he would run off and burst into tears, or David would get frustrated because Will didn't want to spend long hours riding his bike outside with him, instead preferring to be inside building Legos. As Will grew older, on the cusp of the adolescent years, they started regularly butting heads. Every time David asked Will to do his chores, Will resisted, and it escalated into an all-out fight. When David would jokingly tease him, instead of running off and crying, Will would make a cutting, critical comeback.

David was beginning to feel so frustrated. No matter what he tried, he couldn't connect with Will. Even though he loved being a dad and had a strong relationship with his younger daughters, he would secretly admit that he was starting to wonder if he even liked Will anymore.

David began searching for answers and learned about the trait of high sensitivity. Every description fit Will perfectly. It was when David, a non highly sensitive parent, began to understand more about the trait of high sensitivity that he started to understand Will.

When Will didn't want to spend long hours riding his bike with David, it wasn't that he didn't want to spend time with his dad, but that long hours outside were overstimulating for him.

When Will got upset or became aggressive over David's teasing, it was because he found it hurtful (even though that wasn't David's intention). And with his sensitive intuition, Will picked up on his dad's lack of understanding and judgment toward him, becoming angry in an attempt to protect himself.

As David came to understand the way Will felt and processed the world, he made some changes in his parenting. First, he apologized to Will for not understanding him, and he changed the way he joked around with him. He tried to engage in some activities that Will found interesting, and when Will wanted to ride bikes for only thirty minutes, David no longer took it personally.

Within a short time, David saw a complete turnaround in his relationship with Will. When he asked Will to do his chores and take out the trash, Will said, "Sure thing!" and did the chore without complaint. Best of all, David felt like he had a thriving relationship with his son again.

Neurodiversity

If you or your child experiences overstimulation more often and more intensely than others at the same developmental stage, it may be a sign of an underlying neurological difference—that is, the way you or your child experiences and processes the world. Many individuals with these differences experience a lower threshold for overstimulation and a higher vulnerability to chronic stress. In other words, they easily become overstimulated and may need additional support to ensure that they're not living in a state of chronic stress.

Neurodivergence isn't a one-size-fits-all description; it's an umbrella term that refers to many different diagnoses.

- autism spectrum disorder (ASD)
- attention deficit hyperactivity disorder (ADHD)
- dyslexia (difficulty with reading)
- dysgraphia (difficulty with writing)
- dyscalculia (difficulty with math)
- dyspraxia (difficulty with coordination)
- sensory processing disorder (SPD)
- Tourette's syndrome

It's important to clarify here the connection between high sensitivity and early signs of neurodivergence. High sensitivity and neurodivergence are different things. There is often some confusion about this because some people who once thought they were highly sensitive later realize that what they were experiencing was neurodivergence. Although this may happen in some cases, that doesn't mean it's true for everyone. In order for an individual to receive a diagnosis of ADHD or ASD, they have to meet certain criteria through an in-depth diagnosis process with a licensed mental-health professional. One of the categories is "oversensitivity to sensory stimuli." But the individual also has to meet eight or nine additional criteria to receive a diagnosis of ASD or ADHD. Although research is always developing, currently high sensitivity and neurodivergence are considered separate things,[10] meaning that you can be highly sensitive and not neurodivergent; or you can be highly sensitive and also neurodivergent.

Individuals who are neurodivergent have different strengths and challenges from those who are neurotypical. If you or your child has any of these differences, it's important to become aware of them so you can cultivate the support you and your child need. You may be hesitant to pursue a diagnosis, either because of financial cost or because of the potential cost that a label could carry. The process can understandably bring up a lot of worry about what a diagnosis would mean for the future—yet you may also be surprised at how empowering it can be. The fact is, with or without an official diagnosis, the differences will exist; seeking to understand them and advocate for support can allow you to more deeply connect with yourself or your child.

Although the information available online can be helpful to educate us and point us in a certain direction, it's critical to get a personalized, professional diagnosis (as opposed to self-diagnosis). With the overlapping nature of many types of neurodivergence, we need professionals to help us untangle the nuances. We are often too close to the situation, especially when it comes to our children; we may not have a clear perspective about stages of development, and we don't see how our child is behaving at school, church, or other contexts. For example, you might think your child is showing signs of autism spectrum disorder when they're actually dealing with obsessive-compulsive disorder. Or sometimes parents are concerned that their hyperactive five-year-old has ADHD, only to discover that this is simply a developmental stage they're going through.

If you wonder if your child might be neurodivergent, please reach out to a licensed clinical psychologist or psychiatrist for an individual diagnosis and support. Your health-care professional may be able to refer you to someone they recommend.

Mental Illness or Trauma

Jason was a new dad to his baby daughter, Sienna, a six-month-old, black-haired, green-eyed beauty who was all smiles to everyone she encountered. When Jason's wife, Katrina, first told him she was pregnant, Jason couldn't have imagined how much he would love his sweet daughter while also feeling such a fierce sense of protectiveness toward her. There was just one problem: he couldn't handle Sienna's crying.

Despite wanting to be a hands-on dad, and knowing that all babies cry, Jason would find himself trying to escape every time Sienna started crying. Sometimes he gave Sienna to Katrina or placed her safely in her crib while he walked outside. At first, Katrina justified Jason's behavior, thinking, *Maybe dads don't do the comforting thing.* But it began to happen so regularly that Katrina started worrying not just about Sienna, but about Jason. Katrina shared her concerns with Jason about how he was coping with new parenthood.

Diagnosed with clinical anxiety as a young adult, Jason had been working with a therapist for almost a decade. During that time, he had worked through some traumatic past events and found coping strategies to deal with the anxiety that sometimes felt like a regular, unwanted companion.

When he found out he was going to be a dad, Jason spoke at length with his therapist, and together they made a plan to support him. Although he thought he was coping well enough, when Katrina spoke with him, Jason realized that he was dealing with more anxiety than he had first realized.

The truth was, because Jason was already navigating internal anxiety, he had a lower threshold for external stimulation (such as Sienna's cries).

Another contributing factor that limits an individual's capacity for sensory input and stress is mental illness or a history of trauma. This is because so much of a person's capacity is required to manage overwhelming thoughts and feelings.

Think back to the last time you felt really anxious about something. Maybe it was interviewing for a job or waiting for health test results. How did this impact your thoughts, feelings, and behaviors? When we're anxious, we tend to be irritable, on edge, and grumpy toward those around us—and more overwhelmed by sensory input than we normally would be. For some people, high levels of anxiety are temporary or connected to specific circumstances. But if you struggle with mental illness or a history of trauma, these are issues you wrestle with on an ongoing basis.

This is true for children as well. If your child has an anxiety disorder or has experienced traumatic events in their past, their capacity for tolerating sensory input and stress is significantly lowered. Being aware of this allows us to hold space for ourselves or our child as we walk through the journey of healing.

Is It Possible to Expand Your Individual Capacity?

If you or someone you love is more vulnerable to overstimulation and stress, whether due to high sensitivity, neurodivergence, mental illness, or trauma, this doesn't mean you're helpless in the face of vulnerability or that you won't be able to do hard things. Individuals with these vulnerabilities do hard things all the time! They start businesses, build families, hold challenging careers, serve others, engage in their community, overcome health challenges, and navigate relationships. Within the context of individual limits, it *is* possible to expand your individual capacity for dealing with sensory input. We can learn to be even more tuned in to how to handle overstimulation so stressors don't have a negative impact.

Here are some ways we can expand our individual capacity.

Time

As we develop through childhood and into adulthood, our tolerance for what we can handle in healthy ways expands. As your child grows, so will their capacity. For example, a toddler in a crowded shopping center may last only an hour before they have an emotional meltdown and need a nap. But a teenager or young adult may feel fine being there for the whole afternoon before they look for a quieter place to escape.

Self-Care

This means actually taking a break when it's time to. When you notice the feelings of overwhelm and overstimulation, decide to take a short break to calm or interrupt those feelings. (See "Turn Down the Noise Today" the end of chapter 1 for ideas on how to do this.)

No matter our individual vulnerability, if we never take time away from our stressors, they will have a negative impact on us. Highly sensitive individuals can thrive in stimulating environments as long as they have intentional times of rest and recalibration.

Intentional Exposure

The best way to build a higher tolerance for sensory input is through short times of intentional exposure. First, become aware of your current tolerance for sensory input—the amount of time you feel comfortable before you start feeling overstimulated in a specific environment. Then intentionally push yourself to stay in that environment for increasingly longer periods of time.

Many people experienced this when going back into public spaces after being home for so long during the pandemic. For some, returning to crowded stores was overwhelming, and they may have lasted only twenty minutes at first. Yet by consistently putting themselves back in these environments for twenty minutes, then thirty minutes, then forty minutes, they increased their tolerance over time.

Note that this strategy works only when you're using small, incremental steps. It doesn't work if you push yourself or your child into endlessly overstimulating environments (a practice that might end up backfiring).

Therapy

The goal of therapy is to bring healing from your past and equip you with practical tools for your future. A good therapist will walk beside you on this journey toward increasing your window of tolerance over time. Some signs that you might need therapy include feeling stuck in a particular emotional or relational issue, having flashbacks of memories or dreams, consistently experiencing strong emotional reactions or triggers that seem out of context for the situation, or noticing over time that you don't feel like yourself. If this sounds like something you're experiencing, please reach out to a licensed mental health professional. Your health-care professional may be able to refer you to someone they recommend.

Even with all this work, each individual will have their own threshold for what they can handle. While we can be intentional about expanding our capacity, there's also wisdom in accepting that the way we're wired is different from those around us.

Accepting Individual Differences

It took years of heated "marital conversations" between my husband and me about how we navigated parties before we both realized we weren't going to change the other person. He wasn't going to become someone who wanted to leave a party early, and I wasn't going to become someone who wanted to be the last to leave. Instead of trying to change the way we're wired, we finally accepted that we're different.

When we came to this realization, we finally experienced peace in this area of our relationship. That wasn't because the situation had changed or because we instantly knew what to do, but because acceptance is the first step toward emotional health.

You might wish you had a higher capacity for sensory input and stress. It's frustrating to be aware of your limitations, especially when you're in a season of caring for children and navigating the demands of being an adult. It may seem like life would be easier and more peaceful if you had greater capacity.

You might wish your child had a higher capacity for sensory input and stress. It would make the daily activities of life less overwhelming. You wouldn't have to manage as much resistance, and you wouldn't have to deal with as many emotional meltdowns and behavioral challenges. It may seem that life would be easier and more peaceful if they had greater capacity.

But you don't. And they don't.

It is not until we accept our own limits and our children's limits that we can create an emotionally healthy home.

Once Colin and I accepted our differences about parties, it became easier to think of compromises and solutions. None of these strategies are groundbreaking. None of them are hacks you've never heard of or advice that will change your life. Sometimes I stay later at the party if it's important to him, and sometimes he leaves earlier if I'm particularly exhausted. Sometimes we even drive two cars so we can leave when we want to.

Yet our ability to understand each other dramatically reduced the conflict in this area of our relationship. It all began by accepting our differences.

Child Assessment for High Sensitivity

You might be wondering if your child has the trait of high sensitivity. Here's a general guide that may provide some clarity.

1. Is your child a deep thinker?
   - Do they ask deep questions for their age?
   - Are they curious about the world, philosophy, or faith?
   - Do they love learning new things and reading (or listening to) stories?
   - Do they notice details about situations that others don't seem to notice?
   - Do they pause before they respond to a new situation?

2. Is your child a deep feeler?
   - Do they struggle with big emotions more than others their age?
   - Do they intuitively know when someone else is upset?
   - Do they respond to others' words or behavior in heightened ways?
   - Do they notice beauty and make more connections than others their age?
   - Do they have a tender heart or insightful perspective of the world?
   - Do they struggle with a deeply critical inner voice?

3. Is your child sensitive to sensory input?
   - Do they complain about tags on their clothes, dislike wearing socks, or want to change if their clothes get wet?
   - Are daily hygiene routines (such as brushing teeth) triggers for meltdowns?
   - Are they deeply affected by scary media (even when it's age appropriate)?
   - Are they upset by loud noises?
   - Are they overly bothered by music (if it's not their choice)?

4. Is your child more prone to meltdowns than others their age?
   - Do their tantrums seem more like emotional meltdowns from overwhelm rather than attempts to get their own way?
   - Does the number of meltdowns increase when there's an increase in activity or sensory stimuli?
   - Do the meltdowns seem to be connected to transition points during the day?
   - When you increase your child's rest or quiet play, do their meltdowns decrease?

If you answered yes to most of these questions, it's likely that your child has the trait of high sensitivity.

If your child has the trait of high sensitivity, the best thing you can do is to understand and validate their experience of the world. You can do this by learning more about high sensitivity and making small changes in your family rhythms.

Some changes to consider are prioritizing rest and free play time, not overscheduling, and being mindful of the sensory stimulation in their days. (For additional information and resources about high sensitivity, go to www.ResilientLittleHearts.com.)

Parent Assessment for High Sensitivity

1. Are you a deep thinker?
   - Do you think a lot about the meaning of life, art, beauty, philosophy, or faith?
   - When you learn new information in areas of your expertise, do you spend time wrestling with how this new information integrates into what you already understand?
   - Do you notice details about people and situations that others don't seem to notice?
   - Do you find yourself pausing before you respond in a new situation?

2. Are you a deep feeler?
   - Are you highly empathetic toward others?
   - Do you intuitively know when someone else is upset?
   - Do you find yourself deeply affected by emotional trauma, violence, or horror in media?
   - Do you sometimes feel that your heart is too sensitive for our world?
   - Do people come to you for advice because you seem to have wisdom for life?
   - Do you have a rich inner life?

3. Are you sensitive to internal and external sensory input?
   - Are you easily overwhelmed by sensory input (loud noises, crowds, visual stimulation, or heat)?
   - Are you particularly sensitive about and aware of physical discomfort or pain in your body?
   - Do you feel overwhelmed if you have a lot to do in a short period of time?
   - Do you find yourself naturally avoiding highly stimulating situations?

4. Do you struggle with a strong inner critic?
   - Do you struggle with a deeply critical inner voice?
   - Do you hold yourself to a standard of perfection in both your professional life and your personal life?
   - If you don't meet your standards, do you experience extreme shame or guilt?

5. Do you have strong emotional reactions to feeling overstimulated or overwhelmed?
   - Do you find yourself reacting in ways you later regret when you feel overstimulated?
   - Do you feel significantly calmer internally when the physical environment around you is organized and clean?

If you answered yes to most of these questions, it's likely that you have the trait of high sensitivity.

If you become aware that you have the trait of high sensitivity, one thing you can begin to do today is prioritize self-care. Next time you feel overstimulated or stressed, rather than pushing through, try the process described in "Turn Down the Noise Today" at the end of chapter 1 to reduce stimulation in the moment. Making these small changes in your day can add up to a big positive difference in your overall life experience.

CHAPTER 3

THE CHILD'S WORLD

What was wonderful about childhood is that anything in it was a wonder. It was not merely a world full of miracles; it was a miraculous world.

G. K. CHESTERTON

Individual's world

Child's world

"I can do it myself!" My daughter, who was four at the time, was sitting in the driver's seat of our car. Her blonde hair, tied in two pigtails, was swooshing across her face as she shook her head in frustration. Dressed in a pink tutu, she was perched at the very tip of the seat, her little feet stretching to reach the pedals. She was moving the steering wheel back and forth, becoming more and more exasperated about the car not moving.

We were getting ready to go to her dance class, and I was standing at the driver's seat door, asking her to please hop in the back seat so we could put on her seat belt. The problem was, she had decided that she wanted to drive to dance class herself.

If you've ever been in a similar situation with your own child, you know how futile it is to try to reason with a preschooler and explain logically why they can't drive the car. They always win the argument with passion, emotion, and cuteness.

Childhood is a time for exploring the world, embracing adventure and delight, living in a world of imagination and endless possibilities. It's a time for learning how to crawl and walk and run, how to talk and read and add, how to play and make friends.

Children Are Not Adults

We cherish childhood, yet we sometimes forget that children can't handle the same things that we adults can handle. We unconsciously expect them to cope in the same way we do.

In some areas, we are clear on a child's limits. We don't allow a young child to handle a knife or run across the road by themselves. There are legal age limits on alcohol and other substances, and on their ability to drive, vote, and get married. We set those limits because we know that children and adolescents don't yet understand how dangerous or weighty those responsibilities can be, nor can they do them safely yet. We want them to grow in healthy ways until they're mature enough to handle more advanced decisions.

Yet when it comes to stress, pressure, pace of life, and sensory stimulation, we somehow forget that children aren't ready to handle the same things adults can handle. So we might enroll them in a thousand extracurricular activities to fill all their free time, put pressure on them to perform academically (even in early elementary school), or expect a wriggly three-year-old to sit quietly and still in church. Having an understanding of a child's development will empower you to extend compassion and better meet their needs.

Here are three things to remember about how children are fundamentally different from adults:

1. **Their brains are not yet completely developed. Ninety percent of a child's anatomical brain development occurs by six or seven years old.**[1] This growth is particularly significant in the first three

years of life. You do not need to "do" something to facilitate your child's brain development. It occurs naturally (for most children) when they are in a loving, safe, and predictable environment.

A child's healthy neurological development in the early years of their life significantly impacts their future, including their ability to learn, regulate their emotions, and develop social skills. It's also connected to their long-term happiness and health.

This is why one of the best foundations you can give your child for their future emotional and mental health is an emotionally safe environment with deeply connected relationships.

2. **A child's prefrontal cortex doesn't reach full development and maturity until young adulthood.** The prefrontal cortex (PFC) is often called the executive brain—the part of the brain involved in managing attention and memory, regulating emotions, making decisions, and exercising self-control. It's the part of the brain that helps us choose healthy behaviors and interact with the world in a mature way. Although the PFC undergoes some development and is active in younger children (four- to five-year-olds),[2] it doesn't reach foundational maturity until adolescence (twelve years old)[3] and doesn't reach full maturity until young adulthood (up to twenty-five years old).[4]

   This means that, quite literally, children don't have the ability to fully control their emotions. It's developmentally typical for toddlers to have tantrums, for preteens to talk back, and for adolescents to make choices without always understanding the consequences.

3. **Children are more prone to overstimulation than adults because of their developing brains.** A child's capacity to handle sensory input and stress slowly increases as they get older. This is why a newborn can be awake for only an hour or so before they need to sleep again, why a toddler still needs multiple naps a day, and why an eight-year-old can handle a day full of activities better than a four-year-old can. A child's brain *needs* rest in order to

navigate the world; while the child is resting, their brain is undergoing deep restoration, integration, and neurological development. These times of rest allow a child to recover from the stimuli and stress of their day so they can continue to learn and explore their world again.

How Stress and Stimulation Affect Children

Not long after our family moved from Australia to California, we had family visiting who wanted to take our two- and four-year-old children to Disneyland. We'd never taken them there before, but since it was a short drive from our home, we packed everything and planned to spend the day there.

You can probably guess what happened. Let's just say it didn't go the way we'd envisioned.

Within only a few hours of navigating tears and overwhelm, and going on "It's a Small World After All" more times than I could count, we admitted defeat and took our children home. On the way out, we purchased two of those overpriced bubble wands, and that turned out to be the best part of our children's day. After so many tears, it was worth it to see them smiling again. They played with the bubbles for hours in our backyard.

After that experience, I was in no hurry to visit Disneyland again anytime soon. It wasn't until years later when my son, who was now eight, asked to go that we tentatively planned another trip. I was worried it would be another train wreck, but it turned out to be a completely different experience. Now that my children were older, they had the greatest time, wanting to stay all day and into the night, and were still happy when we returned home.

Children have a significantly lower threshold for stimulation and stress than adults do. As they grow older, their capacity to handle stimulation also grows. This is true even if your child has a highly sensitive temperament or is neurodivergent—what they can handle as a younger child will be less than what they will be able to handle as adult.

When our children are young, we have to account for their significantly lower threshold.

In the season of raising younger children, this can often be frustrating, as you may feel limited in how many activities you can do in a day before everyone is upset, or you may have to manage the tension of extended family or friends not understanding why your child is crying after highly stimulating activities. If you're raising a child with a higher vulnerability to stimulation, you might feel that almost any activity ends in overwhelm.

Understanding a younger child's threshold for stimulation doesn't mean that we should never do anything overstimulating for them—there are many important life events and relationships that you will decide to prioritize. Yet this awareness helps us have more empathy for our child when they're struggling in the moment, and it helps us shape the daily rhythms of our lives to be less overwhelming for them.

This was Ashley's experience with her daughter Emily. Even when Emily was a newborn, Ashley noticed that if she had music on in the background, Emily was distracted when nursing and unsettled throughout the day. When she was an infant, if they had more than one outing per day (such as visiting the grocery store or anywhere else with lots of noise or people), Emily would cry for hours in the afternoon and was not easily comforted.

Ashley was exhausted, and although she was a new parent, she intuitively thought that Emily needed a less overwhelming environment. After wrestling with what these limitations would mean for her, she decided to go on only one outing per day, while also reducing the stimulation in their home.

Sometimes this was challenging because Ashley had a lot to do or because she had to deal with the judgment of people who questioned her decisions or told her she was catering to her child too much. Yet with these changes, Emily flourished. She no longer cried for hours at a time, she seemed happier when they went out on their daily outings, and she slept better at night. Despite her new-parent doubts and everyone else's opinions, Ashley had created boundaries to help her daughter thrive.

When Emily was four years old, they went out to the playground in the morning and bumped into family friends who had a daughter Emily's age. After the girls giggled and played on the slides together, the friends invited Ashley and Emily over for lunch and an afternoon playdate. Emily was excited to go, so they accepted the invitation, though Ashley knew it probably meant that Emily would struggle later that day.

After eating lunch and playing dress-up for a few hours, Ashley brought Emily home, bracing for what was to come. To Ashley's surprise, Emily was fine. She played happily with her toys, and although she was more tired than usual before bedtime, she didn't have any overwhelming meltdowns.

Ashley was in shock. After years of watching Emily struggle to cope with stimulation, Ashley almost didn't recognize her own child. But as Emily grew, so did her capacity for stimulation.

The Impact of Chronic Stress

Chronic stress has a negative impact on all of us, but it has a disproportionate impact on children since they're still developing neurologically.

This chronic stress can have long-term effects. The Adverse Childhood Experiences (ACE) study was one of the largest studies conducted on the link between childhood abuse/neglect and the health and well-being of adults.[5] The findings noted a strong link between childhood trauma and poor academic achievement, along with the adult onset of chronic disease and substance abuse. The more adverse experiences a child experienced, the more likely they were to face these negative outcomes. This was found to be particularly true if they had no support or therapeutic intervention.

Although the studies on ACE examined extreme situations such as abuse and neglect, the findings demonstrate that children are uniquely vulnerable to chronic stress because they are still developing and learning to understand the world. By the time we reach adulthood, we have developed the ability to question other people's opinions of the world, recognize people's motives or agendas, and process a specific situation without making it a global problem. Children have not yet developed these capabilities. That's why they often blame themselves for an upsetting event, even when they had nothing to do with it, or why they follow the adults in their world without question. It isn't until they grow into adolescence that these other abilities begin to emerge.

For example, if a seven-year-old is in a high-pressure academic environment and has extracurricular activities scheduled for every night of the week and their parents expect them to be perfectly behaved all the time, they don't have the ability to notice and articulate (like an adult would), "I'm feeling too stressed. If I reduce some of this activity, I will probably feel better." Rather, the child internalizes the situation, feeling ashamed that they are overwhelmed and questioning if there's something wrong with them. This comes out in their behavior, with regressions such as bedwetting, control issues around food, regular tears over small things, physical aggression, or withdrawal into their room for hours at a time.

With adolescents, we see an increase in mood swings and aggressive outbursts and more frequent retreats into their room or behind screens. Parents often see this behavior on the surface and assume their child is being rebellious and needs stronger discipline or boundaries. Yet in many situations, these behaviors are symptoms of a child who is struggling.

Even if a child hasn't faced trauma, they can still experience chronic stress. Ongoing stress can be caused by big life transitions such as adding a new sibling to the family or moving to a new house. It may also result from the cumulative pressure of being overscheduled, having too many stimulating activities, facing academic pressure, and having too little sleep or playtime. During these times, we often see an increase in challenging behaviors. Our child is showing us their stress and dysregulation through their behavior.

This is why it's vital for us to protect childhood as a time of critical development.

Protecting Childhood in This Generation

Childhood has changed dramatically in our world over the past several decades. It has become more pressurized, stimulating, and stressful. These changes include a faster pace of life, lack of free time and creative play, overabundance of choice, and increased access to technology. While I address these changes in detail in part 3 of the book, it's important to discuss here how confronting these differences can significantly impact our children's state of mind and soul.

> Childhood has changed dramatically in our world over the past several decades.

Knowing what we know about a child's neurological development, we need to make the countercultural decision to protect childhood, especially between the ages of zero and seven. This means being particularly mindful of the pace of their lives, what stimulation they're exposed to, and how much pressure is placed on them.

Now, an important clarification: the intentional move to protect childhood is not about trying to save our children from the challenges of their lived experience. People face various heartbreaking circumstances, many of which can't be changed but only lived through. This may include the death of a loved one, a health challenge, a disability, a job loss, or financial insecurity. When children are going through stressful situations, our role as caring adults in their lives is, of course, to come alongside them and support them in processing these events. These unexpected and challenging situations are different from the noise of stimulation that comes from our world's increased pace, pressure, and complexity. To protect childhood is to acknowledge that the latter can be just as detrimental as the former—and therefore we must make decisions as caring adults in their lives to reduce the pace, pressure, and unnecessary stimulation our children are exposed to on a regular basis. This is important for all children, but particularly for children under the age of seven, because they are still developing neurologically and forming who they are. As we respect and protect this time for the children in our care, it becomes a foundation for children to flourish.

Protecting Childhood in Education

Standing in a small crowd of parents, squashed into a narrow hallway with students' art on the walls, Colin and I were trying to catch a glimpse into the classroom while listening to our guide. We were on a school tour, looking for an environment that would be a good fit for our soon-to-be kindergartner.

This school was private and expensive, and it came recommended by many parents in the area. We were grateful to be in a position that enabled us to consider a private education, but this particular school would be a stretch for us, and I wondered whether it would be worth it.

I was still wrestling with the decision when I heard these words from the guide, which made things instantly clear: "We also have an advanced leadership academy for kindergarten." He went on to explain the "high expectations" (aka homework) that would lie ahead for these five-year-olds.

Instantly my mind went back to the stuffy university room where I'd studied to get my master's degree in educational psychology. In the front of the classroom was our professor, a gruff man with strong opinions—and even stronger ways of communicating those opinions. Although he was well respected and incredibly knowledgeable, many of us students were scared to ask questions in the beginning because he seemed so intimidating.

During one particular lesson, he was sharing the research-based evidence that there is no academic benefit for homework in early elementary years.[6] It isn't until later elementary years (grade 5 or 6) that having some homework seems to make a difference to students' academic performance. In fact, in some cases, too much homework for early elementary students can have the reverse effect. This was such a countercultural revelation for almost everyone in the room that it made our minds spin. In a world that assumes that the more you do, the better you perform, the data was telling a different story. I tentatively put up my hand and asked, "But if there's no evidence suggesting it's helpful, then why do so many schools do it?"

He answered, "Because it has been accepted as the cultural norm, and parents who want their children to achieve academically put pressure on teachers and the schools for it. But younger children don't perform well under pressure; they thrive without it."

After my studies, I knew that what I really wanted for my children when they entered their school years was to learn to read and write, make some friends, have fun, play, and create art projects. I wasn't looking for a preparation academy for their future performance. There would be time for that later.

I kept walking with the group, looking for a quick exit, knowing I'd already made up my mind.

Outside the family, one of the biggest influences in childhood is school. Over the past several decades, there have been changes in the educational system that make school much more demanding than it once was.

1. **A higher-pressure environment.** The introduction of standardized testing, with school test scores publicly available, has increased the pressure on schools. Although there are some benefits to this kind of accountability, such as identifying and working to improve underperforming schools, it has also resulted in negative outcomes. Many educators feel increased pressure to get through the set curriculum in more rigid ways. This pressure flows to children who desire to perform well and are stressed about their performance. While in previous generations the focus of elementary school was on schoolwork, students are now thrust into a world of grades, testing, and rankings. As children face higher expectations for their performance, they feel increased pressure.

2. **A decrease in playtime.** Children get far less recess and playtime than past generations. Beginning in the early 2000s, many schools cut back on and even eliminated recess in favor of more instructional time. Since then, the average weekly recess time has declined by sixty minutes.[7] Not only does free-play time give children a break from the stimulation of the classroom, it also

integrates learning in their brains. Decreasing time for play has resulted in increased pressure on children.

3. **An increase in homework.** Studies suggest that the homework load has doubled from past generations, with children under the age of nine seeing the biggest increase.[8] Other research shows that although homework may benefit high school and middle school students, it doesn't provide any noticeable benefit for elementary-age students.[9] Yet the number of hours children spend doing homework continues to increase. This may come from an adult mindset that the more work we do, the better we become. We assume that the more work our children do, the better they will become. It's true that working hard is an important part of learning, but so is free time, physical activity, and time with family—especially for young children.

Education is deeply important. Individuals who give their lives to educating children are doing one of the most important jobs in the world. Our ultimate goal as parents is to prepare our children to go out into the world and thrive. Yet if we don't approach our children's development holistically, we risk them failing to thrive now—and in the future.

Turn Down the Noise at School

If you've pushed your child in the area of school achievement or enrolled them in a plethora of extracurriculars in the name of future success, all hope is not lost. You haven't ruined their childhood or their future. It's still possible to turn down the noise related to education.

The good news is, you don't have to homeschool or "unschool" in order for your child to flourish (unless you want to)—there are many ways to infuse love and safety into whatever educational system they are working within.

For example, if you have school-age children and you have a choice over the elementary school your child attends, look for an option that limits homework in the early years, values curiosity and learning, and doesn't over-focus on grades. If you have a young toddler and it's possible to delay your child from beginning kindergarten until close to six years old, research suggests that starting kindergarten slightly later significantly decreases the instances of attentional difficulties (such as ADHD), especially in boys.[10]

While these are some areas we can make decisions about, there are also circumstances we don't have control over. You may not have options about what school your child will attend or the educational philosophy of the school. It's important to not compare your situation to what you wish you had or the "ideal" you see in other people's lives. Whether you choose homeschooling, private school, or public school, it's possible to find ways for your child to flourish.

Depressurizing school isn't so much about the type or location of schooling but more about the approach and perspective we take. As a family, decide on your values about education and focus on the benefits, not the pressure. For example, when your child is struggling with their homework, a simple encouragement of "We want you to love learning and try your best—that's all!" can go a long way. In many ways, elementary school is for learning the basics of education—reading, writing, and laying the foundations of other subjects; building social skills; and developing interests and strengths. When we orient our approach to school around who our child is becoming—the activities they love, their interests, and the friendships they're making—we allow them to rest and enjoy the journey.

I know this is counterintuitive in today's world. It can be easy to fall into valuing grades and performance—and mistaking those marks as indicators of worth. While grades are helpful in monitoring how things are going at school, they are simply signals, not a reason for correction. If you're concerned about your child not doing their schoolwork, rather than giving a consequence for poor grades, place boundaries around behavior (for example, "You can only have screen time after you've completed your reading") instead of punishing or disciplining.

Children naturally want to grow and learn, so if they're showing more reluctance or if their grades are dropping, it may be a sign that they need additional support. If your child is struggling at school or resisting going to school, this can be a sign of an underlying learning difference.

As your child matures and transitions from elementary school into middle and high school, their education begins to change. One of the key differences during this stage is the expectation that they will take more ownership of their learning and keep up with the expectations of their education themselves. This skill is called executive functioning. If your adolescent is struggling to keep up with school, it may be the result of an undiagnosed learning difference, but it may also be caused by a struggle with executive functioning skills. Getting them support to help with planning and organizing can help them learn this skill.

Another factor that comes into play in education during adolescence is making decisions toward further schooling and a future career. This is the time you and your child may be making decisions to attend schools or colleges to prepare for a specific career.

It's important to name the pressure that comes along with this, both for you as a parent and for your teenager. "What do you want to do after graduation?" is a dreaded question for many teenagers, because many of them don't know yet, and it feels like a weighty decision that will impact the rest of their life.

You can help your teenager navigate this season using your own values and opinions. At the same time, it's important to keep in mind that even if things don't go perfectly—if they don't get into the college you hoped they would or they choose a career direction you're not sure about—there are still many ways for them to have a good future.

It's also important to name the anxiety we feel as parents during this time. Almost all of the pressure we place on our adolescents regarding their education is because we care deeply for them and want them to have the best opportunities for their future. Yet even though we have the best of intentions, our anxiety can place undue pressure on them. Despite their "I don't care about anything" demeanor, teenagers really do care about doing well, their future, and their parents' approval. They care more than they let on.

Developing Resilience

In recent years, we have heard the cultural narrative that this generation needs to be "toughened up." This narrative is based on the belief that this generation is struggling so much because they haven't been exposed to enough challenges to help them develop resilience. The claim is that this generation hasn't been lifting enough metaphorical weights, and therefore they have weak muscles. Like a bodybuilder in the gym, they would develop more strength over time if they lifted heavier weights.

But this is a false belief. Put simply, the reason so many in this generation are struggling is not because they haven't been exposed to enough challenges but because they've been overexposed to chronic stress, without enough times of true recovery.

> This generation is struggling not because they haven't been exposed to enough challenges but because they've been overexposed to chronic stress, without enough times of true recovery.

After giving birth to both of my children, I was experiencing some weakness in my pelvic floor, so my ob-gyn recommended pelvic floor therapy (yes, I'm sharing this—let's hope it's not TMI . . .). As I met with the physical therapist for my first assessment, I cracked a joke about how weak my pelvic floor muscles were in an attempt to make the whole situation a little less uncomfortable. To my surprise, she immediately corrected me, explaining that my pelvic floor muscles weren't weak; in fact, the opposite was true. They were incredibly strong, but they didn't know how to relax. The muscles were chronically holding strong at an eight or nine out of ten most of the time, so when they needed to hold strong, there was only a small gap before they had nothing else to give. Most of the therapy centered around teaching my muscles to turn off when they weren't needed.

This generation lives in a different world from the one we grew up in—one that never allows them to "turn off." They are overexposed to the heaviness and heartache of this connected world, with almost no ability to do anything about it. Adding to this, our global connectivity often comes at a cost to real-life relationships, as parents are increasingly stressed and families are more isolated. This leaves children and adolescents without enough safe relationships to process their emotions.

They aren't like bodybuilders lifting weights in the gym for a few hours a day. They are walking around all day carrying a weight they can never put down. This lack of space to recover is eroding their emotional health and resilience.

This generation is not weak. They don't need to be "toughened up." They are already incredibly strong. Rather, they need more times of true recovery. They need time to turn down the noise of stress in our world. They need time to laugh, play, and take a breath. They need time to connect with people who love them.

Permission Slips to Parent Your Children

In order to protect our children from overstimulation and stress in their environment, we need to give ourselves permission to parent our children. Many times, as we're finding our way in the journey of raising children, we don't realize just how much we're waiting for others' approval or permission. So I'd like to grant it to you now.

- You have permission to place limits and boundaries on your child's life to protect them from chronic overstimulation or stress. You have permission to do this without guilt.
- You have permission to participate in as few or as many extracurricular activities or commitments as you'd like, depending on how it impacts your family. You have permission to make these decisions separate from what everyone else around you is doing.
- You have permission to say no to certain media, video games, smartphones, or social media platforms until you know your child or adolescent is ready for it. You have permission to do this even if "everyone else" is doing it.

- You have permission to advocate for your child with other adults in their life, even when it feels uncomfortable. You have permission to do this even if other adults criticize you.
- You have permission to do what you need to do to support your child and to parent based on your own values and their unique temperament. You have permission to do this in spite of judgment from others and without having to explain yourself.

CHAPTER 4

THE PARENT'S WORLD

> Promise me you will not spend so
> much time treading water and trying
> to keep your head above the waves
> that you forget, truly forget, how much
> you have always loved to swim.
>
> TYLER KNOTT GREGSON

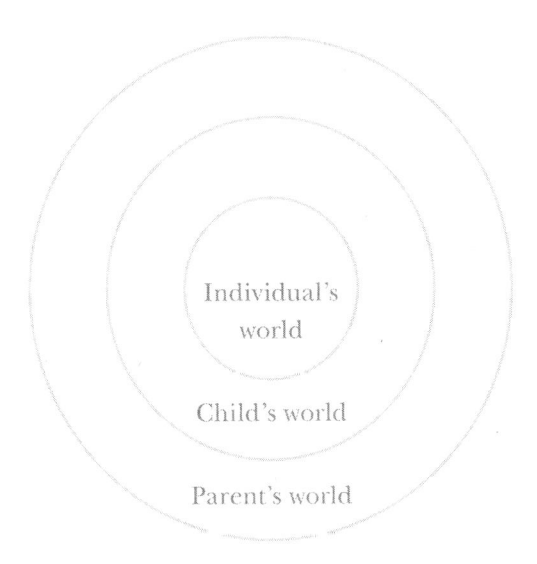

Individual's world

Child's world

Parent's world

Lying on my stomach on my bedroom floor, I had my head under the bed while the rest of my body sprawled across the carpet. The pink duvet rested on my back as I organized my dolls under my bed. I was seven years old and scheming up a new trick that, to my childhood mind, was absolutely genius.

I was playing with a set of Russian nesting dolls. They were a set of five wooden dolls, painted in a pink and gold pattern. The outer doll was the biggest, and each doll inside was successively smaller, down to the last one, which was a tiny wooden baby doll.

Although many people collect these dolls for display and enjoy lining them up next to one another for decoration, that was not my plan.

Under the cover of my bed, I stacked the smallest doll inside the next biggest one. Then I stacked both inside the next one and continued until I'd stacked all the dolls inside the biggest one.

My brilliant plan was to walk around telling my family I couldn't find the baby doll and ask them to help me find it—thinking, to my delight, that I was fooling everyone with this game of hide-and-seek. Then, after they failed to find the tiny baby doll, I would show them with grand gestures and captivating lyrics that the baby was in fact hiding inside the other dolls! (Like I said, absolute genius.)

I might not have fooled anyone in my family, but my young heart loved that these dolls could hide inside the world of the bigger dolls.

This longing is the same one our children have in real life. For parents, our child's world exists within our world—what's going on in our lives, how we feel about and navigate these events, the emotional coping tools we have access to, what our child is exposed to, and how we show up in relationship to them. We can't build an emotionally healthy family without becoming emotionally healthy parents.

This may feel like a lot of pressure at times. It may bring up anxiety about not measuring up or fear of messing up our children. But it also invites us into an unparalleled opportunity to build a healthy foundation for future generations.

Sometimes the pressure we feel about parenting comes not just from theory but from a tender experience of being hurt, scared, or ignored by a parent when we were growing up. Now, taking on the role of parent ourselves, we're deeply afraid that we'll repeat the pain or make our children feel the way we felt. This fear can quickly drive us into self-doubt and overwhelm.

None of us are perfect. Yet when someone with a critical role in a child's life (such as a parent) is consistently hurtful through their words or actions, it isn't just their imperfection that is hurtful. It's their lack of self-awareness, lack of responsibility for their actions, or lack of desire to repair.

If you have pain in your relationship with a parent, it's likely not just because of something they said to you once when they lost their temper. Rather, it's likely because they didn't have the self-awareness to know that those words were deeply painful to you or because they made no effort to apologize, take responsibility, or try to change their hurtful behavior.

It's often the lack of self-awareness or ability to repair that causes harm in a parent-child relationship. This is why perfection is not required to be a healthy parent. You will make mistakes—a lot of them. We all will, because we're human beings. But your self-awareness, your ability to take responsibility for the times you mess up, and your desire to repair will make you an emotionally healthy parent.

> We can't build an emotionally healthy family without becoming emotionally healthy parents.

You need emotional capacity left over for your child.

Throughout the rest of this chapter, we'll look at cultivating a deeper self-awareness of your own emotions in order to cultivate an emotionally healthy home.

Emotional Reactions

"I just feel like a horrible parent, and I worry I'm messing up my kids . . ."

Kristen was sharing her experience of family life with three rambunctious young boys. "I wake up every morning promising to do better," she shared. "Yet every single day, I lose it." Kristen was the primary parent to her three boys. Although her husband was involved, he traveled a lot for work, and most of the day-to-day responsibilities fell to her. In addition, she worked five days a week in health-care administration. Her days were spent getting kids out the door to preschool and school, working, picking up the kids, and doing the nighttime routine by herself most evenings. Weekends were a blur as she tried to catch up on chores and drove her boys to sports or outdoor activities.

Things were going along okay for a while, but recently Kristen had been selected for a promotion at work. It was something she'd really wanted, but it was requiring a lot more bandwidth than her previous position. She'd hoped her husband would step up with the kids, but he seemed unaware or even unwilling to do so, and tension was building in their marriage.

Kristen's oldest son was struggling in school, and his teacher called a meeting to suggest getting him assessed for learning differences. On top of this, her father was in the hospital, and they weren't sure how long he would live. Kristen had a particularly difficult relationship with her father, who had been physically and emotionally abusive toward her family when she was a child. Now that he was on his deathbed, she was experiencing flashbacks from her childhood and wrestling with a mess of emotions.

Is it any wonder Kristen wasn't responding to her children the way she wanted to?

Although the specific circumstances might be different, Kristen's story is not an isolated one.

One of the most common struggles for parents is how to navigate their emotional reactions toward their children.

Parents are often filled with shame and guilt over their big emotional responses. They don't want to react the way they do, but no matter how hard they try, they keep lashing out in impatience, frustration, or anger.

Although it can sometimes feel as if our children are causing our overstimulation and stress—the baby is endlessly crying, the children are always fighting with one another, the teenager is being disrespectful—the truth is, there are often many factors under the surface that drive our intense emotional reactions, as we discussed in chapter 1.

Cultivating awareness of what's propelling our intense emotions is one of the best ways to figure out how to support ourselves and show up for our children with humor and grace.

The Overstimulation Iceberg

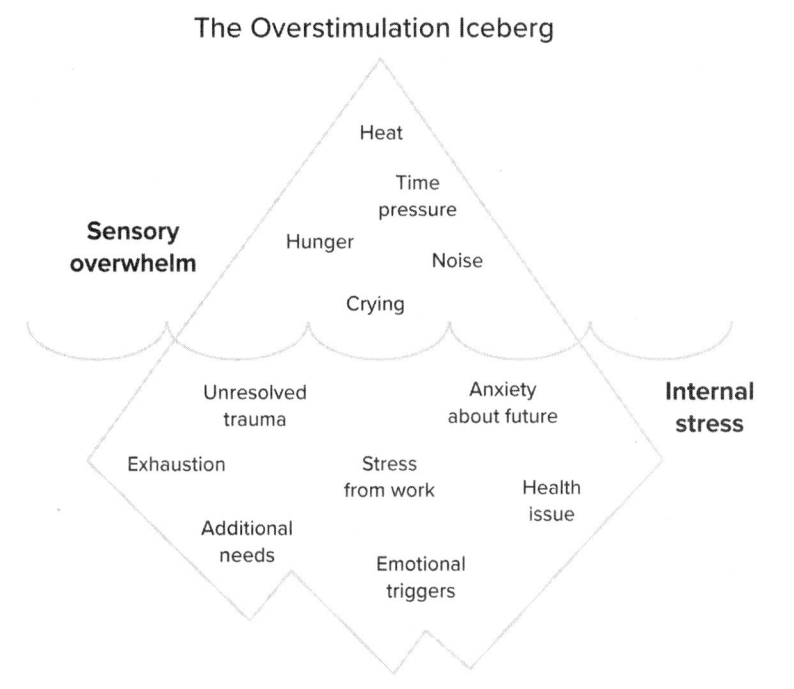

Sensory overwhelm
- Heat
- Time pressure
- Hunger
- Noise
- Crying

Internal stress
- Unresolved trauma
- Anxiety about future
- Exhaustion
- Stress from work
- Health issue
- Additional needs
- Emotional triggers

There are four main areas that drive parents' big emotional reactions.

Factors That Contribute to Parental Dysregulation

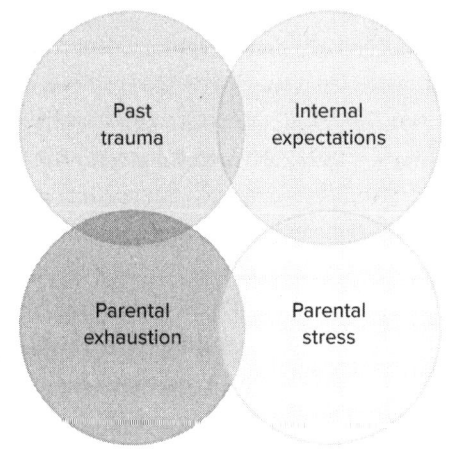

- Past trauma
- Internal expectations
- Parental exhaustion
- Parental stress

Because we're all unique individuals with unique experiences, these drivers will not be equal for each parent. For some, past trauma drives most of their emotional reactions; for others, it may be exhaustion; for others, it may be a stressful situation at work. Note that these can change over time as we navigate different seasons of life.

Varying Factors for Each Individual

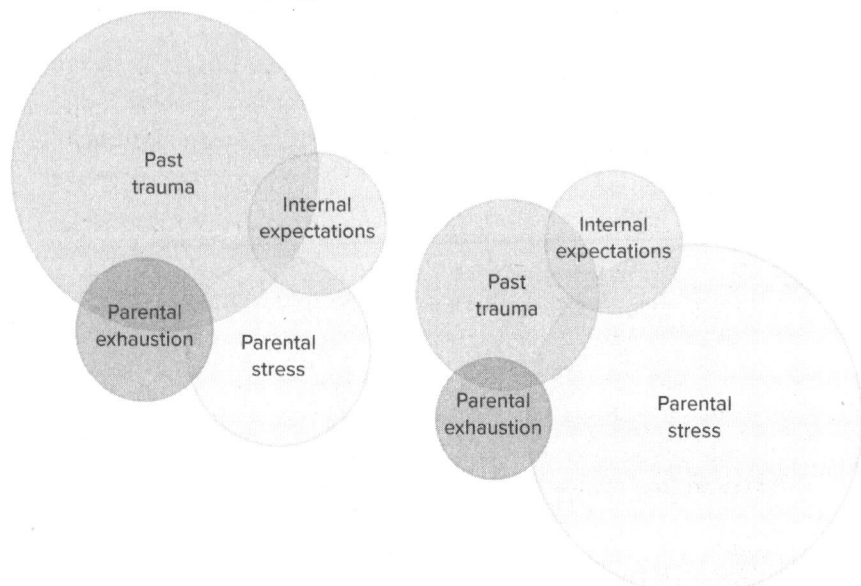

As we become aware of what's driving our heightened emotional reactions, we are empowered to find support in those areas so we can calm our own overstimulation and stress, and then have the margin to respond to our children with patience and grace.

Past Trauma

For years after my cancer journey, I felt on edge and anxious about any type of doctor's appointment, checkup, or test. Even though I'd been given the all clear, I anxiously braced myself for horrible news before any routine appointment.

One evening after work, Colin and I went grocery shopping to pick up some things to make dinner. I left my phone in the car so we could catch up about our day without interruption. We walked back to the car, joking and chatting. While Colin loaded the groceries into the trunk, I sat down in the passenger's seat to check my phone. There was a missed call and a voicemail from my primary care doctor after a routine visit. My heart started racing, and I felt like I couldn't breathe. My palms got sweaty, and the noise around me became muffled.

An after-hours call couldn't be good news—or maybe it was nothing? I tried to calm myself while I listened to the voicemail. Meanwhile, Colin jumped into the driver's seat, still chatting. As he started the car, he asked me if I wanted the fish or chicken for dinner. I screamed (very loudly) at him, "I don't even care! Make whatever you want. Can't you just work it out?" He was shocked by my overreaction.

"Jeez, I was just asking . . . What's wrong with you?"

It wasn't until I heard my doctor say that I might benefit from some vitamin supplements, as one of my levels was slightly low, that my whole body breathed a sigh of relief. It wasn't bad news.

Then came the inevitable cascade of emotions—relief, grief for the journey I'd had to navigate, and guilt about the way I'd reacted toward Colin.

Before being diagnosed with cancer, I didn't have this kind of emotional reaction to medical appointments or tests. But after receiving life-altering news out of the blue, my body was now on high alert, even when it didn't need to be.

Significant situations from our past can influence our emotional reactions in the present. Even when we know rationally that the painful situation is behind us, our nervous system and emotions are often easily triggered by current-day circumstances that remind us of something traumatic from the past. Trauma can stem from a specific event (sometimes resulting in post-traumatic stress disorder, or PTSD), or it can be related to chronic childhood trauma or emotional neglect (sometimes resulting in complex post-traumatic stress disorder, or C-PTSD). We are often more aware of trauma when it's connected to a specific painful event. Complex PTSD is more challenging to disentangle when it's connected to long-term experiences or close relationships with people who loved us and also deeply hurt us.

You might not connect your big reaction toward your nine-year-old's quest for independence and the emotions that override your nervous system with your relationship with your parents. Yet this may be a response from trauma.

When we have significant trauma in our past, our nervous system may be locked in a chronically stressed state, leading to sensitivity to overstimulation.

Past pain and trauma live with us in the present day and affect our relationships, work, and daily life. Yet what many don't realize is that the experience of parenting can trigger past trauma, sometimes more significantly than other life events do. This occurs either because our trauma was connected to our own childhood or because raising children is so overstimulating that the noise triggers our chronically stressed nervous system.

As our child moves through different developmental stages, we might find that certain stages trigger us more than others. For example, we might be coping all right in the early years, but when our child hits eight years old, we might feel flooded with memories or past pain.

Some individuals find it intimidating to even become a parent because of their fear that they will do to their child what was done to them. The process of becoming a parent can be triggering in itself.

If you have a history of childhood trauma, it's important to acknowledge the great courage required to even become a parent. This courage may not be visible to others, but I applaud you for daring to believe in the possibility of goodness, even when what was shown to you was pain. You are bravely writing a new story for the next generation.

> You have the opportunity to bravely write a new story for the next generation.

When you have trauma in your past—particularly if it hasn't been processed yet—it can significantly impact your daily life and your threshold for overstimulation. Without warning, you may become flooded by overwhelming memories and negative emotions, which lead to unconscious reactions. It's normal to be highly reactive to daily life events in the wake of trauma.

The challenge for you as a parent is that your child doesn't know you're internally fighting these memories or emotions—all they know is their experience of your reactions toward them.

As painful as it is, in order to create an emotionally healthy home, we need to face our past and process it with safe people so we can move forward. The good news is that there's a way forward out of the pain and confusion. Don't believe your thoughts when they tell you that what you went through isn't that big of a deal or that you're just not trying hard enough to stop your big emotional reactions.

What you need to deal effectively with trauma is a safe space to process the past. This will help you find closure and integrate a new narrative that will lead to resilience and emotional health in your own life—and in the lives of your children.

Your healing can change the pattern for the next generation.

Therapy

If you've identified trauma in your past, the next step is to find a licensed mental health professional. Try to find someone you feel safe with and who has the background and expertise to support you through your specific challenges. If you have abuse or significant trauma in your past, it's particularly important to process this with someone who is trained to support you through the journey.

Therapeutic Journaling

Research indicates that journaling in a specific way can significantly reduce negative emotions and increase mental and physical well-being. Therapeutic journaling is the process of writing down unedited thoughts and feelings about personal experiences. This practice reduces the suppression of negative emotions and provides a safe space for them to be expressed.

This journaling practice, developed by social psychologist James W. Pennebaker, has been proven to deal with upsetting, stressful, or traumatic life events.[1] Start by choosing one stressful or traumatic experience you'd like to process. Then write about the experience, without editing, for fifteen to thirty minutes. Repeat this process for the next four days, writing about the same experience each time. Studies show that although you may experience an increase in negative emotions in the short term, as the expressive writing brings the traumatic experience to the forefront of your mind, it creates significant positive benefits for mental and physical well-being in the long term.[2]

Parental Exhaustion

Four weeks after having my second baby, I hit a wall. I was sitting in the cool early-morning sun on our apartment balcony, holding my newborn daughter, who was finally asleep after waking every forty minutes throughout the night. My toddler son was upset, pulling on my sweater because he wanted my attention.

And I was in tears. Not the kind of tears that glisten down your cheeks and look pretty in movies, but the red-eyes, nose-dripping, bawling-your-eyes-out, ugly kind of tears.

I felt like I was failing at everything. Parenting was too hard, and I was failing my son for not giving him the attention he needed. I was failing my daughter, who never seemed to want to sleep. I was failing my husband, as I was always short with him, finding myself more and more angry with the demands of this new season. And this was my life now. I needed to look after these children, support our growing business, and somehow manage to shower and keep our house manageable. I was failing at *all* the things I felt responsible for. Life felt very dark.

Colin came out to the balcony to try to comfort me. As he listened to my emotional ranting and realized all his encouragement was falling on deaf ears, he took our baby from my arms and walked me to bed. He closed the door and told me to sleep for a while. After lying in bed feeling guilty about taking a break, I eventually fell asleep. Just over ninety minutes later, I awoke to the sound of giggles from my toddler. As I walked into the living room, I found that both children were happy, the sun was shining, and the world felt new again.

The sleep deprivation that comes from having a newborn is more intense than training for the Navy SEALs. During training, Navy SEALs are sleep deprived for five days.[3] In contrast, the average newborn doesn't sleep through the night until they're three to six months old. Then there's the night waking for diapers, nightmares, wet beds, and sickness, along with all the other demands of life. If you have multiple children, these experiences are layered on top of one another.

The thing that no one tells you going into parenting is that life goes on. So you didn't sleep last night? You still need to get up and go to work today. You still need to look after these children all day. Life doesn't pause because you need to catch up on sleep; it just keeps moving.

Exhaustion can come from sleep deprivation, but it can also come from the nonstop emotional demands of parenting.

Meeting everyone's needs is exhausting.

Staying calm when everyone else is screaming is exhausting.

Organizing home life to make sure there are meals, clean laundry, and a relatively clean house is exhausting.

Doing all of this while managing adult demands is exhausting.

As parents, we tend to beat ourselves up when we overreact or behave in a way we wouldn't normally behave. We condemn ourselves as horrible parents, but the truth is, we're just exhausted. What we need to do is apologize, take a hot bath, and get a good night's sleep.

One of the greatest gifts for children and families is to have parents who take care of themselves.

Short Naps

Most of us know how important it is to prioritize a good night's sleep. Yet when we are in seasons of parenthood that interrupt our ability to get a full night of sleep, we need to consider taking a short daytime nap.

The sweet spot to get the most benefit is to take a short nap of less than twenty minutes or a longer nap of sixty to ninety minutes (naps between thirty and sixty minutes sometimes result in a groggy feeling).[4] Taking a short nap has been shown to increase alertness, memory, creativity, and emotional restoration. So if your children are asleep (or old enough to play alone safely), consider setting an alarm on your phone and taking a short nap.

Mindfulness Practice

Studies show that regular mindfulness practice activates compassion centers in our brains, reduces the risk of depression by 50 percent, and helps guard against Alzheimer's. It's a restorative practice for the brain.[5]

In order to practice mindfulness, focus your attention on the present. You can use mindfulness as you sit, eat, walk, smell, breathe, listen, or see. It's about paying attention to what's happening within you and around you in the moment.

A simple mindfulness exercise is called 5-4-3-2-1. Notice five things you can see, four things you can feel, three things you can hear, two things you can smell, and one thing you love.

A regular mindfulness practice activates your parasympathetic nervous system, causing your body to return to calm. This will give you an increase in focus and emotional capacity to relate lovingly to others.

Parental Stress

It was 8:00 a.m. on a Monday morning, and Claire was racing through traffic to drop off her two teenagers at school. After a weekend of driving them to all their commitments and trying to keep her cool through their back talk and roller-coaster mood swings, she was almost relieved to go back to work.

After navigating school drop-off, Claire started mentally going through her workday as she made the short commute to her office. Working as a marketing manager for a large corporate company, Claire oversaw a large team and a significant budget. She had only three meetings scheduled for the day, but her boss had added another meeting at the last minute. He was looking for an update on a project that wasn't going well.

Arriving in the parking garage a few minutes before work, Claire checked her email for the first time since the weekend. A hundred emails downloaded, including one about a budget oversight and another about a new project with a tight deadline. A feeling of dread hit her in the stomach, as she knew it would take almost all day to answer all the messages. Looking for quick relief, she checked Instagram, where she saw her friend on an overseas holiday, an influencer with a perfect house, and a new product she wondered if she needed.

Realizing that this wasn't helping, Claire took another deep breath and began the walk into the office, anticipating an incredibly busy day. Then she received multiple text messages from her daughter's school, letting her know there would be a special midday performance for the music class on Thursday and that all parents were encouraged to attend—and sign up to bring food. It was only 8:30 a.m.

It's incredibly stressful to be a parent in our world. This isn't to say previous generations weren't stressed and didn't deal with significant challenges, but the addition of technology and interconnectivity brings with it a unique set of challenges that can be particularly overwhelming and exhausting for parents.

The prefrontal cortex of the brain, or PFC (sometimes called the executive brain), is primarily involved in setting goals, making plans, setting priorities, and solving problems. It's also the gatekeeper for our emotional self-regulation and self-control. The challenge is that the PFC has a limit to how much information it can hold at one time—around four to seven pieces of information.[6] It also has limited energy, because it quickly consumes glucose and oxygen. This means there are limits to our clear thinking, problem-solving, and self-regulation. When we hit these limits, we feel exhausted, we can't think clearly, and we have a lower tolerance for managing our emotions.[7] If we can take a break from the amount of information we require our brain to process, the PFC will recharge, and we will regain capacity again.

The sheer amount of information and incoming stimuli we're required to process on a daily or even hourly basis is significantly draining to the PFC. Adding to this, we often don't get the chance to take a break from processing this information, so we're left feeling exhausted, unclear in our thinking, and with a low tolerance for managing our emotions. On top of this, there are all the usual stressors of being an adult in the world—navigating the world of work, managing finances and health, caring for aging parents, or dealing with any number of unforeseen situations that come into our lives. It is no wonder we all feel exhausted.

Becoming aware of our own stress and finding strategies to steer through it leads us to feel healthier emotionally and to have capacity left over to give to our children.

Limits on Technology

One of the best ways we can support ourselves is to create boundaries around technology. This means we intentionally limit how much information we're exposed to when possible. It also means giving ourselves permission to take breaks and come back to problems rather than feeling pressure to keep pushing through.

Limiting technology could look like disabling email or social media notifications on your phone, silencing group messages so you don't get notifications every time someone texts, putting your phone away at night, and not checking your phone first thing in the morning.

Another way to put guardrails around technology is to ignore your phone when you're already overstimulated and stressed (rather than pick it up, as we are all tempted to do!). While we may hope to find something lighthearted and entertaining, we are also being continually exposed to endless amounts of information.

Centering Prayer and Spiritual Practices

A study of Franciscan nuns who practiced centering prayer for more than fifteen years showed that the nuns had increased frontal lobe activity and a decrease in limbic activity on neurological scans.[8] This means they experienced a more peaceful state, with an ability to think more clearly and a higher capacity for regulating their emotions.

Regular spiritual practices are restorative for the brain. Individuals who engage in regular spiritual practices are more focused, alert, empathetic, socially aware, and self-regulated.[9]

In order to practice centering prayer, begin by choosing one word or phrase from Scripture that is meaningful to you, such as *God*, *love*, or *Shepherd*. Then set a timer for five to twenty minutes. With your eyes closed, sit in silence and consider this word. When distracting thoughts come, gently return your focus to that word.

Internal Expectations

"Fine, *I'll* just do it then!" I started wrestling with the trash bag, trying to detach it from our kitchen trash bin. In my frustration and anger, I was being louder than necessary, making a big deal about the fact that I was the one doing this task.

Fifteen minutes earlier, as I was cleaning up the kitchen, I'd asked Colin to take the trash out. He said he would, so I went back to wiping down the kitchen bench.

After ten minutes, he still wasn't anywhere near the trash. I walked out to our backyard to find him cleaning the barbecue—something he'd started doing *after* I'd asked him to take out the trash. My frustration was rising, and my breathing was getting shallower as I tried to ask nicely if he'd take care of the trash. Again, he said he would.

After a few more minutes, I was back in the kitchen, making my frustration obvious to everyone around me.

Colin and I had different expectations. I expected that when he said he'd take out the trash, he would do it immediately. He expected that he could do it sometime that afternoon.

The expectations we hold of ourselves and others are the driving force behind most of our frustration and disappointment. As Anne Lamott says, "Expectations are resentments waiting to happen."[10]

Expectations become even trickier and more complicated when it comes to parenting our children, because we know that in order to thrive, children need both strong boundaries and deep connection with their parents. As parents, our role is to create boundaries that will not only keep our children safe but also help them thrive into adulthood.

There's a difference between boundaries and expectations. A boundary is a clear and communicated standard for behavior. For example, if you say, "We don't hit other people when we feel angry," this boundary creates physical and emotional safety for everyone in the family unit.

Expectations, on the other hand, are internal beliefs that certain behaviors or events will occur. Expectations are often unconscious and not explicitly discussed.

If your family has a boundary of not hitting other people when you feel angry, you may carry certain expectations about this boundary.

Parent 1 might expect that their child will never hit anyone, no matter what. Parent 2 understands that it's developmentally normal for younger children to hit others if they get angry.

Now consider both parents' emotional reactions when their child hits another child. Parent 1 will likely feel shocked, angry, scared, and even worried that their child has anger issues. Parent 2, on the other hand, will likely feel more balanced in their own emotional response because they are expecting developmentally typical behavior from their child. Both parents need to reinforce the boundary that we don't hit other people when we feel angry, yet parent 2 will be in a far calmer state to be able to respond to their child.

We carry numerous internal expectations with us every day, from the way we expect our spouse to co-parent with us to how our home should look or feel to how friendships should work to how our children should act and feel.

Some of these expectations are helpful, as they drive us to create clean homes, healthy meals, and strong relationships. Yet some of these expectations cause us great unhappiness. Perfectionists in particular (yes, my hand is up!) often struggle with unrealistic expectations of ourselves and others.

The Practice of Reflection

The first step in navigating our expectations is to make them conscious. Carl Jung said, "When an inner situation is not made conscious, it happens outside, as fate."[11] The frustrations we experience on a regular basis may hold a key to some unconscious expectations. Start by writing down a situation you are constantly frustrated about.

- What are your expectations of yourself?
- What are your expectations of your spouse?
- What are your expectations of your child?

Once you've written down your expectations surrounding this situation, take a moment to reflect on your expectations.

- Are these expectations realistic?
- Are these expectations appropriate considering the age and developmental stage of your child?
- Where did these expectations come from (family of origin, peers, online sources)?
- Are there real-life limits that make these expectations unrealistic for you in this season?
- Are these expectations beneficial for you and your child?

Many times, the act of bringing your expectations into conscious thought is enough for you to find grace and patience for yourself and others.

After hitting what felt like an emotional breaking point, Kristen reached out to a friend who had mentioned finding a great psychologist. At her friend's referral, Kristen booked a therapy session. In the first session alone, Kristen gained new perspective about why she was feeling the way she was feeling. She was grateful to have a safe space to process her relationship with her father and get professional insight about navigating her son's learning differences.

Kristen's psychologist suggested that she start a personal journaling practice as a way to process painful memories she kept returning to. Through this ongoing practice of journaling, Kristen realized there was too much stress and exhaustion in her daily life and that she needed to make a change. Prioritizing an early bedtime and morning walks instead of late-night Netflix binges, she began to find margin in small ways.

As a result of the support she received in therapy, she was able to share some things with her father, and she found some peace in their relationship before he passed away.

A few months later, Kristen's husband, who was initially skeptical about therapy, agreed to attend a session to support her. Finding the session helpful, he agreed to also do some marital counseling to talk about sharing the load more. Although they had a long journey ahead, they began to have more open dialogue about expectations in marriage and parenting.

After six months, Kristen felt completely different about her life. She was more connected to her family and felt calmer in her everyday life. It was only then that Kristen noticed she had been showing up differently for her three boys. She wasn't losing her patience nearly as often as before, and she even found herself laughing at their crazy antics (rather than wanting to scream). She was walking her son through his learning difference with compassion and sharing bits of wisdom from therapy and journaling with her whole family.

Kristen's boys might not have known the specifics of everything that was going on in her world in the months before, but they could see a big difference in the way she was now. By taking care of herself, Kristen had created a new level of peace, joy, and emotional health for her whole family.

What's Driving Your Emotional Reactions?

These reflection questions can help you cultivate awareness of what may be driving your emotional reactions. You can return to these questions at any time, as your emotional reactions may be driven by different factors in different seasons.

Once you're aware of what area is affecting you most, you can work to resolve it as much as you can.

Past Trauma

- Are there past traumatic circumstances in your life that you still need to process?
- Are there memories that keep looping in your mind?
- Do you feel terrified that you will mess this parenting thing up or hurt your children in the same way you were hurt?

Exhaustion

- When was the last time you had a full night's sleep?
- If you were to lie down right now with no interruptions, how likely would you be to fall asleep?
- When did you last have time off just for yourself?

Stress

- Are there circumstances in your life that are making you worried or anxious?
- Are these worries interfering with your sleep or relationships?
- If you could magically resolve a situation that's causing you stress, how would you feel?
- Are there aspects of your circumstances that you could change?

Internal Expectations

- Are there situations in your family life that you're consistently frustrated about?
- What are your expectations in those situations?
- How realistic are your expectations of yourself and others? Are there areas where you struggle with perfectionism?
- Are your expectations helping or hindering your relationship with others and yourself?

CHAPTER 5
THE STATE OF THE WORLD

> When despair for the world grows in me
> and I wake in the night at the least sound
> in fear of what my life and my children's
> lives may be, . . . I come into the peace
> of wild things. . . . For a time I rest in
> the grace of the world, and am free.
> WENDELL BERRY

Individual's world

Child's world

Parent's world

State of the world

As I looked out our kitchen window, I could see what seemed like our entire neighborhood walking in the same direction.

They were dressed from head to toe in red, white, and blue, and their children rode decorated bikes and carts with streamers and signs.

I quickly gathered our family and followed the crowd. As we walked, I noticed that almost every house had an American flag displayed in the front yard, along with other red, white, and blue decorations.

We turned the corner toward the main road in our suburb and found it shut down by local police as hundreds of people gathered for a neighborhood parade, complete with a marching band, fire engines, and any child who wanted to join on their bikes. Loud music was playing, and people were cheering and generally having a great time.

As the parade finished, we followed the crowd to our local park, which was decked out with bounce houses, carnival rides, and street food. I was shocked because this was just our local neighborhood—similar celebrations were happening in neighborhoods all across the country.

It was our first Fourth of July living in the USA.

I had known about Independence Day, but I had no idea what it meant. Since I didn't grow up in the US, I assumed the holiday would be more like Australia Day (Australia's equivalent of the Fourth of July). On Australia Day, there are fireworks displays in bigger cities at night, but aside from that, most Australians are happy with an afternoon barbecue and a holiday from work and school.

The culture we live in frames our expectations, what we assume to be normal, and what we believe. Many times we don't notice these influences because they're the water we're swimming in. It's not until we visit another culture and immerse ourselves in their way of life that we notice the nuances of the culture we live in.

This is true when it comes to different countries and cultures, and it's also true when it comes to different generations.

Messages from Our Culture

Every generation lives in a different cultural context. What we understand or believe about ourselves, our family relationships, our education, and our faith is heavily influenced by the culture we live in and the generation we're part of.

Just as the child's world is framed by the parents' world, the parents' world is framed by the culture they live in.

Some cultural ideologies in our world have the potential to undermine the emotional health of families. As parents, we need to become aware of these messages so we can be empowered to resist them and help our children live in a countercultural way.

We will explore three messages from our culture in this chapter:

- a culture of fear
- a culture of mistrust
- a culture of self-doubt

A Culture of Fear

The generations born after 1997 (often referred to as Gen Z and Gen Alpha) have sometimes been labeled as fearful generations. Critics say that they're weak, and many young people label themselves as pessimistic. These labels come from their reluctance to get their driver's license or date or be proactive about social engagements. For young adults, this reluctance often plays out in their hesitation to travel, have children, get a job, or buy a house.

If it's true that this generation wrestles with more fear than previous generations, the question isn't why they're so fearful but how could they *not* be?

This generation grew up and went through key developmental years during one of the greatest rates of change in history.[1] We moved from living in a world that was connected locally to a world that's connected globally.

I was born in the early eighties and was part of the generation that got home internet (which took hours to load) when I was in high school. The exciting change in my developmental years was being able to access encyclopedias on the computer rather than going to the library.

With the limited technology my generation was exposed to, there was natural protection from overexposure to information. I had no idea what was going on around the world or what economies were collapsing or who had killed who, aside from what I occasionally saw on the nightly news. These realities felt so far away from my own life that they almost seemed like they were happening in another universe.

Fast-forward to today, and the world events children are discussing with one another in elementary school are far broader and more in depth than what past generations even had awareness of until young adulthood.

It used to be that people had to seek out news about what was happening around the world. But with the development of the internet, 24/7 cable news channels, and social media, we are now endlessly exposed to it.

These sources of information quickly turned into businesses that need to increase advertising to be profitable. This means that sharing information is not purely factual but overwhelmingly driven by a narrative of fear. That's because one of the most addictive forms of sales and marketing is fear. The marketing formula goes like this: tap into a person's greatest fear, then tell them that it's even worse than they think, and then sell them the solution. The voice that wins isn't the one that's the wisest or the most educated or possesses the most proven research; it's the one that's louder than the others (and often the most controversial).

The environment we've been living in for the past two decades has been overwhelmingly influenced by messages of fear—about almost any topic. Fear leads us to avoid what we're scared of, and over time, this avoidance only increases the fear we're experiencing.

Unprocessed fear and trauma ultimately lead to pessimism and despair about the future. If the world (or my world) is probably going to end, what's the point of anything?

One of the unexpected things I experienced in the aftermath of my cancer journey was that for a while, I felt tentative about making plans for my future. Confronting something so scary and traumatic caused me to believe that nothing was guaranteed, and I no longer had a clear, inspiring vision for my future. Sometimes you're hit with the emotions only after the traumatic event because then it's finally safe to process what happened. It wasn't until I was told that the cancer was in remission that I had space to process those feelings.

Many people experienced this globally when the pandemic hit. While our lives were halted, we were overwhelmed with fear and loss, often living in survival mode. It wasn't until the world reopened that we realized the depth of our exhaustion and the lack of vision and passion we felt for the future.

We are constantly bombarded by cultural messages of fear, which often lead to feelings of pessimism about the future without our even realizing what's happening. We need to reframe our thinking with a countercultural message of hope—for ourselves and the next generation.

A COUNTERCULTURAL MESSAGE OF HOPE

When we experience fear or anxiety, it drives us to avoid what we're afraid of. Yet if we consistently choose avoidance, our anxiety grows. The only way to overcome fear is to face it. We must confront the very thing that scares us.

For us as parents, this may mean confronting the cultural narrative that says negative things about our children's generation or makes us fearful about the world they will inherit. Confronting this fear may look like resisting these beliefs through reframing them. For example:

> "My children were created to navigate the challenges of this time and make a positive change for the next generation."
> "This generation is called for such a time as this."
> "My children are resilient and strong. They are problem solvers, good friends, and amazing humans."

We need to encourage our children and teens to face the things that scare them. If they are consistently allowed to avoid what makes them anxious, their anxiety will only grow. As they take small steps with our empathetic support, they can learn to do the things that scare them.

Tackling our own fears or helping our children through their anxiety may feel like an ongoing task. But as we face our fears and reframe the narratives we've been given, we push back the darkness, one day, one decision, at a time.

No matter what we're walking through, there is always hope. It may be hiding in the darkness, beneath fear or grief. But if we keep walking and searching, we will eventually find it again.

One of the biggest mistakes people make about resilience is when they confuse it with mental strength. They mistakenly believe that being resilient means being strong enough to keep going no matter how challenging the circumstances are, without being affected by them. This is apparently the goal: to be untouchable.

The truth is, resilience is a far more complex process than that. It's natural and healthy to have feelings of disorientation, grief, fear, and pessimism when confronted by an emotionally upsetting event. In fact, from a psychological perspective, there's concern when someone doesn't have these emotional reactions, as they are either in shock or emotional suppression, or they may even have a personality disorder (such as being a sociopath).

If your best friend lost a loved one and they weren't disoriented, angry, fearful, or sad, you would be more concerned than if they were expressing these emotions.

I call this the "messy middle" of resilience. No one escapes this stage, where our emotions are strong and unpredictable, grief is present, and uncertainty about the future feels as if it may envelop us. No one can say with any certainty how long the messy middle will last. It depends on how deep the loss is, how disorienting it is, and whether the situation has closure.

> It's the individuals who wrestle with the messy middle who find hope again over time.

It's the individuals who wrestle with the messy middle who find hope again over time. Embracing the messiness may look like feeling your feelings, reaching out for support from therapy and your community, and giving yourself time and permission to explore a different possible future. Over time, these individuals "bounce back" to their previous level of functioning. This is the true definition of resilience—not that you never experience negative feelings but that you choose to face them and continue until you find hope again. Resilience is the resolve to not settle in a season of pain or allow it to be the end of your story. It's a decision to keep moving toward a beautiful future.

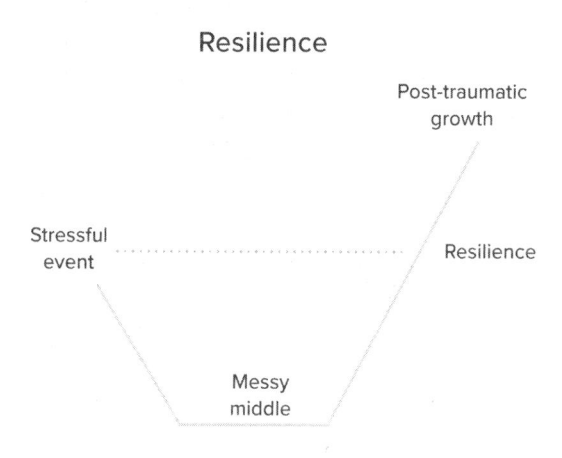

Resilience

- Stressful event
- Post-traumatic growth
- Resilience
- Messy middle

THE GIFT OF POST-TRAUMATIC GROWTH

One of the redemptive things that can happen after we experience pain or trauma and walk through the healing process is personal growth. This is referred to as *post-traumatic growth*.

Individuals who undergo post-traumatic growth report that after going through a stressful or traumatic experience, they developed closer relationships with loved ones, a deeper connection to their faith, more empathy and compassion for those around them, and deeper gratitude as they navigated life.[2] For these individuals, their suffering caused them to grow.

When asked if they could opt not to have gone through the painful experience, they would share that although they wouldn't wish the pain on anyone, they also wouldn't change their past and are surprisingly grateful they went through it because of the inner growth they achieved.

This was Jenny's story. A homeschooling mother to four children, she was shocked and devastated when she found out her husband had been unfaithful for years and wanted a divorce. Being thrown into the grief of her marriage breaking up while also trying to navigate her children's world changing and trying to keep finances afloat seemed like more than she could bear.

For months, she didn't want to get out of bed. She withdrew from many friendships, as others' judgment and lack of understanding hurt too much, and she felt angry at God for allowing something like this to happen.

After some time, however, life began to feel more stable. The divorce was settled with a clear plan for co-parenting, and she found a part-time job as an administrator for an artist. Jenny also talked with her pastor about her questions and the anger she felt toward God. He talked her through her wrestling and pointed her to some helpful books. Although adjusting to this new normal was painful, she was slowly finding her way through.

Almost two years later, Jenny's pastor approached her after church on Sunday, asking if she would be open to meeting another church member who was going through an unwanted and unexpected marriage breakup. Jenny agreed and felt her heart swell with compassion as she heard this woman's story, knowing the depth of her pain and the path that lay ahead of her. Jenny made a decision to support her through this journey, and regularly reached out to her to schedule meetups.

Over the next few months, more women reached out to Jenny to share their stories, and Jenny decided to create a weekly group meeting in her home for these women to support one another. When the group outgrew her home, Jenny approached her pastor to see if she could host the group at their church.

Now Jenny runs a weekly connection group for women who are walking through divorce, and she has helped hundreds of women over the years. Many of these women have shared that the connection group was a lifeline for them in a dark season of their lives.

Although Jenny never would have chosen the circumstances she and her children faced, she is grateful for the deeper connection she has with others and God, her sense of meaning and purpose, and the opportunity to support others in a unique way.

Perhaps you can relate to this feeling in your own life. You may have walked through a situation you would never wish to repeat, but wrestling with the pain led to a deeper and more meaningful life.

If we want to instill hope in our children, we need to find it for ourselves. Hope is found on the other side of wrestling with pain. So if you haven't found it yet, keep wrestling, because that just means you haven't found your way through yet.

One of the gifts of faith and the spiritual life is that we're reminded our pain isn't wasted and the struggles we're walking through aren't the end of the story. For me, as a Christian, I've found that my faith gives me a sense of hope and certainty, and a framework to make sense of the world. In every painful situation I've faced, my faith has both brought me comfort and been something I've had to wrestle with.

Yet it has been my experience that this wrestling, through long seasons at times, has deepened my faith, giving me a sense of purpose and hope for the future. When I was diagnosed with cancer as a young adult, I wrestled with a lot of questions: *If God is good, why did this happen to me? Why doesn't He just take the pain away? Am I being punished for something?* Although I didn't get clear answers to all my theological questions, what I discovered was the reality of a stable, intimate presence that stayed with me as I walked through the pain. I didn't feel alone.

If you're walking through a particularly difficult time, allow the questions of faith to come to the surface. It's often in our most tender and vulnerable moments that we notice faith for the first time or discover an opportunity to deepen our faith.

A Culture of Mistrust

There's a joke circling the internet that says, "There are two types of people I don't trust: (1) those I don't know and (2) those I know." This is tongue in cheek, of course, but it reflects an underlying message of the culture we're living in: to mistrust others.

This generation experiences feelings of loneliness and isolation more than any previous generation. Over 56 percent of Gen Z Americans reported experiencing these feelings on a semi-regular basis in their childhood, compared with 24 percent of baby boomers.[3]

Even when we're surrounded by people, we may feel disconnected from them. These feelings of disconnection may be due to how little we trust the people around us.

Reports show that levels of mistrust of institutions, government, and individuals continue to rise.[4] This is a growing challenge in our society, where different ideologies, political positions, and economic views often get in the way of our relationships.

Mistrust is an automatic, unconscious neurological response. Our brains have a social network that causes us to understand and connect with ourselves and others. This network classifies people or situations as safe or as a threat.[5] Especially if we don't know someone or if we don't have experience in a particular situation, our brain instantly classifies that person or situation as a threat. And what do we do with all threats? Fight, flight, or freeze.

Consider how you felt on your first day at a new job or a new school. You were probably managing a lot of anxiety and stress. And consider your friends—do you have any close friends you didn't like the first time you met them? This is because our brain naturally classifies people we don't know or new situations as threats until proven otherwise.

That's the key—*until proven otherwise*. If we stay at the new job, we get to know the environment, and in most cases, we realize it's not a threatening situation. If we make the effort to get to know a new person, we might discover they're safe—or perhaps even a friend.

So how do we prove this to our brain? We engage in activities that activate oxytocin—the trust hormone.[6] Studies have shown that people who were given a nasal spray containing oxytocin increased their level of trust toward others.[7] When oxytocin is released, it helps us bond with and trust the people around us. You have heard about oxytocin as it relates to nursing an infant, but oxytocin is also released through giving a hug, exchanging a firm handshake, swapping names and information, or discussing something in common (such as the weather or the traffic). These small actions can increase your feelings of closeness and trust with those around you. Trust is the basic fabric of building relationships. You can't share and hold space with someone if you don't trust them.

As parents, if we don't trust the people around us, it's only natural that we try to protect our children from them. This instinct is a necessary part of good parenting. Our instincts let us know when someone is potentially dangerous or when there is a legitimate threat to our children. Yet we are often unaware of our own unconscious beliefs that assume some people are unsafe when they're actually not.

If we don't trust our neighbors, the other parents at our child's school or activities, the other members of our church or community group, then of course we'll be far more tentative about allowing our children to explore the world outside our home.

Online relationships seem safer. Studies show that parents are more likely to feel judged for how they parent in their real-life relationships (such as their spouse, parents, or in-laws).[8] With online relationships, we tend to connect with others who think about the world the same way we do.

It can be a benefit of the online world to find people whose values and belief systems align with ours. But we also need in-person community—real-life, physical people in our physical space. Although online relationships can offer education, information, wisdom, or a place to meet people, they can't take the place of in-person relationships. They can't show up with a meal or drive your kids to soccer practice. They can't sit with you on your back porch and laugh until neither of you can breathe. They can't hold your hand when you're sitting in a doctor's appointment or sit with you during a season of grief. In-person relationships create a social support that acts as a sort of buffer against life's stressors.[9] Without them, we have no models for real-life friendship, marriage, or parenting.

Real-life relationships are hard and messy. They require emotional bandwidth and are in no way perfect. Yet if our only interactions are online relationships, where much of what is shared is a curated version and it's easy to walk away if there's any disagreement, then our children won't have role models for real-life relationships. Children and adolescents need to see others navigating the ups and downs of genuine friendship, marriage, and parenting.

So much of socialization is watching others and practicing. We see this in children on the playground—they test what is appropriate, which sometimes ends in tension, but they learn to resolve it and interact with others.

Watching others in real life normalizes the ups and downs of real-life relationships. If you know it's normal to feel uncomfortable and scared before you ask someone out on a date, you will know it's just part of the process. If you know it's normal to have disagreements in marriage, you won't think you've married the wrong person just because you have a fight over chores. Real-life relationships help us learn conflict resolution, take responsibility, set boundaries, determine what's most important to us, and extend forgiveness and grace. These are core skills that our children need to build healthy families in the future.

A COUNTERCULTURAL MESSAGE OF TRUST

As parents, we need to go first. If we continue to allow our culture to push us in the direction of mistrust, we'll be left with almost no real-life relationships where we can feel safe. We need to lead our families, doing the relational work of deciding and cultivating safe spaces.

This means evaluating what is a real threat and what is merely a perceived threat, such as someone new or someone with different ideologies or opinions. Then, if there's no true threat, we intentionally move past the initial threat response toward a position of trust.

The easy option is to just walk away (and sometimes this is necessary), but in the long term, it's worth the work to stay and get to know the person on a deeper level, to find common ground, to find places of humanity and connection. Many times, we end up building trust with people we initially weren't sure about.

If you don't currently have a strong community in real life, it probably won't happen automatically—you may have to build it yourself. You could start by joining a local church, community group, sporting organization, or extracurricular activity with the intention of increasing your family's relationships and connections. You might decide that on Saturday afternoons you'll play in the front yard as a family (rather than the backyard) so you can interact with other neighbors or children on your street. You might start a group chat with your neighbors to let them know when you're taking your kids to the park so they can bring their children too. You might open your home regularly to family friends who have children the same age as yours and with similar values so you can cultivate these relationships.

Relationships are built through initiative and frequency. This means you have to be intentional about relationships instead of just waiting for them to happen, and then you need to consistently show up. In our busy lives, this can feel like an overwhelming task, but it can be as simple as deciding to stay after church for twenty minutes to meet people or having pizza once a month with family friends or hosting a potluck with your neighbors. Over time, this commitment will build something beautiful.

You don't have to be best friends with everyone. It is still wise to be intentional about who you're vulnerable with. Yet we need neighbors and acquaintances as much as we need our closest friends. They provide a sense of belonging and safety in the places we call home—for us and our children.

As our culture continues to push us toward mistrust and loneliness, building community for our family is not something that just happens. We have to intentionally build it. There's something honorable and beautiful about putting down roots where you live, about building relationships around your children and grandchildren. Even if you relocate in the future, you are still cultivating a heritage of real-life relationships for your family.

A Culture of Self-Doubt

With the rise of the internet, social media, and AI, our culture has seen a dramatic increase in the information that is easily available to us. We can find information on any topic in the world simply by typing a few words on our phone.

This can be helpful information, such as online education, podcasts, or advice from experts on how to live our best lives. It can also be negative information that scares us and makes us worry about our health, the safety of the world, and the traumatization of our children. The problem isn't just the kind of information out there but also the sheer volume.

The challenge with an overabundance of information is that we might begin to falsely believe that we can get everything right. We think we can avoid the discomfort of wrestling with the messiness of life or the challenges we face in parenting (and the fact that none of us really know what we're doing!).

This oversupply of information can be a fuel for anxiety, because it leads us to believe we can get something just right or even perfect. Someone online has without a doubt found the exact right way to get their child to sleep, the best way to feed their child, and the perfect way to talk with their child. We are constantly inundated with tips from experts about how we should do everything from potty training to meal planning to decluttering our closets. This becomes even more confusing when the "experts" share different (and sometimes even opposite) opinions.

The other problem with all this information is that it leads to an increase in self-doubt. We begin trusting everyone else's opinions instead of listening to our own instincts and trusting that we know our children better than anyone else. We're confused when we follow a certain expert's advice and it doesn't work for us or our children, or we feel the incongruency when we follow someone's advice and it conflicts with our personal values and beliefs. Our world is filled with the noise of so many opinions that we live in chronic doubt of ourselves.

Information can be helpful, but even with all the information in the world, we are still imperfect human beings doing our best to raise imperfect human beings. Many times, the generalized advice doesn't take into account our personal context, our culture, our family, or the unique needs of our children.

Education is powerful, and it's the way we rise to a new standard of living. But education should not come at the expense of listening to our own intuition. Both education and intuition are needed to navigate a healthy life.

Too much information does violence to our souls.

A COUNTERCULTURAL MESSAGE OF INTUITION

Mindi had a gut feeling that something wasn't quite right. Her daughter, Savannah, was in second grade and was having some struggles with reading. Savannah was still reversing letters when she wrote, and she kept complaining about stomach pains and not wanting to go to school.

Mindi took her daughter to the pediatrician to rule out physical reasons for the stomachaches. The doctor assured her there was no physical reason, but they might be caused by anxiety. This confirmed Mindi's intuition that Savannah was struggling more than she was letting on.

Mindi wondered if Savannah might have a learning difference. She set up a meeting with Savannah's teacher. During this meeting, the teacher told Mindi that she really didn't think Savannah had a learning difference. Sure, she was in the bottom reading group in the class and got muddled when she read new passages, but she was still young and would learn these skills over time.

Mindi left the meeting feeling uneasy. She started questioning herself—was she just reading into things? Wouldn't the teacher have confirmed her suspicions if they were true? Maybe she was just overreacting. Mindi stopped pursuing the issue.

Yet as the months went by, Savannah was becoming more and more upset about going to school. She frequently came home in tears because she wasn't keeping up with the rest of the class and she thought she was dumb.

After one afternoon filled with many tears, Mindi decided enough was enough, and she booked a professional assessment for Savannah. Following a long process, Savannah was diagnosed with dyslexia and given interventions and accommodations to support her learning. Savannah was relieved to know that she wasn't dumb but that her brain just processed information in a different way. Mindi felt relieved and validated that she had trusted and followed her intuition so her daughter could thrive

Historically, parenting was an intuitive process. Intuition is a way of arriving at a conclusion based on more than just reason. Research shows that intuition is built up over multiple experiences, over time.[10] After enough practice, we're able to quickly recognize patterns and know something on a subconscious level. This means we often have the greatest intuition in areas where we have the greatest experience.

When it comes to parenting, we can cultivate parental intuition through time and experience with our child. In healthy intuition, after we get a "gut feeling" about something, we begin to look for feedback to confirm or deny this feeling.

Pre-digitally, parents would talk to friends with children or older family members about concerns they were having with their child. Then they'd move on to the family doctor or other professionals.

Now parents' social networks are moving toward online experts and communities. There are many benefits to this (for example, if you're socially isolated and don't have the option of real-life support). But the downside of feedback moving online is that we're often not aware of who is truly an expert. On the internet, the loudest voice wins, not necessarily the one with the most education, experience, or qualifications. This can lead to mistakes in either downplaying or overemphasizing our intuition.

> As a parent, you are the greatest expert on your child. There's no one else in the world who knows them better than you do.

Another downside of online information is that we diagnose our child based only on that information. Although this can be helpful in getting preliminary ideas and finding support, it should never replace a professional diagnosis. There is so much nuance in individuals and diagnoses that we may mistakenly give our child an incorrect label or miss what's really happening.

As a parent, you are the greatest expert on your child. There's no one else in the world who knows them better than you do. We need to strengthen and trust our intuition and then look for feedback to find a way forward. This may mean we start online to get connected with professional services.

We don't need to throw out education; rather, we need to bring education and intuition into balance.

Tuning In to Your Intuition

A big part of tuning in to our intuition is paying attention. Many times, we're already experiencing a gut feeling about something, but the noise or pace of our lives is drowning it out.

Here are some questions to help you tune in to your intuition.

1. If you trusted your intuition completely, what would you do differently in your parenting or with your child?
2. What does your child need most in this season?
3. Is there something about your child or their environment that makes you feel unsettled? Why does it make you feel unsettled?
4. What action do you need to take in this situation, even if it scares you?
5. If you were to stop doubting yourself, what would you feel your inner voice is telling you?

PART TWO

Raising Emotionally Healthy Children

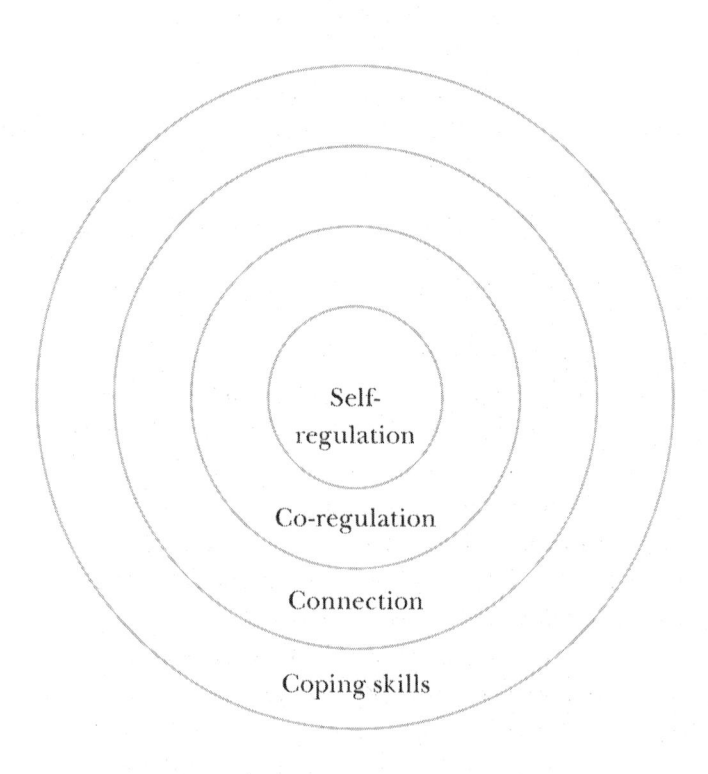

- Self-regulation
- Co-regulation
- Connection
- Coping skills

CHAPTER 6

SELF-REGULATION:
CULTIVATING EMOTIONAL MATURITY

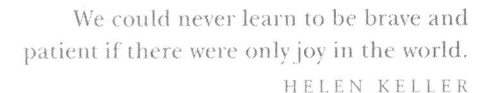

> We could never learn to be brave and
> patient if there were only joy in the world.
> HELEN KELLER

It's 5 p.m. You're exhausted after a long day that followed an interrupted night of sleep. It's still hours before the kids go to bed, and the day is dragging.

In the next few hours, you'll face some of the most demanding parts of your day: making dinner, feeding and bathing children, getting them ready for bed, and then actually making sure they stay in bed and sleep.

The kids are exhausted after a full day. They're screaming, crying, and reactive toward one another.

You might feel like a human taxi, driving them to and from endless activities, all the while attempting to ask them (for the hundredth time) to start their homework. You might be frustrated that your teen is being disrespectful and moody or not talking to you at all. You're breaking up fights and trying to help them calm themselves, all while your name is being screamed over and over and over again.

The exhaustion from your day is rising . . .
The heat from the stove is rising . . .
The crying from your children is rising . . .
It takes just one little thing to send you over the edge.

This is just one of the times in the day when we as parents tend to lose it. We yell, become impatient, say things we wish we hadn't said, and do things we wish we hadn't done. Then everyone else reacts to our reaction, making the situation even worse.

Much later, when we've calmed down and the situation has calmed down, the rage is replaced with a different feeling: overwhelming guilt. We chide ourselves about our failures as a parent until we fall asleep, praying the next day is different.

Is there any other lens through which to see a day like this? If we were to consider this situation (along with the countless other situations that cause us to become overstimulated as parents) with a little more distance—as if our best friend were going through it—would we have more compassion for ourselves? Maybe we aren't a failure as a parent—we just need to be more intentional about our own self-regulation.

The Path to Emotional Health

Self-regulation is "the ability to control your behavior and manage your thoughts and emotions in appropriate ways."[1] It includes being able to handle intense emotions, calm down after something exciting or scary occurs, control your impulses, and focus your attention.

Self-regulation is the foundation of healthy relationships and the cornerstone of physical, mental, and emotional health. It's essentially what helps us become emotionally mature. Without self-regulation skills, we're victims of our impulses and emotions, doing and saying whatever we want, whenever we want. Although this may sound tempting at times, it results in negative fallout and doesn't lead to a meaningful life.

Let me be clear: self-regulation doesn't mean we feel calm all the time, we never get upset or angry, we never feel stressed, and we never experience overstimulation. Rather, we may experience these emotions, but we know what to do so they don't damage our health or relationships in the long term.

As adults, we can cultivate self-regulation in three main areas:

1. Healthy relationships
2. Personal boundaries and practices
3. Strong emotional coping tools

Self-Regulation for Parents

- Healthy relationships
- Personal boundaries and practices
- Strong emotional coping skills

(Self-regulation at center)

Healthy Relationships

I recently had a phone conversation with one of my closest friends. She's someone who has walked alongside me in my darkest moments and celebrated with me in my best moments.

Within minutes of starting our phone conversation, we were laughing our heads off at the ridiculous demands of parenting and adulting in our lives. A moment later, I told her about something complex I was walking through, and she shared about a relationship she was struggling with. Then we were laughing at something again.

It's a gift to have someone in your life who celebrates with you when you're up and doesn't judge you when you're down—to have an uninterrupted conversation with your closest friend. Even if they can't change anything about your situation, just sharing with them lifts a burden off your shoulders and may even enable you to laugh again. This kind of friendship is rare, unfortunately; many people don't know how to give this kind of emotional safety in a relationship. Instead of offering support, friendships are all too often filled with jealousy or negative judgment.

Yet we aren't designed to do life alone—we need others. Safe relationships help us get out of our own head, give us courage during hard seasons, and make life rich and meaningful. Despite all other influences, having close relationships is one of the greatest predictors of health and longevity.

> Having close relationships is one of the greatest predictors of health and longevity.

The Harvard Study of Adult Development is the longest in-depth, longitudinal study on human life to date. Beginning in 1938, it followed a group of participants throughout their lifetime, meeting them at regular intervals for interviews, questionnaires, and collection of health data.[2] The study found that social connectedness at age fifty was a better predictor of physical health than cholesterol levels. It also found that close relationships—not genetics, money, or intelligence—are the factor that predicts happiness levels.[3] As mentioned in chapter 5, social relationships act as a buffer for life's stressors,[4] being linked to stronger immune function and higher quality sleep.[5]

As adults, we have to work at and invest in friendships. My friends and I often laugh at how long it takes us just to set up a phone call or return a message. That's just adult life! But it's worth the effort—prioritizing emotionally safe relationships is one of the best ways we can build our resilience and emotional health.

This may sound great in theory, but it can be challenging to make it happen. You might be in a particularly demanding season when you don't feel like you have energy, time, or margin for relationships. You might not have safe relationships around you, or you might feel lonely despite wanting meaningful connections. This is the reality for many of us at times. There's not something wrong with you—life simply has seasons that ebb and flow. When we're in the season of parenting, we spend far more time with our children, spouse, or coworkers than we do with friends.[6] But as our children mature and grow more independent, we tend to have more time for peer relationships.

Here are some things to keep in mind as you think about prioritizing relationships:

1. **All relationships count toward well-being.** This includes your spouse, children, friends, community, and church—not just your closest friends. Whether it's another parent at preschool drop-off or a coworker you're working with on a project, taking time to connect is beneficial, even if it's just for a few extra minutes.

2. **You don't need a lot of close relationships; you need only one or two.** This may be your spouse or your sibling or a best friend. Brené Brown says, "Social media has given us this idea that we should all have a posse of friends when in reality, if we have one or two really good friends, we are lucky."[7]

3. **If someone's on your mind, let them know.** You don't have to set up a long phone call or a night out together—just sending a quick text to say you're thinking of them and appreciate them can go a long way toward investing in a relationship.

4. **Normalize friendships in context.** You might have some friends you really connect with when it comes to your child and parenting, but you don't have much more in common than that. You might have some friends you really connect with over a sport or hobby but not much else. Give yourself permission to keep that friendship in context without worrying about whether they understand every part of your life.

5. **Leave the guilt.** If your friends are in a similar life situation, they're probably struggling to keep up with their friendships

too. Don't let feelings of guilt for not returning their message or not calling back stop you from reaching out. Most people won't mind—they're just happy to connect with you.

6. **Plan some set times to connect.** Even if it's once a month or once a year for a birthday celebration, try to schedule something. It's more likely to happen if it's on the calendar.

7. **If you're married, keep investing in your friendship with each other.** Your spouse is usually the relationship you spend the most time developing over the course of your life.[8] Having a respectful, loving friendship is a great foundation for thriving through all the seasons of life.

8. **Normalize seasons of loneliness.** There may be times in your life when you don't feel like you have close friends who fully get you or you don't have anyone who feels safe. While this doesn't mean your life is devoid of all relationships, these times can still feel lonely. There's nothing wrong with you if you find yourself in this spot—it won't last forever. During these periods, we can get to know ourselves more deeply and find solace through our faith and our relationship with God.

9. **Acquaintances matter.** Relationships with people you see regularly matter, even if you aren't necessarily close with them. They might be your local barista, the mail carrier, the neighbors down the street, other parents at your kids' school, or your coworkers. Although they may not be your closest friends, research shows that regular contact with these people boosts our well-being and mental health.[9] They're an important part of our relational health.

Personal Boundaries and Practices

I'm not someone who can just go straight to sleep after going to bed. While I envy people with this skill, I've learned that in order to get a good night's sleep, I need about an hour to disconnect from everything, so I like to take a hot bath and slowly ease into bedtime.

I didn't realize how much I needed this routine to sleep well until my husband and I started running a business together. Colin can go to bed and go straight to sleep (so annoying!). Part of his mental preparation for the next day was to run through his upcoming appointments and projects. I would turn off my phone, take a hot bath, and start reading in bed. Then he would enter our room and bring up all the challenges with appointments, projects that needed to be changed, and logistical requests to be addressed. After that, he'd get into bed and go straight to sleep, while I lay there for an hour, thinking about everything he'd just brought up. Let's just say that after many "robust discussions," I communicated that this wasn't going to work for me.

Boundaries are limitations we intentionally place on our lives to help us stay in a place of health. It's the standards that say, "This far, but no further." We all have different boundaries, depending on our values. Our boundaries may include what time we go to bed, what types of food we eat (and don't eat), how much exercise we get, how we allow others to talk to us or treat us, what behavior we tolerate in the workplace, how many commitments we place on our calendars, and the moral decisions we make. Boundaries involve saying no to things that might move us into a place of unhealth.

Practices (sometimes called habits or rituals) are behaviors we engage in on a regular basis that keep us healthy. They may include your morning or bedtime routine, exercise, spiritual disciplines, creative hobbies, journaling, or therapy. Practices involve saying yes to things that might move us into a place of health.

We need both boundaries and practices to keep us balanced and self-regulated. When we keep our boundaries and practices, we are more able to navigate our emotions. When we stay up too late, eat poorly, and overschedule our calendars, and when we stop engaging in life-giving hobbies, spiritual practices, and journaling, we have lower self-regulation and are more likely to behave in ways we will regret.

To find out about other boundaries and practices that support emotional health, you can check out "Practices to Turn Down the Noise" in part 3.

Strong Emotional Coping Tools

When my husband and I first got married, the only tool we owned was a combination hammer and screwdriver. This was okay for a while, because we are both challenged when it comes to home improvement and repair. But as time went on, we began to have a few issues around our home that we couldn't fix. One day my father-in-law came over to help us with a door that didn't close properly. When he asked us for our tools and my husband handed him our hammer (which was also a screwdriver), we couldn't tell if he was shocked, disgusted, or ashamed! The next time we saw him, he gave us an entire box of tools. Suddenly we were able to manage small things more easily because we had the appropriate tools.

No matter how strong our emotions are or how overstimulated we feel, if we have strong emotional coping tools, we are more likely to be self-regulated and able to navigate our feelings. You probably already have some emotional coping tools that you use on a regular basis. The goal is to continue to expand our toolbox of skills so we're equipped to handle whatever overstimulation and stress come our way.

Skills for Your Emotional Toolbox

Consider the emotional coping skills in this section as extra tools to add to your toolbox. These skills have been found to reduce our emotional reactions and increase our ability to deal with overwhelming situations. When we use these frequently, they strengthen not only our self-regulation but also our emotional maturity.

Here are eight coping skills that increase self-regulation. Note that they require practice. As with any skill, they need to be repeated on a regular basis for us to master them and experience the positive impact.

Interrupt the Buildup

When we hit the point of overstimulation or big emotional reactions, our feelings have typically been building for some time.

We've probably been experiencing frustration and stress that we pushed down and managed to stay on top of. But if these feelings keep piling up, they will eventually explode.

Rather than trying to control the moment of explosion, consider interrupting the buildup so you prevent the moment of explosion altogether.

If you consider the moment of explosion to be 10 out of 10, pay attention when your stress levels have built up to around 6 out of 10 or 7 out of 10. This is the moment to intervene.

Interrupt the buildup of stress by doing something that temporarily removes you from the situation and helps you change your emotional state. It's challenging to regulate your stress level while you're still in the situation that's causing you stress. When possible, remove yourself for a moment (while making sure your kids are safe). This might look like locking yourself in the bathroom, hiding in the pantry, or walking into your backyard for a few minutes of peace.

Then intentionally do an activity that changes your emotional state. This might include drinking a glass of water, running your wrists under cold water, watering the garden, texting your friend, reading funny memes, or escaping to watch a short clip of your favorite comedian.

If you notice a pattern that you're consistently being overstimulated during certain times of day, try to put this tool into practice before you hit that time.

Name Your Emotions

When you name what you're feeling, you're giving language and expression to your emotional state. You may have heard the phrase "name it to tame it." Not only does this strategy increase your self-awareness, but it has also been proven to neurologically decrease your stress response.[10]

When we name our emotions, we're activating our prefrontal cortex (the seat of self-control and self-regulation), reducing the unconscious control our feelings have over us.

There's a specific part of the brain that neuroscientists call the brain's "braking system" (the right ventrolateral prefrontal cortex). When this part of the brain is activated, it slows down the stress response. Studies show that naming emotions helps activate this area of the brain.[11]

We can label our emotions by naming how we're feeling, whether to ourselves, to our spouse or a friend, or in a journal. It can be as simple as saying, "I'm feeling stressed right now because I'm overwhelmed by all the demands on me."

Feel Your Feelings

Feeling your feelings may seem counterintuitive to self-regulation, but giving ourselves permission to experience our emotions leads to a regulated nervous system and emotional health.

It should be noted that feeling our feelings isn't always appropriate in the exact moment they're occurring. Regulating an outburst of words or emotions can save our relationships and our jobs. This is particularly true when it comes to parenting our children. It's not wise to vent all our emotions with our children, as it places them in the relational position of caretaker, assigning them the responsibility to comfort us. That's not our children's job.

This doesn't mean you have to completely hide your feelings from your children or feel guilty for bursting into tears in front of them. It's more about how you narrate to them what's happening. Instead of sharing every feeling you're having in that moment, you might say, "Mama's feeling sad today because I miss my friend, but I will be okay" or "Dad got angry at that driver on the road, so I'm just going to calm myself down now." This allows you to share your feelings so you're not hiding them, but the narration helps your child see that they're not responsible for fixing your feelings.

Then, when you have some space and time by yourself or with other close adults, give yourself permission to feel your feelings so you can process and heal.

You may have heard of the expression "feel it to heal it." This means giving ourselves permission to feel all the emotions—grief, anger, sadness, rage, and frustration. We don't invalidate ourselves or the way we feel; we hold space for it.

Many studies show the harmful impact of chronically suppressing of our emotions.[12] When we push down our feelings, never giving ourselves permission to feel them, the emotions don't go away. Rather, they build up and come out in other (unhelpful) ways—often toward other people. In the long term (over the course of years), emotional suppression can increase our internal stress response, cause us to become more aggressive,[13] and make us more vulnerable to chronic health problems such as cardiovascular conditions and even cancer.[14]

We need safe spaces to feel our feelings, such as in emotionally safe relationships, in therapy, or through a journaling practice.

Reframe Your Thinking

When we go through challenging situations, it's not always the situation that determines our emotional response but the meaning we make about the situation.

Situation + Meaning = Emotional Response

The meaning you make from the situations you walk through is one of the most important factors in navigating adversity or trauma.

While reflecting on his own experience in a Nazi concentration camp, Viktor E. Frankl wrote, "Everything can be taken from a man but one thing: the last of the human freedoms—to choose one's attitude in any given set of circumstances, to choose one's own way."[15] We don't always have control over the situations we're going through, but the one thing we always have influence over is our perspective and the meaning we make about the situation.

Reframing means we intentionally manage the meaning we take from a situation. It's when we actively interpret the meaning of a situation or an emotion. Essentially, it's seeing the same situation from a different perspective.

Reframing has been proven to activate the brain's braking system in the prefrontal cortex and to slow down the

> When we go through challenging situations, it's not always the situation that determines our emotional response but the meaning we make about the situation.

stress response. This strategy has been found to be one of the most effective ways to deal with situations we can't change.[16]

For example, let's say you're telling yourself the reason you're going through this painful experience is because you're a failure, you deserve it, and you should be ashamed of yourself. Compare that to believing this painful experience happened simply because life isn't always fair, rather than seeing it as a reflection of your worth or value.

These different meanings don't change the painful situation, but they do change the intensity of your emotional experience in the situation.

Here are some examples of reframing in parenting:

"I can't deal with another meltdown from my child today."
Reframe: "My child is blessed to grow up in a home where I know how to help them through an emotional meltdown."

"I can't cope with the stage my child is in."
Reframe: "This is an opportunity for me to grow in ways that will help my child and others."

"I feel stuck in the daily demands of looking after everybody else."
Reframe: "What's the opportunity hiding in this situation that I haven't seen yet?"

Stand in a Power Pose

If you've ever watched a superhero movie, you know the powerful stance the superhero takes when they're on top of a building or when they're saving the world from evil. Their feet are wide apart, their hands are on their hips, their shoulders are back, their chest is out, and their head is pointing up to the sky. Superman or Wonder Woman, here to save the day!

Research has shown that standing in this physical position (called a "power pose") can impact your emotional state and even your hormones. In the studies, individuals reported feeling both more powerful and calmer. Their saliva samples showed that after doing the power pose for only two minutes, they had a 19 percent increase in testosterone and a 25 percent decrease in cortisol.[17] This effect continued for hours afterward.

You can use power posing for yourself, or you can do it with your children: "Let's all stand like superheroes for two minutes!" (Depending on their age, this may elicit giggles or groans.)

Use Metacognition

Metacognition is a psychological term for being aware of your thoughts and feelings. It means that when you're overreacting, you notice it. When you're worried about a situation, you're aware that your thoughts are racing and may even be a little irrational. In other words, it means watching your thoughts rather than getting caught up in them.

After my cancer journey, I started noticing that I had some anxiety when it came to my health. If I received an unexpected call from my doctor, my thoughts would start cycling through all the horrible things it could be. If I had a blood test or appointment for anything (not necessarily related to the cancer), my mind would immediately go to the worst-case scenario.

Because I had an awareness of my thoughts and feelings (metacognition), it helped me manage them and not get as caught up in them. I calmed myself by naming how I was feeling and validating that this was normal, considering what I'd been through. I also leaned on others' opinions in this area rather than trusting my own thoughts. I would tell my closest family members and friends, "This is what my brain is telling me is probably going to happen, but I'm aware that because of what I've been through, I can lean toward overreacting. What do you think this situation means?"

Studies show that when someone has strong metacognition skills, they also have strong mental and emotional regulation skills—these skill sets go together.[18] Strengthening an awareness of your thoughts and feelings in the present moment has been found to change brain patterns, reduce stress, and even reduce the risk of mental illness.[19]

The good news is that metacognition is something you can strengthen over time.

The first step is to tune in to an awareness of your thoughts and feelings. You may do this naturally without much assistance. On the other hand, if you struggle with being aware of your thoughts and feelings, it helps to talk openly with a close friend or a therapist. Another way to see what's going on in your mind is to journal your thoughts and feelings, unedited.

Then hold this awareness with curiosity, not judgment. Many times we're aware of what we're thinking and feeling, but we criticize ourselves for thinking and feeling that way. Rather than invalidating yourself, practice normalizing and accepting your thoughts and feelings. It's understandable that you're feeling this way. What would you say to your closest friend if they were experiencing these thoughts and feelings?

Finally, decide how to respond to these feelings and navigate through them. You may recognize that this isn't an area you should unequivocally trust yourself in (like my situation with health appointments), or you may realize that you're feeling this way because you need to do something.

Metacognition is a powerful tool to manage your thoughts and feelings.

Seek Grounded Hope

Holding on to grounded hope doesn't mean ignoring reality with fake optimism or toxic positivity. Rather, it means facing the hard reality of your situation and the limitations within it, and then seeking the genuine hope within it.

Studies show that when individuals who have gone through trauma are asked to think deliberately about how it impacted them, what it now means for them, and how they can move forward, they are significantly more likely to experience post-traumatic growth.[20] This process allows them to face the reality of their situation as well as look for hope in the future.

Grounded hope means asking yourself, *Given where I am now, how can I build the best future possible?*

When I was walking through my cancer journey, I wasn't guaranteed healing or a definite positive ending to my story, so I found grounded hope in small places. I was grateful to have loving people around me and excellent surgeons and medical teams. On days when I felt less fatigued or when I was able to read or journal, I tried to focus on the progress.

I did small things that brought beauty to my day—buying a bunch of flowers or watching a favorite movie.

Practice Loving Detachment

If you tend to border on overthinking or being a "control freak" (my hand is up here!), you may benefit from an emotional coping tool called loving detachment.

When we over-function, we move into controlling or stressing rather than supporting and releasing. Loving detachment means that we stop trying to hold everything together for everyone in our world. This may be one of the most loving things we can do for ourselves and others.

Over-functioning is a nuanced topic when it comes to parenting, because it's often hard to tell the difference between over-functioning and good parenting. With young children, we almost have to over-function in order to care for them. As they get older, the idea is that we train them to do tasks for themselves and gradually release them to look after their own lives. But for many reasons—sometimes because of our children or sometimes because of us—this can be a hard transition. One way to practice loving detachment is to consider how you end the day.

For women in particular, we often end our days going over all the things we could have done better, thinking about the million boxes of things we need to do, wondering if our children are going to be okay. In these moments, we have the opportunity to practice the skill of loving detachment and remind ourselves that when we've done all we can do, we need to surrender the rest.

This is where your faith can add depth and support. When I'm feeling worried about my children and all the things I can't control, I remind myself that God loves my kids even more than I do, and I can trust him with their lives. I surrender the burden of worrying about my children into his hands.

You can't make your child healthy, successful, or happy. Even if you do all the right things, they are still influenced by life circumstances beyond your control and have their own free will. All you are called to do is provide a loving relationship with them, do your best, and find joy in the rest.

As we practice loving detachment over time, it develops in us a light-heartedness that allows us to take seriously what we need to take seriously and then surrender the rest. This is where joy enters our lives—not from white-knuckling everything because we're scared for the people we love most in this world, but from the knowledge that we've done all that we can and that is all that is required of us.

Emotional Coping Skills to Try Today

If you want to put some of these emotional coping skills into practice, here are a few ideas to get you started. Don't do these all at once—choose one or two that really resonate with you and give them a go. You can add more when you feel ready.

1. **Interrupt the buildup.** Next time you feel your frustration rising, pay attention to when it's at a 6 out of 10 or a 7 out of 10 and change what you're doing. Anything that provides an interruption from the mundane routines of our lives can quickly change our emotional state.

    - Drop the housework and sit down for a cup of coffee.
    - Put the kids in the car to go for ice cream.
    - Load your baby into the stroller and go for a walk.
    - Give up on making dinner or checking your email and lie down for ten minutes.
    - Put on your favorite music and have a dance party with your kids.

2. **Name your emotions.** Take a moment to tune in to how you're feeling. If you were to label your emotional state, what would it be (e.g., happy, sad, fearful, overwhelmed, anxious, contemplative, frustrated, guilty, stressed)? Then give a short explanation as to why.

Self-Regulation: Cultivating Emotional Maturity

- "I'm feeling stressed because I'm overwhelmed by all the demands on me."
- "I'm feeling relieved because the kids are finally in bed."
- "I'm feeling guilty because I just lost my temper."

Practice this a few times throughout the day. You may not notice a difference when you first do this, but as it becomes a regular part of your life, it will strengthen your self-regulation.

3. **Feel your feelings.** Think back to the last time you had a strong emotional response, especially if it's something you keep thinking about. Pull out a journal (or even just a piece of paper) and write, unedited, exactly how you feel about that situation. Don't judge what you're writing—allow it to be a place of expression. Or ask your best friend or spouse if you can just talk awhile (first explain that you don't want them to fix you; you just need to talk), and share, unedited, how you feel about the situation.

4. **Reframe your thinking.** Bring to mind a situation that has been consistently challenging and that you don't have a lot of control over. Now ask yourself (or journal about) these questions:

   - What's the good hidden within the bad?
   - What's an opportunity here that I haven't seen yet?
   - How is this situation growing me in my emotional maturity and character?
   - In twenty years, how much is this situation going to matter?

5. **Stand in a power pose.** Find a space where you are comfortable. Stand in a power pose, with feet hip-width apart, hands on hips, shoulders back, and head up to the sky. Set a timer for two minutes while remaining in this position.

6. **Use metacognition.** Think about a situation that has been frustrating you. Pull out a journal (or just a piece of paper) and write down how you're thinking or feeling about that situation. Now look back at what you have written, and ask yourself these questions:

    - What do you notice?
    - If your best friend were thinking or feeling that way, what would you say to them?
    - Are there any understandable reasons your thoughts or feelings might become irrational in certain situations?

7. **Seek grounded hope.** Try to identify a situation that's making you feel hopeless or despondent. First, acknowledge the grief, pain, and unfairness you've had to walk through in this situation. Then ask yourself, *Given where I am, how can I build the best future possible?* Talk about this question with a close friend or your spouse. Brainstorm ideas in your journal. It might feel hard to get started because of the real-life limitations of your situation, but start with small ways, and these will eventually grow into bigger ideas.

8. **Practice loving detachment.** At the end of the day, take a moment to surrender all the heaviness you feel. You might do this through journaling, prayer, or meditation. Bring to mind all the things you did today to serve others, all the ways you looked after your family, all the ways you did your job well, and all the ways you cared for your environment around you. Acknowledge a job well done (not perfect!). Now take a breath and remind yourself that you are not God—it's not your job to hold the universe together. Surrender all the people, projects, and places that are weighing on you. And remember: you're just one person, and your job has come to an end for the day.

CHAPTER 7

CO-REGULATION:

BEING YOUR CHILD'S SAFE PLACE

> You've always had the power, my dear;
> you just had to learn it for yourself.
> — GLINDA THE GOOD WITCH,
> *The Wizard of Oz*

One Monday afternoon, Amy picked up her kindergartner from school. After getting Henry strapped in and settled into the car, she began the drive home, striking up a conversation.

"How was school today, hon?"

"Good."

"What did you do in class today?"

"We did math and reading."

"What about lunchtime—did you get to play with anyone?"

"Yep."

Over their fifteen-minute drive home, Amy noticed that Henry was becoming more and more annoyed by her questions, so she decided to pause them for the rest of the trip.

When they arrived home, Amy parked the car in the driveway and asked Henry to bring in his backpack.

"No!" Henry shouted.

"Henry, you know this is your job. I have my own bags to carry."

"Why can't you just carry it? Everyone else's mom carries their bag for them."

Amy started questioning whether she was being too hard on him, but at the same time, she wanted to teach Henry some routines to look after himself.

"Maybe that's true, but in our home, you need to bring your backpack in from the car."

Henry burst into tears. "Fine!" he yelled, grabbing his backpack. "You are the meanest mom ever!" Then he ran into his bedroom and slammed the door.

Like anyone, Amy didn't like being called a bad parent. But she knew she hadn't done something to cause Henry to be this upset in this situation. She wondered if something had happened to Henry at school.

Amy unloaded the rest of her belongings from the car and went to check on Henry. She knocked on his door and asked if she could come in.

Henry said, "Yes, but only if you're going to stop being so mean!"

Amy opened the door to find Henry sprawled across his bed, crying. Aware that her previous more direct approach had only made things worse, Amy sat down on Henry's bedroom floor next to his bed and started playing with some of his toys. They sat there quietly together for a few minutes.

Amy could tell Henry was beginning to soften toward her, so she asked, "Are you okay, Henry? You don't seem like yourself . . ."

"No, I've had the worst day! But you wouldn't care."

"I care a lot, Henry. What happened today?"

Through tears, Henry shared a story of an incident that happened at lunchtime with some other boys in the class who had called him a baby because he didn't want to play soccer. Henry told them to stop being so mean, but they only continued to tease him.

After the whole story poured out, Amy said, "You're not a baby, Henry. Lots of people don't like playing soccer for different reasons. When your dad didn't want to play soccer with his friend last weekend, did that mean he was a baby?"

"No, I guess not," Henry agreed.

"Sometimes people just say mean things because they're frustrated, but it doesn't mean it's true."

"It doesn't?"

"No, buddy, just because someone says it doesn't make it true. You're not a baby at all. Think about all the ways you've grown—you've been helping Dad take out the trash bins, and you're in school now. I know it hurts when people call you mean names. I would feel hurt too. These boys obviously don't know you that well. But I know who you really are. You are strong and capable and a great friend to others."

Henry sat up from his bed and came to sit next to Amy on the floor.

"Do you really think so, Mom?"

"I know so, Henry. Dad and I are proud of you, and we love you so much."

Henry grabbed Amy in a big hug.

"Thanks, Mom. I'm sorry I said those things before. You're not a mean mom. You're the best mom!"

These moments don't happen every time, of course. And yet when they do, there's something significant and wonderful happening: you are offering your child co-regulation. In doing so, you offer them even greater gifts—gifts they will carry for a lifetime: resilience and emotional health.

Emotional Regulation Is Learned

Children aren't born with the neurological development or skills for self-regulation. It can be particularly difficult to remember during the middle of a child's meltdown, but the reality is, children don't have the capacity to appropriately deal with, cover up, or process their emotions until around age six or seven. This is because their prefrontal cortex (the part of the brain involved in self-regulation, emotional control, and decision-making) takes longer to come into full maturity than other parts of the brain—sometimes up to twenty-five years! (See chapter 3 for more on childhood brain development.)

Babies will cry; toddlers and preschoolers will have irrational meltdowns; elementary school children will talk back and roll their eyes; teenagers will be disrespectful or test boundaries. We need to expect these behaviors—they are a typical part of child and adolescent development. At each stage, they present opportunities for us to set boundaries for our children and teach them healthy ways to deal with their emotions.

Children need the empathetic presence of their parents to calm their emotions. When babies are crying or when toddlers are upset, they look to their primary caregivers to soothe them and help them calm down. The parents' presence and caretaking actions teach the child that everything will be okay. As we consistently bring our own calm to our child, we are teaching them that the world is a safe place and that there are people who love them. This is co-regulation.

In co-regulation, your child's nervous system is calmed by *your* nervous system. As you enter their world, listening and responding with empathy, warmly embracing them, and sitting with them for as long as it takes for them to return to themselves, you are teaching them how to emotionally regulate. Over time, they will develop the capacity to regulate themselves.

Similar to adults, children learn to self-regulate in three ways. (We will explore these concepts in more detail later in this book.)

1. Having warm, connected relationships with their primary caregivers
2. Having boundaries and practices that create an emotionally safe environment
3. Developing emotional coping skills

How Children Learn to Regulate Their Emotions

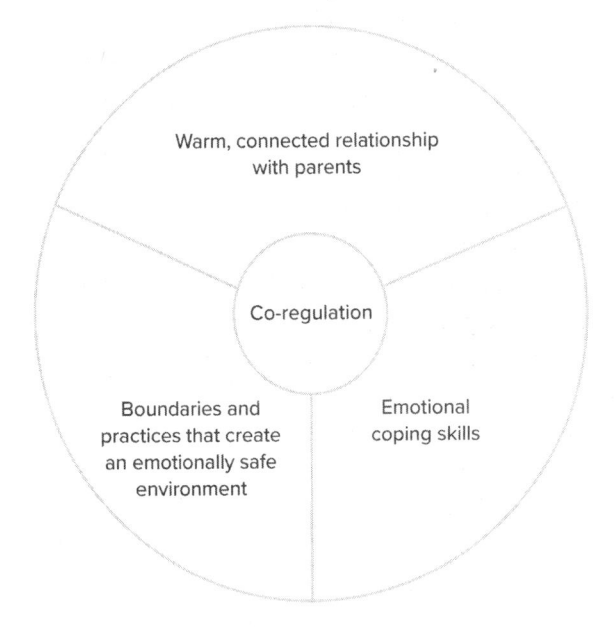

- Warm, connected relationship with parents
- Boundaries and practices that create an emotionally safe environment
- Emotional coping skills

(Center: Co-regulation)

Our role as co-regulators changes over time. As our children grow and develop, so does their capacity to self-regulate. The need for co-regulation is greatest when children are babies, and it slowly decreases as they mature—although more support is needed during the turmoil of puberty and adolescence (ages twelve to seventeen). And, of course, all children need more intentional co-regulation during complex life transitions or when they are emotionally overwhelmed, regardless of their age or stage of development. Yet we are there for them in this way to empower them to be there for *themselves* in this way as adults.

This is why we, as parents, must prioritize our own emotional health. If we have no capacity left over for the emotional lives of our children, how will they learn the healthy self-regulation they need?

Children learn and cultivate emotional health as they grow—and so can we. Co-regulation is recoverable; emotional health can be established again. As we gain what we need to increase our own self-regulation, healthy co-regulation can be rebuilt. And as we find health and healing, it *will* naturally benefit our children too.

Foundations for Co-Regulation

So what do we do? We intentionally build our capacity for co-regulation by expanding our own capacity for emotional maturity, resourcing ourselves with a variety of coping tools to regulate our own emotions (see the list at the end of chapter 6).

Becoming an Emotionally Healthy Parent

When I was pregnant with my first child and preparing to become a parent, I thought I was ready. I had read all the books about what to expect for pregnancy and birth, we had prepared our home for this new arrival, and I even had a degree in child development (which I thought would make this whole endeavor pretty straightforward).

But of course, nothing actually prepares you. The only way to learn how to parent is to become one. I didn't anticipate just how much I would need to grow and mature emotionally along the way.

Whether you become a parent by conscious choice or not, whether you waited until your career was stable or you were barely just an adult yourself, all of a sudden, you are the adult in the room—and another human being is looking to you to teach them what it means to be a mature, healthy human being. (No pressure!) When it comes to the decisions and demands of parenting, Colin and I often jokingly wonder where all the adults are so they can tell us what to do!

Parenthood is one of life's greatest opportunities for spiritual and emotional growth. In no other experience are you consistently presented with situations that require you to react and make decisions when you're exhausted, touched-out, sleep deprived, and juggling so many other priorities. Even though it may feel as if you have to immediately become mature (the way you immediately became a parent), this is actually a process of *becoming* over time.

We *learn* to give when we have nothing left to give, learn to love when someone else's words or behaviors hurt us, learn to respond rather than react. This is emotional maturity. I'm not suggesting that parenthood automatically makes us grow in emotional maturity. After all, we all know people who are older in years and have been raising children for a while who are emotionally immature. And we know, maybe through experience, how hurtful it is when these adults aren't emotionally mature enough to have a healthy relationship with us.

Whether you're continuing a cycle of generational health that was passed on to you by your parents or you're a generational cycle breaker and the first in your family to commit to this kind of growth, emotional maturity is one of the greatest gifts you can give your children and future generations.

Becoming a Non-Anxious Presence

Family systems therapist Rabbi Edwin Friedman suggested the term "non-anxious presence" to describe someone who avoids being drawn into the chaos and anxiety of the environment around them.[1] He suggests that this individual provides a calm and steady presence, empowering others to become more relaxed amid the chaos around them.[2]

Have you ever been in the presence of someone like that? Someone who instantly lets you take a deep breath and believe that life is going to be okay? Someone who makes you laugh, makes you feel normal, and makes you feel as if you can get back up and face the world again?

As I drove to my friend Lee's house, my mind was racing with all the situations that were weighing on my mind—getting our new business off the ground, reentering life and work after my cancer diagnosis, being newly pregnant with our first child. The world felt full of problems and things I needed to take very seriously, and I was feeling worried about the future. Yet even as I parked my car outside her beautiful home among the trees, I could feel my whole body relax.

> Emotional maturity is one of the greatest gifts you can give your children and future generations.

Lee has been one of my closest girlfriends for years. She is funny and kind, creatively gifted, and hospitable. She is who I want to be when I grow up. She has also walked beside me throughout a wide range of seasons, good and bad, and has been a loyal, trustworthy friend.

When I walked into her home, she cracked a joke and gave me a big hug. As I sat down on her couch, I noticed that she'd already organized a lavish charcuterie board (even though it was just the two of us). We sat and talked for hours, sharing all the heavy things on our hearts and laughing so much I kept forgetting what we were talking about. After a few hours together, I felt like a different person.

Lee hadn't changed anything about the circumstances of my life, but being in her presence had changed how I was feeling about life.

Essentially, this is who we aim to be for our children.

When the chaos of an emotional meltdown occurs, we respond calmly and maturely.

When the chaos of friendship drama occurs, we respond calmly and maturely.

When the chaos of an adolescent issue rears its head, we respond calmly and maturely.

As a non-anxious presence for our children, we become the place they can go to find rest and lightheartedness away from the seriousness of the world and be reminded that they are deeply loved and that everything's going to be all right.

We give them the gift of our emotional maturity.

Wrestling the Guilt

When it comes to co-regulation and becoming emotionally mature parents, all of us (that's right—*all* of us) can immediately think of times we missed the mark. We lost our temper, we yelled, we responded unkindly, we spoke harsh words. It's easy to think we're failing at this and not doing a good enough job or that in our attempts to give our kids the gift of co-regulation, we're actually making things worse.

We've all been there, facing the parent guilt, the mom guilt, the fear that we're going to mess up or traumatize our children.

As an Australian (now living in the US), I grew up watching TV shows where famous people (who may have missed the healthy fear gene) wrestle crocodiles. They would grab the crocodile from behind in an attempt to stop it from going into a death spiral. Once they had the creature from behind, they would be able to pin it to the ground.

This is how guilt can feel—it spins and spins, telling us we've wrecked everything, saying we're just like the person who hurt us, calling us a failure, and accusing us of not having what it takes to do this parenting thing.

This is what guilt (and crocodiles!) do. If you find yourself in this death spiral, you need to grab the guilt from behind.

The reason you're wrestling with these feelings is because your children are so important to you, because you want to do a good job at parenting, and because you're still growing in this. You may need to repair a breach with your child (as we all do at times), but try to remember: even the act of repairing is a form of wrestling the guilt and a way to change the narrative about your parenting.

> Progress, not perfection.
> Momentum, not perfection.
> Growth, not perfection.

One way to wrestle with the guilt and stop it from spinning around in your head is to create a mantra to repeat to yourself:

Progress, not perfection.
Momentum, not perfection.
Growth, not perfection.

When we sit under the guilt, we don't have the opportunity to grow, and we end up eroding our confidence and peace in the process. Your child doesn't need a perfect parent; they just need a healthy one. There's no way to do this parenting thing perfectly, but there are many ways to grow. And as we grow, we give our child the gift of our emotional maturity.

So wrestle with the guilt. Give yourself permission to be imperfect and to repair with your child. And know that even as you do these things, you're creating emotional health for generations to come.

Practical Ways to Soothe Your Child

Here are some practices you can use when your child is feeling dysregulated to soothe them and help them return to calm. Different strategies work well for different children, depending on how old they are, what their temperament is like, and how upset they are. Experiment with different strategies and see how your child responds.

Embrace them. Hugging and embracing your child gives them a sense of comfort and reminds them that they're loved. It also activates oxytocin, a neurotransmitter that promotes bonding and social attachment.[3] When someone is emotionally dysregulated, a big bear hug can help them return to calm. (Tip: Let them be the first to let go!)

Lie side by side. Try lying down beside your child, either on the floor or on their bed. You might also try holding their hand. This gives them the assurance of your presence without being too physically overwhelming or requiring direct eye contact. This can be an effective calming strategy for many ages or temperaments. A variation on this is to go for a walk or a drive together. Being side by side, without direct eye contact, can help your child feel calmer and make them more comfortable to open up in conversation.

Sit with them. You can sit next to your child, rubbing their back or playing with their hair. This gives them the assurance of your presence and cultivates connection while their nervous system calms down.

Be in the same space. Sometimes when a child is highly dysregulated, it can feel overwhelming for them to be physically close to you. Even though your intention is to help them, physical touch can increase their emotional dysregulation. If you're sensing this from your child, try to remove them from other people (for example, by taking them to their bedroom). Then just sit on the floor near them, in the same physical space but not touching. This shows you're there for them but gives them the space they need to calm down. Sometimes once the child begins to calm down, they will come physically closer to you and will eventually be ready for a hug or embrace.

Give them space. When a child moves into adolescence, if they have a highly anxious temperament or if they're neurodivergent, they might want space from everyone (including you) to calm down. We don't want to make the child feel punished for having a big emotional response, but sometimes what they need most is time alone. If this is the case, allow them their own personal space (such as their bedroom) and tell them where you'll be and that you're there for them. For example: "I'm in the kitchen if you want a hug or want to chat." For younger children who need space, you can check on them in five- to ten-minute intervals, knocking on their door and asking if they're ready to connect.

Sing to them. You don't need a great voice to do this—just sing a song your child likes. This is particularly calming for younger children. Having a special song you regularly sing can provide a grounding, calming experience for them. Humming is effective too, as it has been found to activate the parasympathetic nervous system and help children return to a place of calm.[4]

CHAPTER 8

CONNECTION:

BUILDING HEALTHY ATTACHMENT

> You will teach them to fly, but they
> will not fly your flight. You will teach
> them to dream, but they will not dream
> your dream. You will teach them to
> live, but they will not live your life.
> Nevertheless, in every flight, in every
> life, in every dream the print of the
> way you taught them will remain.
> ATTRIBUTED TO MOTHER TERESA

Thomas was a curious young boy who loved science and mechanics. He enjoyed figuring out how different things worked and whether he could improve them.

Yet despite his natural curiosity and love of learning, Thomas found school a challenge. After being in the classroom for a few months, he was struggling to pay attention, and his teacher was becoming more and more frustrated.

One day, Thomas overheard his teacher talking about him to another teacher. The teacher said that Thomas was "addled," inferring that he was mentally deficient and probably shouldn't even be in school.

Understandably hurt by these words, Thomas went home in tears. His mother was so enraged that she marched to the school to tell the teacher that they didn't know what they were talking about, that Thomas was smarter than they were, and that she was withdrawing him from the school to educate him at home.[1]

Under her instruction, Thomas began to thrive. He developed a deep love for reading and learning, and as an adult, he began his career as an inventor.

Thomas Edison became one of the most prolific and genius inventors of all time. He is credited with creating over one thousand inventions (either by himself or with others), including the record player, the light bulb, and the motion-picture projector.

Describing his relationship with his mother, he wrote, "She came out as my strong defender. . . . She was the most enthusiastic champion a boy ever had."[2] He went on to say, "My mother was the making of me. She was so true, so sure of me."[3]

The Power of Connection

The most influential relationships in a child's life are with their parents.

The health of these relationships has a significant influence on the child's academic performance, physical health and development, and emotional health. But we also see that a close, attached relationship between a parent and a child is one of the greatest predictors of the *future* resilience and emotional health of the child. Studies on extreme child neglect show that when children don't have a warm relationship with a caregiver, they don't experience healthy neurological development. As they grow older, they have significantly higher levels of cortisol (a stress hormone), and they are more likely to struggle with mental illness and substance abuse as a teen or an adult.[4]

It may not seem like a revolutionary idea to prioritize cultivating a healthy relationship with your child. You might even think it sounds too simple, too obvious. But as we discussed in chapter 7, the single best way to teach your child to calm their emotions is through your physical and emotional presence with them. This process of co-regulation, repeated over time, will lead to the development of your child's self-regulation skills.

It may not be easy, but it is simple: your relationship with your child matters.

Building a Foundation of Healthy Attachment

Children are neurologically wired to connect to their parents or primary caregiver. This is what psychologists call attachment. Attachment occurs when the child's relationship with their caregiver provides them with a secure base of love, safety, and comfort from which they can explore the world.

When a child has a strong, healthy attachment to their caregivers, they show significantly reduced behavioral challenges, increased academic performance, and significantly greater mental and emotional health outcomes in their future.[5] The relationship between parent and child lays the foundation for a child's future resilience and emotional health.

This can feel like a lot of pressure. You might find yourself questioning whether you've done enough to build healthy attachment with your child, or you might worry if something they're struggling with is your fault because of inadequate attachment. It's important to qualify here that you just need to be a "good enough" parent (not a perfect parent) for healthy attachment to form.

Studies show that parents only need to get it right 50 percent of the time in their response to their child in order to develop a healthy attachment relationship.[6] Many times, an unhealthy relationship attachment between parent and child is due to abuse, neglect, substance abuse, or unsupported mental illness, not a parent who is giving their all and occasionally loses their patience. If you are reading this book, it's because you care deeply about parenting well—and it's likely that you're already doing a far better job than you give yourself credit for.

It is also important to know that a child's experiences early in life don't automatically determine their future. It's never too late to build a close, connected relationship with your child.

They can still develop emotional and relational health through corrective

> Parents only need to get it right 50 percent of the time to develop healthy attachment with their child.

experiences and relationships with supportive people. As psychiatrist Dr. Bruce Perry says, "The more healthy relationships a child has, the more likely he will be to recover from trauma and thrive. Relationships are the agents of change and the most powerful therapy is human love."[7]

Attachment as the Child Grows

People often talk about attachment being most important in the first three years of a child's life and then losing significance in the stages following toddlerhood. While it's true that the first three years are a critical time of development, the truth is, your child needs your love and connection *throughout* their life.

When her oldest daughter, Kara, turned fifteen, Taylor felt like she almost didn't know her anymore. As a little girl, Kara followed Taylor around everywhere, wanting to dress like her mom and do everything she was doing. Taylor loved the closeness she experienced with her daughter in the younger years, as Kara regularly poured out her heart to her mom about everything that was going on in her life. She constantly wrote her notes saying she was "the best mom ever!"

But things changed as Kara hit adolescence. Kara became closer friends with the "cooler" girls at school, and although Taylor didn't think they were a bad influence, it was obvious that Kara was changing after spending more time with them. Kara started criticizing the clothes Taylor wore and pushing the boundaries about when and where she could go with her friends. Then there were the mood swings—from screaming to crying in a short period of time. Taylor never knew if she was responding to these episodes properly, as they kept coming like waves.

But this wasn't even the worst part. Taylor felt like Kara didn't want a close relationship with her anymore. For weeks, Taylor had been trying to talk with Kara and find activities for them to do together, but her attempts were ignored so blatantly that Taylor felt rejected. She questioned whether she mattered in Kara's life anymore.

One night, after this had gone on for weeks, Kara came home crying after one of her friends had told the boy she liked about her crush. Kara was humiliated—embarrassed that her secret had been revealed and hurt that her friend had betrayed her trust. Taylor sat with Kara on her bed as she shared through tears about all that had been happening over the past few weeks.

Taylor could sense that this was not the time for lectures or opinions. Instead, she listened and related to Kara's emotions, sharing a story about how something similar had happened to her when she was a young adult and how hurtful it was. Then she reminded Kara what an incredible person she was. After their long chat, Taylor suggested they have ice cream for dinner and watch Kara's favorite movie. Later that night, as Taylor was getting ready for bed, Kara tentatively came into her room and said, "Thanks for tonight, Mom. I hope you know that I really love you."

It would have been easy for Taylor to read Kara's behavior as rejection when in reality, Kara was wanting to navigate the world independently, stretching her wings toward adulthood. When things got painful (as they often do), Kara knew she still had a safe place to retreat to.

The way our children need us will change as they grow, but the fact that they need us never will. The parent-child relationship is unlike any other. That's because we're attempting to cultivate a close relationship with a child who is rapidly changing while also holding boundaries for their safety and their healthy development. My friends and I often joke that the moment you start to feel as if you've gotten one age or stage of development down and your confidence as a parent is rising, your child changes again and you find yourself back at the beginning of the learning curve.

At each developmental stage, it is possible to create a healthy and lasting attachment with our kids.

The Unconditional Love of Early Childhood

Most of us expect to have an emotionally close relationship with our infant and child. Although these relationships are never perfect (there are disagreements and personality clashes), relationships with younger children tend to be more straightforward. Developmentally, younger children still think you're the greatest person to ever live, and they haven't yet started noticing your imperfections. As you spend time with them, encourage them, and take an interest in what is interesting to them, you will often find that your relationship flourishes.

This begins to change as your child grows older and moves through the developmental stages into adolescence. During these transitions, we sometimes misunderstand the changes that are occurring because we misread our child's behavior or buy into cultural narratives. Parents of teens may wrongly assume their child no longer needs them, when the truth is, they need their parents more than ever.

The Peer Group Stage

"But everyone else is doing it!"

I was folding laundry in my bedroom, having a conversation with my then-ten-year-old that was beginning to feel like a regular occurrence. There was always some new thing—media, technology, fashion, books, activities—that "everyone else" was doing and our family wasn't.

I would counter with the annoying parental response "Is *everyone* really doing it? What about _____?" Thus began the dance of deciding whether I was okay with this new thing and navigating my child through the tender emotions of wanting to fit in while holding steady to our family's values.

Around ages eight to thirteen, children start looking outside their family and toward their peers for their sense of acceptance.

Parents sense this change. As children move toward adolescence, they often struggle with friendship drama, desiring to fit in with certain groups and be accepted by them. As a result, this is also a time when parents feel as if their child is pushing them away in their desire for independence.

During this time, it can be easy to think that the best solution is to back off from the relationship, to "give them space" as they are gaining independence. Many parents assume their child doesn't want or need them much anymore. Yet nothing could be further from the truth—they actually need you more than ever. They are going through one of the most turbulent developmental times of change in their life!

If parents back away during this stage, the child will be primarily influenced by their peers. These same-age friends don't provide the healthy modeling children and adolescents need, the maturity to hold their big emotions, or the wisdom to guide them. Children aren't designed to raise children. Developmental psychologist Dr. Gordon Neufeld suggests that when parents make the mistake of backing off from their relationship with their child, it results in relational disconnection and behavior issues, including higher aggression and early sexualization.[8] While it's true that children moving toward adolescence have an increasing need for autonomy and independence (which we need to respect), it's also a time when they need our influence, boundaries, and proximity. Although they may push you away, the reality is that underneath it all, they also truly want you to be there when they need you. Your kids may think you're uncool or that you don't understand their technology or culture, but they still deeply desire your love, support, and connection. So keep showing up; your presence matters.

The Adolescent Stage

Brian was the father of thirteen-year-old Sophia. When she was younger, Brian would constantly give Sophia hugs and have tickle-fights until she laughed so much she couldn't breathe. Yet over the past few years, Sophia's body had changed and she'd matured physically. Not wanting to make her feel uncomfortable, Brian wasn't sure how to interact with Sophia anymore. He wanted her to know he still loved her, but he also wanted to respect that she was changing.

> Your kids may think you're uncool, but they still deeply desire your love, support, and connection.

When a child moves toward adolescence and their body begins to change, the physical and emotional changes can cause parents—especially the opposite-gender parent—to back off from the relationship. A dad may pull back as his daughter matures and leave the emotional topics for Mom to handle. Similarly, a mother might feel close to her son when he's young, but as he gets older, she might begin to pull away, not wanting to "over-mother" him.

The truth is, a teenage girl still needs her father to hug her and tell her she's beautiful. A teenage boy still needs a hug from his mom (even if it's a shoulder hug or a scruff of his hair). We need to remember that teens feel uncomfortable in their newly changing bodies—even though their bodies *look* older, they are mentally stuck in between childhood and adulthood. We may need to change the way we physically interact with our developing children, but it's important that we continue to interact with them and find new ways to connect.

During this stage of development, a child may begin to gravitate toward the same-sex parent in an effort to learn what it means to be a man or a woman. This shift should be embraced, but it doesn't mean the opposite-gender parent needs to disappear from the child's life. Girls who continue to have a close relationship with their fathers are more self-confident, and they have stronger boundaries in their personal relationships. Boys who continue to have a close relationship with their mothers learn how to relate to women in a healthy, respectful way.

The "Finish Line" of Parenting

When a child is eighteen and has finished school and may be preparing for a job or further education, many parents assume they are done with their parenting role. After all, as we're often reminded on social media, we only have eighteen summers with our children, so we need to make sure we cherish the time and make it count.

While I understand the sentiment, I don't think we need to subscribe to such a fear-based narrative. It may be technically true that we have only eighteen years with our child living full-time under our roof—eighteen years when we're the ones responsible for navigating their boundaries and decisions—but that doesn't mean it's the end of our relationship with them! Our relationship simply changes.

As we discussed in the previous chapter, cultivating an emotionally mature, non-anxious presence is a foundation for co-regulating with our children. Even when our child is an adult, we can be a non-anxious presence in their life, providing a calm environment where they can take a deep breath and be reminded that everything is going to be okay. We can be someone who makes them laugh, reminds them that everyone feels this way sometimes, and reassures them that they can get up and face the world again.

Causes of Relational Disconnection

Mike, a single father, was feeling stuck with his daughter, Rose. She was consistently resistant to doing the basic things he asked her to do. These daily situations quickly turned into all-out battles in their home.

One particular day, feeling tired and stressed after a long day at work, Mike picked Rose up from school. Once they were home, he asked her to do her homework while he made dinner.

Rose ignored him.

Mike instantly became frustrated, saying that if she didn't do her homework, there would be no screen time later.

"Fine! I don't care!" Rose shouted, crossing her arms in defiance.

"Look, I've even got it out on the table for you. It's only one worksheet. Just come and do it . . ."

"I'm not doing it."

Within minutes, Mike and Rose were yelling at each other, until Rose ran off and slammed her bedroom door. Mike was left in the kitchen, feeling both frustrated and guilty.

It's easy to talk about the importance of connecting with our children; it's harder to actually *do* it. The primary factors that undercut the connection between a parent and a child are overstimulation and chronic stress. An overstimulated, stressed-out parent will often overreact to situations, have limited emotional capacity to notice their child's struggles, and wish for some time away from their child. An overstimulated, stressed-out child will often display behaviors—becoming overly emotional, aggressive, reactive, resistant to instructions, unfocused—that make it difficult for their parents to connect with them.

And when *both* the parent and child are overstimulated and stressed, it's a recipe for disconnection.

If you're stuck in a cycle of reactivity and disconnection, it may seem daunting to know where to begin to change this pattern. Even in our hardest seasons, we can make intentional decisions to turn down the noise of overstimulation and chronic stress in our own lives and in the lives of our children so we can increase our connection with one another.

Rupture and Repair

Mike walked out into the cool air of his backyard and took some deep breaths to calm down, acknowledging that he was probably more exhausted from his own day than he realized.

Then, after knocking on his daughter's door and asking if he could come in, Mike sat on Rose's bed and said, "Hon, I'm sorry for getting angry and raising my voice. I shouldn't have done that. Will you forgive me?"

Rose sat up and gave Mike a hug. "Yeah, I forgive you. I'm sorry too."

Mike asked Rose how her day at school went. Tears came to her eyes as she explained that she didn't understand the ideas the teacher was presenting and she wasn't keeping up in class. Mike finally understood why she was so resistant to doing the homework.

"How about I make some dinner and we sit down together with the worksheet?"

Rose nodded through her tears.

Small moments of disconnection, like the one here between Mike and Rose, are considered ruptures in a relationship. As parents, we may be tempted to ignore these ruptures, glossing over their impact and hoping they will eventually fix themselves. But if we follow this temptation, we will find that we eventually have a distant, disconnected relationship with our child. If Mike hadn't addressed the conflict with Rose, leaving her alone with her struggles and getting angrier at her behavior, it would have led to disconnection over time.

Take heart: we're all imperfect human beings, and we all make mistakes in relationships. Ruptures are a normal part of relationships, and therefore the repairing of those ruptures must be too. Repair is the process of mending and healing the relationship after a rupture occurs. If repair is done well, these ruptures won't pull apart the fabric of our relationship with our child. Repair restores connection with our child.

So what does the process of rupture and repair look like?

1. **Acknowledge and name the rupture.** Do this as specifically as possible. For example, you might say, "I yelled."
2. **Take responsibility and apologize.** As parents, we need to normalize apologizing to our children for our behavior when necessary. If we expect them to apologize for their behavior, we must lead by example. Taking responsibility means that we don't blame our reaction on their behavior. For example, you might say, "I'm sorry I yelled—I shouldn't have done that. Will you forgive me?"
3. **Move forward.** Focus on what you will change in the future. For example, you might say, "I will work harder to not raise my voice in the future."

Again, this sounds a lot easier than it is. Many times, in the complexity of a parent-child relationship, the process of rupture occurs at the same time your child is crossing a boundary:

We raise our voice because our child is hitting another child.

We overreact because we've lost our patience with our child's inappropriate behavior.

We say things we later regret because our child isn't listening to what we're asking them to do.

It can be so easy to lose sight of our own behavior in the heat of the moment, to feel so frustrated that offering repair to our child seems permissive or unjust.

But the truth is, we can't teach the boundary until we mend the connection.

Sure, we *can* teach fear and compliance without connection. We can scare them into submission. But if we take the time to repair the connection first, we restore the true influence we have on our child's heart. This way, we're far better positioned to revisit the boundary.

In the heat of the moment, when your child isn't listening to you and is pushing all your buttons, say over and over to yourself, *Repair, then teach boundaries.*

"I'm sorry I said you were being annoying. I shouldn't have said that because it's not true. You're not annoying. Mom is just very tired today, and sometimes when I'm tired, I say things I don't mean. I'm sorry—will you forgive me?"

Then, later: "Now that we've all calmed down, I want to talk to you about hitting. Even when we feel angry, we don't hit because hitting hurts other people. Do you understand? If you hit them again, you won't be allowed to play that game anymore."

Yes, this process requires more emotional work for the parent than using fear-based tactics. But your child will learn far more in the process: by slowing down, you're giving your child an example of emotional maturity, you're providing co-regulation as you de-escalate the situation, and you're creating clear boundaries for the values and behaviors you want in your home.

Practical Tips to Connect with Your Child

Connection with your child can be challenging at times, but the long-term payoff is well worth it. Here are some ways you can deepen your connection with your child.

- **Take an interest in what interests them.** This may be sports, art, music, or their collections.
- **Work to find combined interests.** These are activities or pastimes that both of you enjoy. The shared love will make your time together even more enjoyable.
- **Tell them stories about your life.** Children love hearing what you were like as a child or funny stories from your childhood.

- **Show up.** Make an effort to be present at the things that are important to them—whether it's a sports game, a dance recital, or a play. Your presence during these moments in their life is a vital way of showing them your love.
- **Plan some one-on-one time with them regularly, even if it's just for ten minutes.** This gives them your focused attention. This might be reading together before bed or having breakfast together while everyone else is asleep.
- **Plan some longer intentional time with them on a weekly or monthly basis.** If you can, aim for an hour or two. This could be going out for breakfast together or going on a walk or a bike ride together.
- **As they grow older, consider taking a solo overnight trip with them.** This doesn't have to be flashy or expensive; the key is to have extended time to connect. This could be going camping together or going to a concert or gathering that you both have an interest in.

CHAPTER 9

COPING SKILLS:
GIVING CHILDREN EMOTIONAL TOOLS

*Anyone who has never made a mistake
has never tried anything new.*
ATTRIBUTED TO ALBERT EINSTEIN

When my children were in upper elementary school, Colin and I decided it was time for them to unload the dishwasher as one of their household chores. They agreed that it was a good way to earn extra pocket money.

They had watched us do this task hundreds of times. They'd been in the kitchen countless times as we pulled out the cutlery drawers and opened the cupboard doors for our crockery. Yet despite being familiar with the activity, when it was time to do it themselves, they didn't know where to begin.

We took the kids through a few clear lessons—start here, look out for the sharp edges—and gave them instructions about where the different dishes live. After two or three sessions when we unpacked the dishwasher together, Colin and I stepped back and allowed them to do it themselves.

We stayed nearby and answered their questions. After only a few days, they were confidently unpacking the dishwasher without instruction or supervision from us.

This process is often called *scaffolding*. It provides a framework for learning and follows four steps:

1. I do; you watch.
2. I do; you help.
3. You do; I help.
4. You do; I watch.

There are some skills our children just pick up intuitively, based on their temperament, desires, and observations. But often they need our clear, direct instruction and support to gain mastery over a skill. If we assume that children should automatically know how to do something, it can lead to frustration when they don't do it (much less do it the way we would've liked them to). It would have been easy to think my children should have known how to unload the dishwasher, but the truth is, they didn't. I could feel frustrated all I wanted to, but it wouldn't change my children's competency at the task.

This is true also when it comes to our children's self-regulation skills. Sometimes a child hasn't developed self-regulation skills because of their age or stage of development, but other times it's because they need supportive, clear instructions on how to build these skills. In recent years, some schools have added emotional skills and self-regulation as part of their curriculum—and yet there is much more we can be doing, even at home, to give children what they need to navigate overstimulation and stress. At the end of the day, this isn't something we as parents can completely rely on someone else to do; it's something *we* need to be intentional about teaching our children.

Emotional Literacy

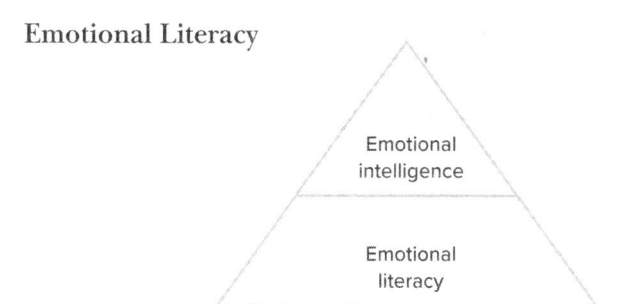

Pyramid diagram: Emotional intelligence (top) / Emotional literacy (base)

If you don't understand what emotions are, what they mean, or what to do with them, it's difficult to navigate through them, no matter your age. This emotional literacy—the ability to understand and navigate emotions—is the foundation of self-regulation and emotional health.

As you might imagine, the process of teaching children about emotions looks different from how you might approach teaching adults. That's because adults come to the conversation with some understanding of emotions, while children need to learn the basics first. Just as a child can't learn to read until they've learned the alphabet and can recognize letters, a child can't navigate their emotions until they know what the different emotions are.

Emotional literacy involves three main skills:

1. Naming emotions
2. Noticing emotions
3. Understanding emotions

Venn diagram: Naming emotions, Noticing emotions, Understanding emotions

Naming Emotions

Emotions can be taught as early as two years old. If you know a two-year-old, you know they have *plenty* of emotions to start with! Giving language to these feelings can be so empowering. For these younger children (under the age of five to seven), you can begin by teaching and talking about the four main emotions:

- happiness
- sadness
- anger
- fear

Most children at this age don't understand more complex emotions (for example, jealousy or disgust). This is why Fred Rogers in *Mister Rogers' Neighborhood* (a television show intended for young children) used simple phrases such as "What do you do with the mad that you feel?"[1]

Once your child has an understanding of these four core emotions (usually around five to seven years old), you can begin to introduce more complex emotions, such as

- surprise
- disgust
- jealousy
- excitement

When your child has a clear grasp of these different emotions (around eight to twelve years old, depending on the child), you can freely talk about the nuances of all the emotions. For example, fear may be categorized as worry, anxiety, fright, overwhelm, or panic.

Naming emotions will look different at every stage. For a toddler, you can point out emotions matter-of-factly (the same way you'd point out a tree or a rainbow), narrating the world around them:

"That boy is stomping his feet and shaking his head. He must be feeling angry."

"Mama is smiling because I feel so happy."

"I know you feel sad about losing your toy. It's okay to cry."

For an elementary-age child, you can reflect back to them their own emotions in addition to narrating the world around them:

"I can see you feel very happy we're having ice cream for dessert."

"Dad is feeling angry because a driver cut him off on the road. But he is calming his anger now."

"Sometimes I feel scared when I watch scary movies. They make me want to hide in my bed."

For a teenager, you can reflect back their own emotions, but it's important not to make assumptions about their feelings with the same confidence you would with younger children:

"It seems like you might be feeling worried about your upcoming test."

"If that happened to me, I would feel really angry. How does it make you feel?"

"Most people would feel really disappointed if they didn't get invited to the party."

Noticing Emotions

Evan threw the game board across the table at his parents and brothers. A few minutes earlier, it had seemed like he might win the game, but at the last minute he had an unlucky roll and ended up losing.

"I hate this stupid game!" He ran off to his room and slammed the door.

A few minutes later his mom went to his room. "Evan, are you okay?"

"What do you think?"

"I think you're feeling very angry that you lost the board game."

"Yes, I am! I was so close to beating you all, and now I'm just the loser."

"I've noticed that board games in particular mean a lot to you. You seem to get angry when you don't win."

"Yeah, I suppose so . . ."

Once your child has names for the different emotions, you can begin teaching them to become aware of and notice emotions. This includes feelings they are personally experiencing and feelings they observe someone else experiencing.

When a child is younger (under the age of five to seven), they aren't always aware of what they're feeling. This provides an opportunity for us to reflect their emotions back to them:

"You seem so happy today!"

"Do you feel sad about losing your toy?"

"It's normal to feel angry when someone calls you names."

As you point out emotions for your younger child, they will learn to notice emotions, and over time, they'll be able to recognize them for themselves.

When your child is older, they may still struggle to notice their emotions at times. When you see them struggling, you can reflect back to them what you notice, ask them how they're feeling about a specific situation, remind them of how they felt in similar situations in the past, or encourage them to start a journaling practice for their feelings.

Understanding Emotions

Once children have learned to name and notice their emotions, they need to know what to do when they feel a certain way. This includes the messages behind the emotions, how those emotions make them feel in their body, and what they can do to process the emotions.

It's important to keep this simple, especially for young children. Here are some ways to help children frame and understand the four main emotions:

HAPPINESS

- **What it feels like:** light, warm, bouncy, sunshine, rainbows, blue skies, bright colors, fireworks, glitter, ice cream, balloons
- **What makes you feel happy:** sunshine, hugs from people you love, doing activities you enjoy
- **What to do with happy feelings:** enjoy them, savor them, share them with others
- **Message of happiness:** "It's good to feel happy for no reason."

SADNESS

- **What it feels like:** heavy, blurry, shrinking, tears, energy zapping
- **What makes you feel sad:** toys getting lost or broken, friends moving away, losing something important to you, someone saying words that hurt you
- **What to do with sad feelings:** cry, share with someone you love, do things that make you feel cared for
- **Message of sadness:** "It's okay to cry when you feel sad" and "We should share our sadness with someone who loves us."

ANGER

- **What it feels like:** boiling, ready to explode, tight chest, volcano about to erupt
- **What makes you feel angry:** when something isn't fair, when something is taken away, when an expectation isn't met, when things don't work out as planned, when you're trying to control something you can't control
- **What to do with angry feelings:** take a break from what's making you angry, tell someone who can help, get out the energy in healthy ways, such as physical exercise or screaming into a pillow
- **Message of anger:** "Feeling angry is a normal part of being human" and "We must choose healthy ways to deal with our anger."

FEAR

- **What it feels like:** shaky, jittery, jumpy, shrinking, stomachache, racing mind, heart beating fast
- **What makes you feel scared:** the dark, bad guys, monsters, going to the doctor or the hospital, being alone, feeling smaller than the challenge
- **What to do with scared feelings:** tell someone who loves you, be near people you love, face fear as the way to grow bigger than it
- **Message of fear:** "It's normal to feel scared sometimes" and "Who you are is bigger than what's scaring you."

Emotional Truths to Live By

One Saturday afternoon, I took my two children to our local playground in an attempt to give them an energy outlet. The playground was full of kids, and I sat on a bench next to a mother and an older man, who turned out to be her father.

My kids were yelling, "Mom, look at this!" and "Mom, watch me do this!" so constantly that I didn't even have a chance to say hi to them before their child/grandchild, who looked to be around six years old, ran up crying. Through his tears, he said that he'd been playing a game of tag with some other children, and in his frustration over their unfair play, he had burst into tears. One of the other kids started teasing him that he was a baby, because "only babies cry."

Instantly, the grandfather said, "That's enough of that crying. Don't be so sensitive about it. Just get back out there and start playing." This comment caused the boy to cry even more.

Then the mom got up and moved her body so she was shielding her son from the other kids' view. She gave him a hug and said, "It's okay to cry, honey—you're not too sensitive. Everybody cries. I cry. Even Pops cries sometimes. But not everyone understands crying, so it's good to cry with people you feel safe with."

At this point the grandfather rolled his eyes. My kids noticed that the little boy was upset and came over to see if he was okay. They invited him to play on the spinners with them, and he happily agreed.

The consistent messages children hear about their emotions are internalized and become the blueprint for what they believe about emotions as adults. In an otherwise ordinary moment, that mom gave her son a significant gift for his future.

We all grew up with different messages about emotions. These messages frame how we navigate our emotions, relationships, and careers as adults.

Many of the messages we received about emotions were negative ones that don't serve us well:

"Boys don't cry."

"Get over it—stop being so sensitive. You need to toughen up."

"Why would you be scared about that? It's nothing."
"You shouldn't be angry at anyone—it's a sin."
"Stop flaunting your happy life in front of others."

These messages cause us to feel ashamed of the emotions we experience, so we may push them down and try to hide them. We believe the messages that emotions are bad, rude, and inappropriate.

As children, we observed the emotions that were expressed (or not expressed) by our primary caregivers, as well as their responses to our own emotions. Our parents unconsciously modeled these lessons to us—in most cases, because that's what they learned about emotions from their parents.

In order to cultivate an emotionally healthy home, we need to examine our own beliefs about emotions so we can pass on healthy messages to our children.

Here are six healthy beliefs about emotions.

Emotions Are Normal

The truth is, emotions are a normal part of life for every human being. Whether you recognize it or not, every person experiences the highs and lows of an emotional life.

If you grew up in an environment that invalidated your feelings, it's likely you've internalized a belief that emotions are bad. You may not have had a safe person to mirror back to you that your feelings are valid.

Your child doesn't need to be told the same story. When we acknowledge and affirm our child's feelings, we share the message that emotions are normal.

"I understand why you feel that way."
"I would feel that way too if I were in your situation."
"Of course you feel that way! I felt the same way when I was your age."

When we work to create an environment where it's normal to talk openly about feelings, we give children the gift of knowing that their emotional experience of the world is real and normal.

Consider a typical family dinner where everyone is discussing their day. Maybe your toddler is screaming about the pasta not being the exact type they want. Validating their emotions might look like this: "It's understandable you're frustrated about the pasta. We can have the pasta you like another night, but tonight we're having this kind." Silencing their emotions, on the other hand, might look like this: "They're exactly the same—just eat the pasta!"

Your child might share that a teacher was "mean" to them and told them off for something at school. Validating their emotions might look like this: "That sounds like a hard day. It's upsetting when something like that happens." Silencing their emotions is saying, "Serves you right—you shouldn't have misbehaved for the teacher!"

Your teen might complain about having to put away their phone during dinner. You could validate their emotions by saying, "Yeah, I find it hard to put my phone away too. But we appreciate you doing it so we can have some family time together." Silencing their emotions is saying, "You're on that thing all day—can't you just sit for a few minutes without it?"

Remember: while it's good to validate your child's emotions, don't fret if you don't get it right every time. "Good enough" is good enough.

All Emotions Are Good

We often distinguish between good and bad emotions. We assume that happiness is good and anger is bad. It's true that what we do with our emotions can be positive or negative, but all emotions are good because they all serve a purpose.

It's healthy to feel happy when good things are happening.

It's healthy to feel sad when we experience loss.

It's healthy to feel angry when someone has wronged us.

It's healthy to feel scared when we're facing something overwhelming.

The problem comes when we communicate that only "positive emotions" are okay and we're uncomfortable when someone expresses anger, sadness, or fear. We lose sight of the fact that it's not the emotion itself that's harmful; it's what we choose to do with the emotion.

The church hasn't always done a good job with this in the past. Some Christians share Bible verses out of context to promote a world that says emotions are evil and that we need to live

> All emotions are good because they all serve a purpose.

by logic and willpower alone. But that's not how God created us. He designed us to feel the depth and breadth of our emotions. All emotions are good because they all serve a purpose. And life would be pretty boring without them!

That's why we place boundaries on behaviors, not emotions, with our children.

For example: "It's normal to feel angry. You're allowed to feel angry. But when we feel angry, we don't hit other people."

We can normalize the expression of emotion while also communicating that we need to learn healthy behaviors to deal with the emotion.

Emotions Are Signals

Somehow it always seems to be when I'm running late for an appointment or I have a long drive in front of me that the low fuel light in my car comes on.

This warning light is not an instant directive. You don't have to drop everything you're doing and attend to it immediately. Yet if you ignore it for an extended time, it *will* begin to affect your ability to drive the car.

We can think of emotions as functioning in a similar way. They are signals to pay attention to.

They show us what's most important to us.

They show us where our boundaries are.

They show us what we are and are not okay with in relationships.

They show us when we're exhausted or in need of rest.

They show us when our child is struggling with something they're unable to articulate.

Kate was counting to ten in her head to try to keep her cool. After asking her four-year-old son to put on his shoes and hop in the car,

Noah was still sprawled across his bed, screaming that he didn't want to go. With her baby daughter on her hip, Kate was trying to reason with her son.

"But it's going to be fun, honey. There will be games, activities, and lots of things to learn. And we can see your friend Matthew there."

"I don't care. I'm not going."

"We have to go—I have an appointment with baby Nellie."

> Emotions show us what's most important to us. They show us where our boundaries are.

"Can't I just come with you to the appointment?"

"Not this time—I'm sorry."

"Well, I'm not going!"

By this point, Nellie was starting to get upset, and Kate realized she wasn't getting anywhere with Noah. She grabbed Nellie's playmat and set her down nearby with some soft toys while she sat next to Noah.

"I can see you don't want to go to preschool today."

"I never want to go to preschool," Noah said in a huff.

"Why not?"

"Because I always miss you, Mommy!" Noah said, bursting into tears.

By taking the time to understand what her son was feeling, Kate was able to recognize that his resistant, aggressive behavior was just a sign that he was struggling with the big emotions of leaving her to go to preschool.

Emotions Need to Be Felt

My husband is a surfer, so all our married life we have lived near the ocean or spent a lot of time traveling to places with waves. Now, I'm not a surfer, but I do enjoy sitting on the beach. There's something calming about being near the water, watching the waves roll in and out.

Emotions are like waves: they flow in and out. When we feel a big emotion come, it can seem totally overwhelming, a tsunami wave threatening to envelop us. But if we *allow* that wave to flow—if we ride along with it—it *will* eventually subside. As my husband will tell you, fighting the waves only leads to getting yourself into trouble in the water. Instead, he leans into the wave and lets it carry him to shore. It's only when we resist this flow that we struggle to move forward.

Similarly, if we want to have a healthy relationship with our emotions, we can't stuff them down. Emotional health means giving ourselves permission to feel our emotions. We need to "feel it to heal it." This looks like compassionately letting our emotions in, even when they're uncomfortable, without judgment or shame. We simply allow them to come, and we allow them to go.

Emotions don't define us. They don't determine how good or bad we are. They're a part of life that keeps us healthy, if we allow ourselves to feel them. This is one of the hardest parts of parenting—allowing our child to feel their emotions without trying to fix them or the situation.

As a mom, every time one of my children is upset, I am naturally inclined to try to fix the situation and help them feel okay again as quickly as possible. (This is especially true if one of their peers has been mean to them—it takes all my self-control not to give the other kid a piece of my mind!) But although this may make my child feel better in the moment, it won't help them in the long term. So most of the time I'm internally talking to myself as I'm talking to my child.

"It's okay to feel upset."

"That would make me upset too."

"You can feel upset for as long as you need to."

Sometimes the wave is short lived, and other times it takes a while, but if these feelings are given space, they usually resolve.

You can use the metaphor of waves to talk to your children about emotions: "Emotions are like waves. They feel big at times—so big it seems they will never end. But if you let yourself feel them, they will eventually resolve."

Emotions Drive Behavior

Whether we like it or not, emotions don't just stay inside of us; they are drivers for the way we act. If we feel angry, we might say or do something we later regret. If we feel sad, we might withdraw from a relationship. If we feel scared, we might avoid a situation we need to face.

It's not always a negative thing. Consider the mother who is so frustrated by the inadequate care at her child's preschool that she takes action and removes the child from that environment in order to help them thrive. Or the father who, after an angry outburst, feels scared that his reactions might be hurting his children and decides to go to therapy to work through his past. Emotions can lead to positive change!

The key is slowing down: we must ensure that there is *space* between our emotions and our behavior. In the moment of heated emotion, our prefrontal cortex gets overridden by our emotional brain. We experience the emotion with such intensity that we may temporarily lose control over our actions. We're not thinking clearly; we're not making good decisions with our words or actions. We need to take a break so that our emotions can back off the threshold. If the emotions remain, they may drive us to make a decision or take action in a way that's positive and productive.

The main way we teach younger children the connection between emotions and behavior is through the boundaries we set:

"It's okay to feel angry. But when we are angry, we don't hit."
"It's normal to feel scared. But when you're scared, you still can't run away from Mommy."

When your child is older and moving toward adolescence, you can teach them how to create space between their emotions and choices. This might include encouraging them to sleep on the problem and decide what to do in the morning or to move their bodies to help them regulate or to take a few days to think about what they want to say to a friend. When it comes to bigger life decisions, this might include urging them to share their feelings with people they trust to gather some wisdom.

Making space between our emotions and our behavior is not invalidating our emotions; rather, it helps us to be wise with the choices we make. Strong emotions are good—they can drive healthy change and can be directed into creativity and innovation when they're channeled with wisdom.

It's Good to Share Emotions with Safe People

In a crowded mall, my friend and I huddled around a small table in a coffee shop. Karen was a decade ahead of me and was like a big sister and mentor. From the first time I met her, I instantly felt like I had a friend. She was lighthearted and kind, interested in my life without prying, and made me feel validated about anything I shared with her.

That particular day, I was visibly upset. I shared with her about a situation I was navigating that I'd only told two other close friends about. I felt confused about it, struggling to think clearly, because it was a situation not many other people I knew had encountered. I didn't want to feel judged or shamed by people who didn't understand what I was going through.

Yet I felt safe with Karen, which is why I wanted to speak to her about the situation. She listened to everything and normalized my feelings while also speaking truth into the blurry places in my mind. Her nonjudgmental wisdom was balm to my soul, and I left our time together, as I always did, feeling more loved, encouraged, and empowered than when I'd arrived.

Emotions can be overwhelming at times. Being vulnerable by sharing them with the safe people in our lives helps lift the burden from our shoulders, process what the signals may or may not mean, and feel a little less alone.

A safe person is trustworthy, encourages what is good about you, respects your boundaries, and accepts you.

An unsafe person invalidates your emotions, is judgmental about your thoughts and behaviors, makes you feel there's something wrong with you, and walks all over your personal boundaries. When you're teaching children about safe people, it's also important to let them know that safe adults don't ask you to keep secrets from others.

We can teach our children about safe people by sharing about our own friendships (maybe without names!) and whether they've been safe or not. We can help our children ask:

"Can we trust them?"

"Do they make us feel better or worse about ourselves?"

When we share our emotions with safe people, it makes us feel better.

Raising Emotionally Intelligent Children

There's so much pressure on parents when it comes to raising our children. We are bombarded with advice about how to make sure our kids excel at reading, math, sports, music, and countless other areas. But we rarely hear about the importance of emotional intelligence. Some people may not register the need at all, and others assume kids will just pick up these skills along the way. But if we want to raise kids who are resilient and healthy, emotional intelligence isn't optional; it's something we need to be intentional about teaching them.

Ways to Teach Emotional Literacy for Younger Children

1. Take note of your child's age and stage of development as you talk about emotions. For example, if they are a toddler, stick to the four main emotions. When they're in elementary school, you can introduce a few more complex emotions. When they're in middle school and high school, you can talk about all the different emotions.
2. If you have younger children, read picture books about different emotions or characters who experience different emotions. Point out what the emotion is and what feelings or behaviors the character shows in response to that emotion.
3. Practice naming different emotions as they arise in daily life. For example: "It seems like you felt mad when your toy was taken away" or "Look at your friend—they seem so happy on the swing!"
4. Teach through an art activity what different emotions look and feel like. For example: "If we were to draw sadness, what do you think it would look like? What colors would you use? What makes you feel sad?"
5. Use emotional-regulation teaching aids such as emotion color wheels or visual posters of the emotions you're trying to teach. (Check out our website, www.ResilientLittleHearts.com, for these visuals.)

6. Narrate your own emotions (in an age-appropriate way) to your child. When you're narrating your emotions, be sure to bring resolution for them so they don't feel emotionally responsible for you. For example: "When my friend moved out of town, that made me feel sad. I'm going to rest a little while, and I will feel better again."
7. Use emotional check-ins with your child: "How are you feeling today?"
8. Use empathy in conflict resolution: "How do you think the other person might be feeling right now?"

Ways to Teach Emotional Intelligence for Older Children and Adolescents

1. Talk openly about emotions. Allow conversations about thoughts and feelings to flow freely in your home, without shaming or punishing your child for what they share. By talking openly about emotions, you are normalizing their emotional expression. If your child doesn't naturally share, you might begin these conversations with sharing about your own emotions in age-appropriate ways.
2. Validate their emotions. If you can validate them by saying, "It's understandable that you feel that way" or "I would feel that way if I were in that situation," it normalizes their emotional experience of the world. It also makes them feel safer to share again in the future.
3. Talk about emotional coping skills. You might share some of your own emotional coping tools, such as naming emotions, reframing the meaning of emotions, or doing physical activities to reduce the stress that comes with heightened emotions. (See chapter 6.)
4. Encourage them to start a journaling practice. Journaling can help your older child or teen pay attention to their emotions and notice what these emotions might be showing them. Promise them that you won't read their private journal unless they share it with you (and keep your promise!).

5. Together with your child or teen, brainstorm activities you could do to help support different emotional states. For example, when you feel angry, you could take a break, go for a run, punch a punching bag, scream into a pillow, journal your feelings, etc.
6. Place boundaries around behavior rather than thoughts or feelings. This creates an environment of emotional safety in your home so your child can explore all their thoughts and feelings without fear of punishment or shame.
7. Normalize attending therapy. Whether your child needs therapy now or not, the way you talk about it will frame how comfortable they are to reach out for therapeutic support in the future. You might talk about attending therapy as seeing a doctor for our thoughts and emotions and explain that almost everyone needs therapy at some point, or multiple points, in their lives. This removes the stigma from getting therapeutic support if they need it.

PART THREE

Developing Practices to Turn Down the Noise

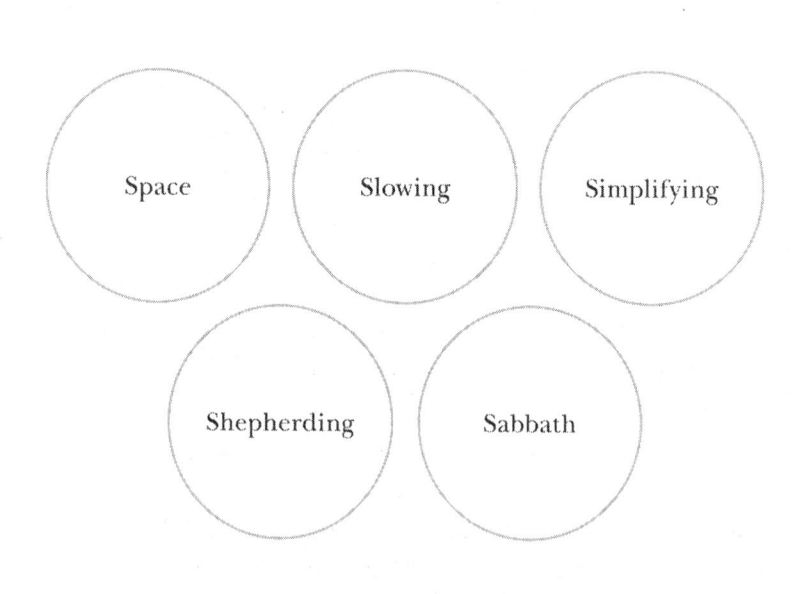

- Space
- Slowing
- Simplifying
- Shepherding
- Sabbath

CHAPTER 10

SPACE:

MAKING ROOM FOR CREATIVE PLAY

> His house was perfect, whether you liked food, or sleep, or work, or story-telling, or singing, or just sitting and thinking best, or a pleasant mixture of them all.
>
> J. R. R. TOLKIEN

"Bluey!"

As the theme song played, the whole room of children started singing along.

We'd had a group of families with children around the same age at our house for lunch. After a long afternoon of eating and playing, the kids were now watching some episodes of *Bluey* while the adults had some space to talk.

The kids were giggling and calling us over to watch different scenes as the cartoon family of Australian blue heeler dogs played games with one another.

"Dad, that's just like what you do!"

"We played that game of Keepy Uppy!"

"Let's be grannies!"

The children's television show *Bluey* gives a window into family life with young children through a family of dogs that play (many!) games together. One of the reasons it has become so popular is because it shows the kind of playful, heartwarming relationships families deeply desire. (As a bonus, it also offers a peek into Australian culture!)

Play as a Joyful State of Mind

If you were to broach the topic of play with the parent of a young child, you'd likely get an exhausted or even exasperated reaction about how much their children ask them to play and their desire for a break. But the true definition of play goes far beyond board games, Legos, and Barbie dolls.

Play expert Dr. Stuart Brown defines play as "a *state of mind*, . . . an absorbing, apparently purposeless activity that provides enjoyment and a suspension of self-consciousness and sense of time."[1]

Play is less about the activity we're engaged in and more about a *state of being* when we're relaxed and enjoying something purely for enjoyment's sake. Play is the opposite of productivity. In a culture that prizes efficiency, it seems almost wasteful to do something "just because," with no particular output intended.

> Play is the opposite of productivity.

Ingrid Fetell Lee, author of *Joyful*, says that play "is the only known activity that humans engage in solely because it produces joy. . . . The only metric of success for play is how much joy it produces."[2] The true definition of play is any activity that brings us joy.

Joy is confetti and balloons, laughing so much your belly hurts, twinkle lights and cake, rainbows and cartwheels, giggles and hugs, parties and sunbeams.

These are things we deeply desire for our children when they're young. But once we become adults, they can seem frivolous, as if joy is only for children, not grown-ups. After all, as adults, we have lived long enough to know that horrible things happen in this world—and we've had to walk through some of these things ourselves. This awareness of the heaviness of life has somehow convinced us that joy is no longer available to us. We sometimes make the mistake of thinking play is only something we wish our children would go and do on their own so we can have a break or get something productive done. We want our children to experience joy, but we remove ourselves from that equation.

But play isn't just for children; play is for us, too.

When was the last time you laughed so hard you started crying?

When did you last lose track of time because you were engrossed in a good book or an activity you love?

When was the last time you felt a moment of joy in your daily life?

These questions may bring up feelings of anger or disbelief for you. Many of us can't remember the last time we experienced this kind of true play and enjoyment. If you're going through a season of grief or a particular hardship, it's even more natural for the joy of daily life to feel absent for a while. But we often don't pay enough attention to the nonstop seriousness of our lives and the way our focus on productivity and achievement slowly drains the joy from our lives. This comes at a cost to us and our children, mentally and emotionally. As play expert Dr. Stuart Brown says, "The opposite of play is not work—the opposite of play is depression."[3]

Joy is a core human need, for both children and grown-ups. Joy is a sign that our nervous system feels safe and at rest. It provides the recovery we need mentally and emotionally after going through stress. Joy bolsters our creativity, courage, and resilience for hard times. It reenergizes us and gives us the motivation to keep persevering.

> Joy bolsters our creativity, courage, and resilience for hard times.

Joy also fuels connection. When we have playful times with our children, it deepens relational bonds. Parenting is not full of joy all the time—but if there are *never* moments of joy, the relationship with our child begins to feel as if it's always hard work. Joy refills our hearts with the reserves to get through the more challenging moments.

Of course, joy may look different for grown-ups than it does for children. We may feel joy when we watch our sleeping child, when we're doing an activity we love, at the end of a long chat with a loved one, during times of family fun and connection, or when we're looking at the stars at night. Joy is when our heart swells with gratitude at the grandeur of the life we've been given.

As a family, we love the card game Uno. We started playing it together when our youngest was five, and it has become a regular event in our household. One evening after dinner, when my kids asked if we could play a quick game, I saw that the table with the cards was already laid out, and I knew it wasn't really a question. The only problem was that I'd been writing all day, and my brain was more than a little frazzled.

I wasn't sure I felt like playing, but everyone else wanted to, so I figured I just needed to persevere for their sake. I told myself that it was a simple game, assuming I would get through it despite my mental exhaustion. So when I put my wild card down (which can change the play of cards to any color) and announced confidently that the color would be nine, the whole family looked at me strangely for a moment, then burst into laughter. I didn't understand what was going on until, through breathless laughter, they started teasing:

"Mom, nine is a number, not a color!"

"I think Mom is a bit confused about her numbers and colors. Do you know your letters?"

"Okay, let's all choose our favorite color—mine is four!"

It wasn't long before we were all in stitches over my exhausted comment. Even though I'd played the game for the kids, I ended up laughing so hard at myself that I felt joy too. What had started as a basic card game turned into a hilarious family memory that is still brought up to this day.

Joyful play isn't only for children. As adults, we also need it for our own resilience and emotional energy, as it helps us get through the hard, serious parts of life. We may think we don't have time to play, but as we allow space for it in small moments, we are also modeling for our children what it means to have a meaningful, joyful life.

Why Children Need Play

Play is foundational for the emotional health and development of a child. It's one of the main ways they learn. On the outside, it may look as if a child is just running around or playing make-believe, but these activities are stimulating their brain to make connections about how the world works. They are learning problem-solving and adaptability, and increasing their empathy for and understanding of others.

We can see how foundational play is in a child's life when we note what happens when children don't have enough opportunities to play. Studies show that moderate to severe play deprivation during childhood (under ten years old) is linked to significant emotional dysregulation. This includes inflexible thinking, lower impulse control, less self-regulation, poor management of aggression, and a higher incidence of mental health issues.[4] Severe play deprivation can occur in abusive family environments, but it can also occur in hyper-strict families that never allow for free play or any type of personal expression.

The Power of Free Play

There are many different types of play, but the two broad categories are structured play and free independent play.

Structured play is when adults set up play opportunities for children to engage in or when they enroll their children in extracurricular activities such as sports, music, or scouts. Structured play often involves a group of other children. This is the primary type of play we think about in our culture—something parents organize for their children.

Structured play is an enjoyable, healthy part of childhood, but it's not necessarily the type of play that reduces a child's stimulation. In fact, for some children, it may increase stress (such as when the involvement in extracurricular activities exceeds the child's stimulation threshold).

Free play is when the child has space to initiate the play activity themselves and define the parameters for play. This is what you see when you stumble across your child engrossed in an activity that you didn't suggest to them. It's also what you see when a group of children start an imaginary game on the playground. This type of play, when the child has time and space to initiate, has the greatest potential to reduce their stimulation and stress levels. Time for free play increases emotional health in childhood.

In our culture, we often lean too heavily on structured play. We do this with the best of intentions, wanting our children to have opportunities to do all the activities they enjoy, discover new skills, and build their confidence. But in the process, we've created so much structured play that it comes at the expense of free play.

During free play, children calm themselves and process their day. This reduces their cortisol levels and regulates their nervous system. This is especially true for highly sensitive children, as it helps them decompress and process the stimulation from their day. If your child has a highly sensitive temperament, one of the best ways to support their resilience and emotional health is to protect their free play time.

Children need times in their daily and weekly rhythms that are unscheduled, unrushed, and under their control so their nervous system can relax.

Free Play Guide

If your child struggles with free play, take heart. This is a skill that can be learned, and you can support them in developing this skill.

Let's begin by assessing how much free play your child is currently doing. A lot, some, or none at all?

If your child is already spending a good deal of time in free play, they likely have the ability to initiate it independently. If this is the case, your main role is to pay attention to when they may need more at different times.

If your child isn't doing much free play or they're not doing it at all, here are some tips for helping them grow in this area.

1. Choose an activity they enjoy that they can do alone (based on their age).
2. Get out the activity so it's easily accessible to them.
3. Sit down and begin to do the activity yourself, without necessarily inviting them to do it.
4. Within ten minutes, they will likely begin doing the activity alongside you.

5. Once they're engrossed in the activity, say something like, "I'm going to do the laundry. I'll be gone for ten minutes and then I'll be back." Then leave them with the activity.
6. If they come to find you before the ten minutes, begin with a shorter period next time. If they don't come to find you before the ten minutes are up, re-enter the same space, but don't re-engage with the activity. Note how long they're engrossed in the activity. For example, if it's twenty minutes, that's their current threshold.
7. Start having regular times of free play during the day. Set a timer for their threshold (for example, start with twenty minutes), and tell them they can choose anything from the craft or game cupboard or anything in the backyard. Be sure not to interfere with the play unless they're about to physically hurt themselves. (Note: It's important that they have access to toys, craft supplies, Legos, and outdoor activities. They need to know they won't be in trouble for making a mess or touching things they shouldn't touch. If they're tentative about engaging in free play, you want to encourage any initiative they show.)
8. Incorporate this as a regular practice in your family life, and slowly increase the time periods. After a few weeks, notice how they begin to initiate play without you having to put structure around it.

Play vs. Entertainment

Play is different from entertainment. Play is something we're actively involved in, whereas entertainment is something we passively consume.

The advancements in technology over the past several decades have gradually moved our leisure-time activities from active participation to consumption. We've slowly lost the joy of free time.

Entertainment certainly has its place, but it's not usually regenerative. Think about how you feel after reading a good book, working in your garden, playing pickleball with friends, building something, drawing, or cooking. There's something about being involved in the process that fills our souls in a different way from watching a movie or scrolling on social media.

But with the exhaustion of our lives, it often feels like too much work to "do" anything. We think it will be relaxing to just watch something and be amused. But the more we do this, the more we lose the muscle of play.

One of the core problems with the surge of technology and entertainment is that children today are never bored. Ever. They are constantly stimulated by things to consume, looking for the next hit of dopamine. Yet boredom is the precursor to creativity. In studies on creativity, neuroscientists found a repeatable pattern in brain wave activity prior to moments of insight.[5] This state of insight occurs especially often when the brain is relaxed and alert, such as when we're taking a shower, praying, meditating, or doing a mundane task. So if our children are never bored, their imagination and creativity don't have the chance to blossom.

Many musicians, artists, authors, and entrepreneurs began their journeys being bored as children, such as prolific writer Agatha Christie, who credits boredom in her childhood as the prompt for her to become a writer.[6] It was boredom that caused other people to pick up a guitar or pen or paintbrush and start playing around with something they later realized brought them joy and fulfillment.

Developmentally, imaginative play for children typically stops between the ages of eight to twelve years old. This doesn't mean their need for play ceases; rather, it moves toward hobbies and activities or social interactions and games.

But a child can lose interest in play (at any age) because they have access to so much entertainment that they lose the muscle of active play. With increased access to technology, children are trying to be teenagers at a younger and younger age.

Will You Play with Me?

This is the question that haunts many.

A child's question "Will you play with me?" is often their way of seeking connection and time together. A five-year-old doesn't usually have the self-awareness to articulate, "I don't feel connected to you, so I would like you to give me some focused time." They communicate this need by asking to play.

When we sit down with our child to draw, or build Legos, or kick a ball together, or give our full attention to a conversation about their card collection or sports or dancing, we are sending our child a message that they matter to us.

As parents, we often underestimate just how much our child wants to be with us and finds comfort in our presence. Even just ten minutes of focused playtime with our child (with no phones or distractions) can significantly increase feelings of connection.

Yet many parents feel as if they've played with their child endlessly and are still being asked this question. When this occurs, it may not always be because the child is seeking connection. As children have more access to entertainment and less free time, their muscle for playing independently weakens. Sometimes the question "Will you play with me?" is your child's way of articulating their boredom and lack of ability to initiate an activity themselves.

When this question comes your way, you first need to be honest with yourself.

- Have you truly given your child focused attention for a period of time (without your phone or other distractions)?
- Is their need for connection time higher because of stress or exhaustion they're experiencing?
- Has your weekly or monthly schedule been so busy that you've had less time together overall lately?

If you've given your child focused attention during playtime but you sense they have a higher need for connection, consider involving them in your daily chores and tasks (if they're old enough) so you can still get things done and they also get to spend time with you.

If you've given them focused attention during playtime and they're not interested (or not old enough) to engage in your chores or tasks with you, it may be that your child needs support in learning free play (see "Free Play Guide" earlier in this chapter for practical ways to help them develop this skill).

As a parent, you are not responsible for keeping your child entertained. Part of play is learning to be independent and initiate activities (even if that means being bored sometimes!).

Why Families Need Play

It was 6:14 p.m., and I was rushing to get dinner on the table. Watching the clock, I was mentally running through the list of things that still needed to be done for the night: homework, showers, reading, preparing for the next day. My thoughts were becoming more anxious and pressured as I considered all the activities we needed to get through before bedtime.

Then my daughter came into the kitchen and handed me a small orange piece of paper the size of a business card. The card said, "You are invited to a talent show" and was decorated with pictures and stickers.

"Mama, we're starting straight after dinner, and everyone is going to perform!"

"Everyone? As in, I have to perform in the talent show?"

"Yes!" she said, running out of the kitchen to set up the upcoming show.

I instantly felt the weight of another thing on my to-do list, wrestling with whether we had time to do this tonight. But she was so excited that right after dinner, we all headed for the lounge room, where she'd set up the talent show.

For the most part, the talent show consisted of everyone doing silly dances to music the kids chose. After just a few minutes, as the kids giggled and we all laughed at my husband's ridiculous dance moves, I felt the whole energy of the house change.

It has been said that laughter is the key that grace has arrived.[7] When our approach to family life is lighthearted and playful, it cultivates an emotionally healthy home. Research shows that families with playful environments have more connected relationships and lower levels of anxiety.[8]

Cultivating a playful, lighthearted family environment doesn't mean you have to be a comedian or constantly play with your child. Rather, it means keeping a lighthearted perspective when interacting with one another. When you are clear but playful in your approach, your children know the boundaries in your home without having to walk on eggshells, scared they'll make a mistake or fail at keeping those boundaries (which children do multiple times a day).

Being lighthearted might look like chuckling at your nine-year-old's back talk before saying, "Would you like to try saying that a different way?" rather than harshly correcting them, or laughing (rather than crying) when your two-year-old smashes their juicy peach into your living room carpet (speaking from personal experience!), or making fun of yourself when your teen criticizes you before reminding them about using words carefully.

So much of parenting is outrageous and ridiculous. It's why those parenting memes are so funny—because they're true. Raising children is challenging, but it can also be joyful—and hilarious.

When You Don't Feel "Fun" or "Funny"

Maybe the idea of being playful seems impossible at this stage of your life. With so many tasks on your to-do list, it seems like fun has to wait for an elusive day when all your work is done. Or maybe you don't see yourself as a fun person and, in fact, you feel intimidated by play. You see your personality as more of the responsible type, the dutiful type, the type A achiever. You aren't usually the life of the party, telling funny stories or jokes. The idea of play can seem like a lot of work and can even make you feel guilty.

But if play is a core need for *everyone*, then it isn't something to do only on vacation or when all your chores are done; it's something you have to be intentional about carving out time for. This could look like giving yourself permission to do activities you love, even if you haven't yet achieved everything on your to-do list. This could look like making space for hobbies or sports or recreational activities, even if they don't always make sense practically. It could also mean allowing yourself permission to find joy and rest as much as you do for your children.

Play also doesn't mean you need to fit a specific personality profile. No matter the responsibilities on your plate, no matter your temperament, you can cultivate a lighthearted attitude and engage in joyful activities where you lose track of time.

You don't need to become a different person to be an incredible parent to your children; you simply need to get in touch with what brings you joy and then share that joy with your family.

Something I love to do in my free time is read a good book. I love the slower pace of sitting or lying down and getting lost in a story or an interesting nonfiction read. I love learning and having conversations about interesting topics. I've sometimes wondered if this makes me boring (when people ask what you do for fun, reading isn't typically at the top of the list of exciting hobbies!). Yet when I became a mother, I was able to share my love of reading with my children.

Since they were little, we've had reading time before bed. When they were young, we'd climb into bed together and read picture books; when they got a bit older, they would wiggle around next to me on the couch, getting distracted one moment, then looking at the pictures in graphic novels the next. Now they draw or do other activities while I'm reading chapter books.

We've visited imaginary worlds together, wondered about suspenseful endings, and compared characters in the books to people we know in real life. Not only is this reading time something I genuinely enjoy, it has also cultivated some really special moments of connection along the way. This feels like play for my children and me. The details and activities will vary for you, depending on your interests and your family dynamics—the important thing is to try different ideas and find something that feels playful for you.

Protecting Free Time

If we want to create space for creative play, it needs to be something we value and plan for. Our lives get so busy that unless we put boundaries in place to protect our family's free time, it will get scheduled over.

I recommend taking out your calendar and scheduling in free time. If possible, try to create a repeatable rhythm (for example, early afternoons on weekdays or on Saturday mornings). If this isn't possible, begin by carving out one space of time in the next week.

As you do this, you might discover that despite your best intentions, you don't have time or space left for free time. Sometimes this is because you're in a season of unusually high demand, such as when work is particularly busy or a child has a health concern or aging parents need your care. If this is the case, be gracious toward yourself—some time is better than no time. Try to release yourself from high expectations, and take the small pockets of space you can find.

But if you find that your calendar has no space just because of the number of "good" activities you've scheduled, this might be an opportunity to reconsider these commitments and decide which ones to limit, either now or in the future.

How to Add More Joy and Play into Family Life

- Reflect on things that feel like play for you. What did you do for fun before having children? What activities or hobbies did you enjoy as a child?
- Make a "joy list" of small things you enjoy. How can you add these into your life on a daily or weekly basis?
- Make a "joy list" with your children. Ask them what simple things they love and plan how you can incorporate them into your life more.
- Consider using some of the time when your child is sleeping or engaged in free play to do something you enjoy (rather than working or getting chores done). This might not be plausible every day, but even if you start doing this once a week, you may find this practice life-giving.
- Invite your child into your joys and interests. Do you enjoy surfing, riding bikes, building things, gardening, reading, or cooking? Inviting your child into these activities can increase the amount of time you get to do the activities you enjoy while also connecting with your child.

- Consider your child's natural interests and create some resources or space for them to safely do these activities. For example, if they love painting, consider setting up a spot for them to do this in the garage. If they enjoy building, make sure there's space on the floor or shelves to display their creations. You don't need to go overboard, but the physical space will invite the child to play.
- Curate a playlist of fun songs that you and your children enjoy and have a dance party.
- Find some age-appropriate joke books and tell your child some jokes.
- Blow up colorful balloons and play balloon volleyball.
- Laugh at yourself and take a lighthearted view when things go wrong or when people make mistakes.
- Start a gratitude practice on your own. Each night, write down three things you're grateful for.
- Start a gratitude practice with your child. Each night, have them share three things they're grateful for as you're putting them to bed.

CHAPTER 11

SLOWING:

REDUCING THE PACE OF FAMILY LIFE

> Hurry is the enemy of love. Love means
> giving someone your full attention.
> STEVE BIDDULPH

The carpet was brown shag, like in many houses built in the 1970s. I was in my school uniform, sitting tentatively on a chair in the hallway, all alone. Grasping my books, I could feel my heart beating so fast it seemed like it would thump through my chest. Just behind the closed door ahead of me, I could hear another student playing and the teacher correcting them.

It was a Tuesday afternoon, and I was nervous. I was about to have another piano lesson with a teacher who scared me, and yet again I hadn't practiced all week. I quickly tried to come up with an excuse to avoid being told off.

The door opened, and the other student walked out with their piano books, eyes down. I mustered a smile and a "hello," walked into the next room, and sat at the piano. Fumbling with my books, I shared reasons I hadn't been able to practice much that week. Sensing the teacher's disapproval, I quickly opened my book to the song I was supposed to play.

Realizing that I'd last laid eyes on this music exactly this time last week, I placed my hands on the keys and attempted to play the song, very slowly. As I came to the end of the song with only a small mistake here and there, I felt relieved that by playing the song so slowly, I'd convinced my teacher that I had done the expected practice.

When the song ended, she didn't say anything. She stood up and walked to the corner of the room. Picking up a small box, she brought it over and placed it on the piano, right above me. She explained that this was a metronome, a device that creates a steady clicking noise to help musicians play at a certain pace.

She set the metronome at a slow speed: *click . . . click . . . click*.

Quietly taking a deep breath so I wouldn't give away my sense of relief, I put my hands on the piano keys to play the song again. Then my teacher decided the metronome wasn't fast enough, so she adjusted the speed to a much faster pace: *click, click, click*.

My heart started racing. As the speed increased, so did the demand on my piano skills. My stress level rose as I was no longer convinced that I could play the song at that pace.

"Now let's play the song at the proper speed," she said.

An Increased Pace of Life

In the past several decades, it feels like the metronome determining the pace of our lives has been sped up several clicks, and we're racing to keep up. Actually, the pace of life began to increase long ago with the industrial revolution and its focus on productivity and efficiency. But in recent years, the pace has increased even more as a result of technological advances. The interconnectedness that was supposed to make our lives easier (because we could read our emails at home or message people whenever we wanted to) has actually led to us feeling that we are "on" all the time, racing just to keep up.

We feel this daily as we constantly rush from one thing to another.

In our own lives, this may look like an overcommitted calendar, endless to-do lists, and days when we feel like we're hurrying from one activity to the next. It may also look like frustration at our child for not moving fast enough or a lack of patience for other people who are moving more slowly than we are.

Whether we have young toddlers at home or school-age children, we as parents feel so much pressure to get things done. We wish we could just "get it together," finally becoming organized enough to feel on top of things, to maximize our time and create a peaceful, efficient home.

If you're the parent of a school-age child, you probably experience this mindset in full force at the beginning of each school year. As summer comes to a close and fall approaches, the preparation for the new year begins, with the scramble to get school supplies, new clothes or uniforms, and backpacks, and to sign up for sports, clubs, and extracurricular activities.

Every year, armed with new hacks and calendar reminders, we promise ourselves that *this* is the school year we'll stay on top of everything. We tell ourselves, *If I just push myself a little harder, I won't forget anything* or *If I just had a better system, I'd be organized enough to stay on top of everything.*

But as the days turn into weeks, and as the year turns toward the holiday season, our hope for "getting it together" fades. The parent group chat explodes with hundreds of text messages each day, and the school office announces last-minute dress-up days, not to mention homework, extracurricular commitments, and all the sicknesses the kids bring home.

It is a falsity, of course, that we should be able to do it all, and almost everyone is going through the same experience. Despite this, in all our introspection, we never stop to question *the pace of our culture*. Instead, we blame ourselves or our children for our inability to properly "keep up." Instead of looking at what needs to change in the broader system, we just keep trying harder and pushing our kids more relentlessly, often burning out in the process.

We're trying to do too much in too short a time.

Why It's Hard to Slow Down

There are many reasons it's hard to slow down our pace of life. Here are some common challenges we face when trying to create a more manageable rhythm.

- **Sometimes we legitimately can't slow down.** This may be because of pressures related to finances, a sick family member, or a child with additional needs. You may desperately desire a more slowed-down life, but you're currently not in a position to make that happen.
- **We desire to build a better life for ourselves and our children.** This isn't inherently a bad thing, but in doing so, we may lose sight of the greater goal. We want our children to have opportunities for activities, experiences, and education. This impulse is good, but sometimes we end up overscheduling and overstimulating our children in the process.
- **We're part of a culture that determines the pace.** If we're surrounded by people who are living at a fast pace, this starts becoming normalized to us. Our pace is also influenced by the school, church, community group, or extracurricular activities we're committed to.
- **We tend to focus on visible metrics rather than invisible health.** There are obvious metrics that are easy to measure, such as salary, finances, calendars, extracurricular activities, and education. Relationships and emotional health, on the other hand, are often less tangible, unless they become problematic.
- **We may never have questioned our pace.** We're so caught in our culture that it feels normal to us. We may never have questioned whether our pace is helping or harming our family.

Despite how challenging it is to slow down the pace of family life, and despite how countercultural this is, it's still worth the effort to pursue a slower pace for the health of our souls. It's not just a matter of preference; it's an essential part of cultivating an environment for our family's resilience and emotional health.

Resisting a Culture of Hurry

Wednesday morning began as most weekday mornings do. The alarm went off, and I woke up the kids and got them fed, dressed, and organized so they would make it out the door and to school on time. That morning they were tired and required multiple reminders to hurry up because if they continued stalling, they would be late.

As soon as I got them out the door, I changed to go for my morning walk before starting work. Putting in my earbuds, I turned on a podcast to listen to while I walked (so my time would be additionally productive).

My pace quickened as I mentally ran through the list of all the things I needed to get done that day. I was caught up in my thoughts—alternating between my to-do list and the ideas they were talking about in the podcast—when I turned the corner and was stopped in my tracks.

A little boy, about two or three years old, was crouched down on the strip of grass in the median. His father was standing by him, waiting protectively and patiently, as he gave his son space to explore. They must have been walking from their house to the local park when the boy found something that caught his attention—a dandelion to wish upon, a snail making its way across the pavement, or a rock he wanted to keep for his collection.

The father was just standing there, waiting. He wasn't rushing his son along to the next activity but was allowing him a moment to examine the world at his own pace. Amid the frantic pace of my internal and external world that morning, encountering the slow presence of this father and son interrupted my cadence in a profound and beautiful way.

As I walked by, I smiled at the little boy and said "Good morning" to the father. I wondered if the father knew what a precious gift he was giving his son that morning. Did they know that their unhurried presence along the side of the road served as a sacred interruption to the frenzied rhythm of my day?

In our world, speed is almost an addiction. When life slows down and we aren't experiencing the high of efficiency and productivity, we face "time anxiety"—the feeling that we're wasting our time. One symptom of time anxiety is the feeling of agitation that comes if anything gets in the way of what we need to do. This elevated sense of urgency has also been called "hurry sickness." The anxious belief that we constantly need to be in a hurry increases our daily stress level and can, over time, lead to chronic physical and mental health problems.

Rushing also places undue stress on children. We struggle with this pressure as adults, but at least we're already fully developed, physically and neurologically. Children, on the other hand, are still developing and therefore more vulnerable to this stress.

If we are constantly hurrying children throughout their days, it not only reduces opportunities to meet their developmental need to explore the world and learn through curiosity but also doesn't allow them times of recovery when they can rest and recalibrate their understanding of the world. This is true for older children and teenagers too. If they're constantly hurried from one demand to the next, with no downtime, they may experience an increase in mental health struggles and problematic behaviors.

Love and Connection

In order to cultivate the emotional health of our souls, we need to slow down. If we're constantly rushing through our days, every day, we do harm to our inner life. It's no wonder we aren't able to show up as the parents we desire to be.

One of the primary reasons for disconnection in family life is that we don't slow down enough to be present with those we love most. We're so busy rushing from activity to activity, commitment to commitment, that we forget to make time to connect.

You simply can't give another person your attention and presence if you're in a hurry.

Our souls have a speed that is emotionally healthy. They hold the pace of love and connection.

Theologian and writer Kosuke Kayama writes, "Love has its speed. . . . It is a spiritual speed. It is a different kind of speed from the technological speed to which we are accustomed. . . . It goes on in the depth of our life, whether we notice it or not, . . . at three miles an hour. It is the speed we walk and therefore the speed the love of God walks."[1] Although our inner life has an ideal speed that serves our emotional health, life is often significantly faster than this pace. But we weren't created to constantly live at a fast pace or try to keep up with the speed of technology. This is why we feel out of sync when we are living in this cadence for an extended period of time.

Children have a way of reminding us what's most important in life. They are often far more in touch with their souls than we are as stressed adults. One of the gifts of children is that they are slower than we are. This can be frustrating when we have things we need to do and schedules to keep, but if we take the time to see the world from their perspective, we recognize the value of a slower pace. Rather than trying to teach them to hurry up, maybe we can let them teach us to slow down. When we slow down, we have time to look into the eyes of those we love, have meaningful conversations with them, and make lasting memories together. When we slow down, we give ourselves the space to breathe, process what we've experienced, and bring alignment and health to our inner life. Slowing down also opens up creative ideas that we would never discover when living at a frenzied pace.

> Children give us the gift of paying attention.

Beauty and Wonder

In the slowing, children notice things that we don't notice—the fall leaves, the butterfly on the flower, the rainbow on the wall when the sun shines in. Children give us the gift of paying attention.

Young children slow us down so we can engage in the wonder of tiny things. This is part of the beauty of childhood. Without young children around, we'd be unlikely to crouch down to watch a snail move across the pathway. Yet when we're with a young child, we're reminded of the wonder around us that we would otherwise miss.

There are seasons of our lives when the way of wisdom is to intentionally slow down—whether by saying no to some things so we can say yes to others or by following the lead of our children. But other times our lives slow down by no choice of our own.

Suffering has a way of forcing us to slow down against our will. When you're walking through the darkest days of your life or your child's life, your days can feel very slow.

When I was diagnosed with cancer in my late twenties, the eighteen months of treatment significantly reduced my capacity to work or do much activity at all. The fatigue I experienced from the treatment was so intense that just walking to the mailbox felt like an accomplishment. Then there was the emotional toll, as I came face to face with the fragility of life. Grief surrounded me like a fog—grief not just about my specific diagnosis, but about the loss of my naivete about the future. Between my physical limitations and wrestling with grief, my daily life slowed dramatically.

It's an odd experience when you're walking through grief, chronic pain, a medical diagnosis, or an intense season of caregiving: your daily life slows down while everyone else's pace of life stays the same.

While I was walking through a season of grief and loss, my life slowed down and something unexpected happened: I began to notice beauty. Not the kind of beauty you see online in perfectly curated pictures, but the beauty of tiny, ordinary things—the flowers blooming on my back porch, the way the light danced on our apartment walls in the midafternoon, a line in a movie that made me tear up, music lyrics that encouraged my heart.

All these things had been a part of my daily life before my cancer diagnosis, yet I hadn't noticed them. I had seen them, but I hadn't really paid attention . . . until grief and fear brought my life to a standstill.

These small moments of beauty are less about seeing something and more about receiving the voice of God speaking to your soul, reminding you that although you feel tiny and insignificant, he is present alongside you in this suffering, and goodness can still break through in the darkest of moments.

After my cancer went into remission (it's been more than fourteen years now), my pace of life increased to what it was before. Although I can't say I live with a constant awareness of beauty and wonder, that season of suffering profoundly changed me, and I am now more intentional about slowing down. There is a treasure to be found, something of deep importance to my soul, when I slow down.

Slowing down lets us return to the pace of our souls, connects us with the beauty and wonder in the world, and allows us to cultivate deep connection with those we love. You might find that the slowing of your life has happened through circumstances outside your control, or you might find yourself wondering how you could ever slow down. No matter where you find yourself today, you can make an intentional decision to welcome an unhurried life.

Embracing Times of Slow Living

When you think about slow living, maybe you envision images of #slowliving on social media, with pictures of beautiful houses that are uncluttered by mess and filled with nature and candlelight. But this is little more than a fantasy, especially if you have anyone under the age of twenty-five living in your house.

Maybe you feel like the only way to slow down is to move to the country because it feels too challenging to slow down right where you are. Or maybe you think the only way to decrease the pace is to homeschool and remove your family from extracurricular activities. But the reality is, changing your environment doesn't automatically slow down your pace of life. Even if we make a big change to where we live or how we educate our children, we can still find ourselves exhausted by the pace of family demands and commitments or the overwhelm of technology.

> Slowing down lets us return to the pace of our souls.

So before you go off the grid, consider this: What if it were possible to stay in your current neighborhood, your current job, your current school situation, and still slow down?

Can you stay in the loud, messy, demanding world of family life and still live at a slower pace?

Our goal for ourselves and our children is to live at a pace that cultivates emotional health and deep connection with others. Living slowly in this world is not always realistic, as there will be certain days and seasons that are more intense than others. Our nervous system is designed to move between stress and rest, demand and recovery. Without times of challenge, we don't grow as individuals. But the same is true if we don't have times of slower pace. The key is to find a balance between stimulation and rest that is best for our temperament and our family.

This begins with a countercultural decision to prioritize our soul's health over productivity.

Listen to Your Longings

One of the downsides of our busy pace of life is that we have less time to reflect, and we lose touch with our longings. Our desires can be instructive to us, because they show us what we value that we may not be making space for right now.

Take some time to reflect on some what-if questions to help you discover what you're longing for and how those underlying values can help direct your decisions as a family.

1. Imagine you moved your family to the countryside or by the sea for a slower life. What would be different about your life? How would your daily activities and routines change? What would you have time for? What would you have more of? What would you have less of?
2. Imagine you quit your job, you pulled your kids out of school, or you said no to all extracurricular commitments. What would this freedom give you? What would you want to do with your

children or invest in their hearts? What would you do more of? What would you do less of?

Begin by writing your answers to these questions unedited. Once you're done, review what you wrote and look for themes. Then consider how you could make these changes within the parameters of your current life. Whether or not you make a big change in your family life, adding these practices into your current life will ground you right now and prepare you for the next season.

Slow Yourself Down

Are you living at a pace in your daily life that makes it possible for goodness and beauty to speak to your soul?

If you want to slow down the pace of your life, here are some practices to consider:

- **Start journaling.** Take some time to reflect and journal on a regular basis, writing down your thoughts and the things you're wrestling with. This will help you slow down and pay attention to your inner life.
- **Implement physical practices.** This may include walking, bike riding, gardening, swimming, cooking, having a cup of tea or coffee outside, lighting candles, or turning on your favorite music. We often can't "think" ourselves into slowness; we need a physical pattern to help us change our emotional state.
- **Choose slowness.** This means purposely putting yourself in situations that force you to slow down. For example, you could intentionally drive in the slow lane on the highway or get in the longest line at the grocery store or reduce conveniences for a short period of time, such as by not using a microwave or walking somewhere instead of driving. These practices may feel painful, especially at first, but regularly placing ourselves in situations where we slow down strengthens our patience and peace.

- **Follow your child's lead.** If you have a young child in your life who notices the little things with wonder, follow their lead. Rather than rushing them along to the next thing, decide that they'll be your teacher in that moment. Let them show you what's amazing in the world.
- **Practice savoring.** This means slowing down, paying attention to the present, and finding joy there. This plan can be implemented while eating a meal, watching a sunset, or embracing your child. Take a deep breath and become present to the gift that is before you.

Slow Your Family Down

As the leader of your family, you are the pacesetter—the one who makes sure your family is moving at a speed that allows all of you to thrive. Here are some ideas for slowing the pace.

- **Set boundaries on your calendar.** This may include being intentional about how many extracurricular activities, sports, and school commitments your children participate in. Get clear on what's most important to your family and be realistic about what is manageable for your family in this season.
- **Protect the gaps.** When there's free time in your day, whether early in the morning or later in the afternoon, use this time slowly. Rather than trying to be more productive during this time, protect it as sacred.
- **Be intentional about setting goals.** As a family, agree on what's most important to you and why you're saying yes to something. As parents, we may tell ourselves we're taking on extra work or commitments to give our children a better life. But if your child's basic needs are being met, remember that what they want most isn't more financial opportunities but more time with you.
- **Practice awareness of the seasons.** When we pay attention to the seasons, it gives our lives a cadence for slowing down and noticing. This practice isn't about adding things to your to-do

list or overwhelming yourself with seasonal home decorations (unless you love that!). It's about paying attention to the current season through small practices such as picking flowers in the spring, collecting leaves in the fall, sharing a cool drink on a summer afternoon, or looking at Christmas lights together in the winter.

Practices for Facilitating Family Connection

One way to protect slowed-down connection time with your family is to make it a regular routine or an appointment on your calendar, the way you'd schedule any other commitment. If you can get these times on your calendar before all the other priorities, it helps your family preserve the slowness to create connection with one another.

- **Daily family rituals.** Daily rituals don't have to be long or elaborate; the key is consistency. Maybe your family could read a book together at bedtime, go for a walk after dinner, or say prayers or blessings in the morning.
- **Weekly family rituals.** When possible, prioritize at least one time a week for your family to have fun and connect. This may be going to the park or building a fort (with younger children) or going out to eat or having a family movie or game night (with older children).
- **Yearly family rituals.** This could include going on a family vacation or camping trip, creating holiday traditions, and going on special outings together. If your child is old enough (around six to eight years old), try to plan a one-on-one trip together. It doesn't matter what the activity is, the important thing is to spend time connecting.
- **End-of-the-day rituals.** When you are wrapping up your workday or your child is ending their school day, it's helpful to have an intentional time of transition to shift your focus from work to your family and to help your child shift from school to home. Even if you work from home, it's helpful to have a ritual to tell your body

that work is finished for the day. Maybe that means gathering your computer and phone and putting them in another room for the night. Maybe it means changing into more comfortable clothes, taking a short walk around your neighborhood, or going outside to water the garden. For your child, it may mean having a snack or playing with their favorite toy or talking to you about their highlights and low points of the day. These small practices will help you catch your breath and transition to a slower pace.

- **Technology-free rituals.** Engagement with technology (especially email and social media) keeps us in an emotional state of hurry and time anxiety. Having times during the day or week when we intentionally turn off our devices or put them in a lockbox helps us slow down. It may be that you put your devices away when you get home for a time of connection and family dinner. Or maybe you have one afternoon or a full day each week that you declare a technology-free zone. Removing ourselves from technology for a while helps us slow down the pace of our lives.

CHAPTER 12

SIMPLIFYING:

DE-STIMULATING YOUR HOME

> The ability to simplify means to eliminate the unnecessary so the necessary may speak.
> — HANS HOFMANN

"I just don't know what to do. We've tried everything!"

Amanda was overwhelmed trying to figure out how to deal with her five-year-old son, Simon, whose behavior had become so challenging she was starting to wonder if there was something deeper going on.

Amanda recounted that when he was home, Simon constantly had meltdowns, kicking his brother and screaming at everyone in the family. They'd tried giving time-outs; they'd tried creating extra connection time; they'd tried withholding privileges, but nothing was changing his behavior. Amanda was completely at her wit's end in knowing how to help her son.

Amanda and her family lived in a three-bedroom home. Simon and his brother shared a bedroom so one of the rooms could serve as a playroom for the boys. Yet to her frustration, the boys hardly played there.

The playroom was packed from floor to ceiling with activities and games. It was constantly so cluttered that it was hard to even walk into. The boys' bedroom wasn't much different, with two bunk beds, crates full of toys and books, lamps that projected flashing lights onto the ceiling, and bright posters and decor of the boys' favorite action figures.

One factor that Amanda hadn't considered was how Simon's home environment was impacting his behavior.

How Visual Noise Affects Us

Whatever stimuli our brain is exposed to, it has to process. We aren't usually aware of this processing, as most of it happens unconsciously. Yet this still requires energy. Before we're even conscious of something, our brain has already decided what we need to pay attention to and what isn't necessary.

This is an important role of the brain; otherwise, we'd be constantly overwhelmed by the awareness of our heart beating, our lungs breathing, and our observations about everything in our environment.

Once our brain has filtered what to pay attention to, the conscious part of the brain begins to process it. Is this a threat, or is it safe? Is this important or unimportant? How does this new information connect with our current view and understanding of the world? How do we feel about these new stimuli?

This processing happens quickly—almost automatically—in the prefrontal cortex. Our prefrontal cortex, or executive brain, is in charge of our self-control, decision-making, and emotional regulation. But the prefrontal cortex has a very limited capacity. It can focus acutely for a short period of time before it needs to rest. Once it has exhausted its capacity to work well, it must get refueled.

Your brain's limbic system (which keeps all your organs working unconsciously) is like a steady family car on a long road trip. In contrast, the prefrontal cortex is more like a nitro engine on a racing car—it performs well for short distances, but you wouldn't necessarily want it for a long trip.

Where I live in California, rain is rare, so much of the infrastructure and many homes in our area aren't built to handle significant rainfall.

So when it rains, it often causes mini-floods in people's backyards and on the streets. There's not much capacity to process the rain.

The same is true of the brain. Our brains have a limited capacity to process stimuli each day. There are differences in how much each individual can handle: some can handle more, and others (such as those with highly sensitive temperaments, those who are neurodivergent, and younger children) can handle less. We aren't machines or supercomputers; we are humans. One of the realities of being human is that we have limited capacity to process stimuli each day.

One way we can guard against overstimulation and chronic stress is to reduce the amount of daily stimulation we're exposed to. Simplifying our home and family life is one of the best ways to decrease the load on our brains and support thriving for our whole family.

In this chapter, we'll look at different areas in which we can practice simplification. This is not a checklist of everything you need to do; rather, it's an invitation to reflect on the way the visual noise in your world affects you and your family, especially when you notice signs of overstimulation in your children and your own soul.

Simplifying Toys

As I walked into our family room, I felt instantly overwhelmed. It was as if someone had placed every toy we owned into a confetti cannon and exploded them all over the house. My children had only been home on break for two days, and already the house had been turned upside down by toys, puzzles, Legos, crafts, and fort-making paraphernalia. As I felt my agitation rising from the overwhelming mess we would now have to clean up, I wondered how my children felt looking at this room. If *I* was overwhelmed by the toys everywhere, how would it make them feel?

The number of toys children have today has dramatically increased from previous decades. Surveys show that the average ten-year-old in Western countries owns 238 toys. Meanwhile, children play with only 12 toys daily.[1]

The volume of toys in our homes is a challenge to navigate, even when you're committed to limiting it. Children are given toys at birthday parties, holiday gatherings, doctor's appointments, and school activities. This is on top of what you buy for them and what they buy with their own money.

> It's possible to have too much of a good thing.

Children are sweet (and often hilariously frustrating) when it comes to their attachment to things. Whether it's the train set they haven't played with in years or the little "treasures" they collect on their outings to the park or the rocks that somehow find themselves in the laundry, kids have a hard time parting with their belongings. It's difficult to keep things simple when you have a child who resists getting rid of any toy they've ever owned.

But as adults, we know it's possible to have too much of a good thing. Studies on food sales show that when a consumer has too many "good" options (for example, thirty breads to choose from), they often experience "choice paralysis," where the overwhelm causes them to get stuck making a decision, and they sometimes walk away. When the number of choices is reduced (for example, to five breads), the consumer's confidence and satisfaction increases.[2]

Choice paralysis impacts children as well—it's one of the reasons they say they're bored and don't know what to do. When you hear your child make a comment like this, you may be shocked because they have *so many options* to choose from. But the truth is, all those options may be the very thing that's blocking them from initiating an activity.

The number of toys may also contribute to your child's resistance to cleaning their room. If you walk into their room and feel overwhelmed, imagine how your child feels. If you reduce the number of toys, and therefore how much they have to put away, they feel less overwhelmed and may be more likely to participate in cleaning up.

> Choice paralysis impacts children—it's one of the reasons they say they're bored and don't know what to do.

The toys available to children today are also significantly more stimulating than they used to be. Building blocks and dolls have been swapped for toys with screens or light and music shows. This adds to the overall stimulation they have to process each day.

If you reduce the number and type of toys your child sees on a daily basis, you will lower their level of stimulation and may increase their willingness to initiate free play in the process.

Practical Tips for Simplifying Toys

Most of us have felt like we're drowning in toys at some point. But it can be difficult to know where to begin in solving this problem. Here are some ideas for getting started.

1. **Create systems of organization.** You could use storage boxes or designate a game cupboard or a craft corner. The goal is that if you were to pack away all the toys, everything would have its own space in the house and everyone would know where they live.

2. **Set regular times to purge.** There is no storage system in the world that can keep up with too much stuff. That's why we need to set aside regular times to get rid of toys that have broken, are no longer played with, or have been outgrown. Depending on your child's age and temperament, you can involve them in this process or you can do it for them.

3. **Devise a toy rotation.** If you have a lot of toys that you don't necessarily want to get rid of, consider doing a toy rotation. Begin by dividing your child's toys into three groups. Then pack away two of these groups and put them out of your child's sight and reach. Let them play with the first group for a week or two, then put that group away and bring out another group. This often makes the child feel as if the toys are new and reduces their overwhelm.

4. **Consider low-stimulation toys.** When you're purging or reorganizing toys, or when you're purchasing new toys, consider whether they are low- or high-stimulation. High-simulation toys make noise, have lights, or activate a response from a button. Low-stimulation toys don't have lights, noises, or buttons. Depending on your child's temperament, you might consider removing all high-stimulation toys or reducing the number of them.

5. **Incorporate both open-ended and close-ended toys.** Open-ended toys encourage a child to engage their creativity (such as Legos, paint, and marbles). Close-ended toys have a specific goal in mind (such as a puzzle or a board game). Having a blend of open- and close-ended toys encourages children to develop their creativity and carry a task to completion.

A Note on Children with Differences

The process of simplifying your child's toys is more challenging (and emotional) when your child has ADHD, autism spectrum disorder (ASD), sensory processing disorder (SPD), OCD, or anxiety. These children tend to be overwhelmed by change, and they typically have a strong attachment to their things.

If you think your child would struggle with being part of the decision-making process, it might be better to simplify for them while still respecting their most treasured possessions.

Tell them you're going to organize and clean up their room so they know a change is coming, but let them know you'll make sure they have all their most important items. As you simplify their toys and remove things you think they don't want, keep them in storage (or out of sight) rather than throwing them away or giving them away immediately. Then if there's something specific your child is upset about not having, you'll still have it. After a few weeks, if your child hasn't asked for the items, you can get rid of them.

Parents sometimes feel intimidated about doing this for their child, scared of an emotional reaction if their child realizes something has been removed or thrown away. But the child is often so relieved at the simplified environment that they don't notice what's gone.

Simplifying Clutter

Our homes are the place where we retreat after a long day. For many children, particularly younger ones, it's the place they spend the most time. Yet our homes can be overstimulating because of the overwhelm of our physical stuff.

As a culture, our consumption of material goods has dramatically increased over the past several decades.

- The average size of the American home has almost tripled over the past fifty years.
- There are 300,000 items in the average American household.
- One out of ten Americans rent off-site storage for their belongings.[3]
- Nearly 25 percent of people can't park their car inside their garage because it's full of stuff.[4]

We now have bigger spaces and more items to organize, put away, and make decisions about. This has a big impact on the way we feel. Some studies suggest that a higher number of household objects correlates with higher cortisol levels.[5]

Talking about reducing clutter is almost comedic when it comes to family life. Despite what some people depict online, I don't know anyone with children whose home is clutter-free. Children are naturally messy. If you have an expectation that they will be otherwise, you're setting yourself up for constant stress and frustration. At the same time, living in complete chaos is stressful, for both you and your children. So we have to find the balance; rather than seeking a perfect house that's never messy, we need to find a way to reduce the clutter and visual stimulation.

Practical Tips for Reducing Clutter

If you're looking for a sustainable way to handle messes in your home, here are some ideas to get started.

1. **Decide you don't want to live in overwhelm.** Clutter often builds up on us, and it feels like just another thing to do. But when we recognize how overstimulating clutter is and decide we don't want to live that way, it can motivate us to make the changes we need to make.

2. **Make sure everything has a place.** If you were to put everything away, would there be room for it? Once you've ensured that all your things have a spot, make sure everyone in the family knows where it all goes. This may mean labeling storage containers, cupboards, or shelves to give direction to children who struggle with executive functioning.

3. **Choose what areas will be clutter-free every day.** This may be a small space, such as your kitchen countertop, or a larger space, such as your bedroom. Having some areas that stay clear and tidy removes the pressure of feeling your whole house needs to be clutter-free all the time.

4. **Have regular times of purging and reorganizing.** You may go through the whole house in a set period of time or just focus on a small area here and there when you have smaller windows of time.

5. **Involve your children in tidying up the house.** When your child is two to three years old, they can learn to pack away their toys when they're done playing with them. When your child is four to five years old, they can start "helping" with chores around the house. When children are in upper elementary school, they can be responsible for cleaning their own rooms and helping tidy common areas. Tweens and teens can be responsible for cleaning their own rooms, cleaning the kitchen, unloading the dishwasher, or doing laundry.

6. **Have regular cleanup routines as a family.** You might do this at the end of each day or once a week. Put on some fun music and work together to tidy up a space. The biggest factor to consider with children and tidying up is the amount of work for you and your child. For example, if you walk into a space and you're overwhelmed as you think about tidying up, it's likely your child feels this same way. If your child is younger than seven years old (or it's not working to involve them), try reducing the size of the space they're responsible for (for example, the top of the coffee table) or the difficulty level of the task (for example, packing away the

puzzle and the craft). As they practice doing smaller tasks, you can begin to increase what they're responsible for.

Simplifying Visual Stimulation

Visual stimulation is the cumulative effect of the wall color, how many decorations are displayed, the kind of lighting, and the amount of clutter (including toys!) in our homes.

We all have different styles of decor we love. Some people are naturally minimalist, others are maximalist, and still others fall somewhere in between. It's beneficial to take time to consider how the style of your home makes you feel and how it makes your child feel.

You don't necessarily need to create a minimalist environment in your home (if that's not your style), but it is wise to consider how the spaces where you spend the most time support your family's ability to thrive.

Consider your temperament and that of your child. Are you or your child easily overwhelmed by visual stimulation? Are you or your child highly sensitive? If so, you may need to be more intentional about your decorating choices in your home. In particular, consider making the bedroom a calming space. Small, inexpensive changes can make a big difference in the way we feel.

Practical Ways to Reduce Visual Stimulation

When you're decorating your space, here are some ideas to consider.

- Use softer colors on the walls instead of bright tones.
- Use simple textures on the walls rather than busy wallpaper.
- Reduce the amount of furniture in the space.
- Choose lighting with a warm glow instead of cold light.
- Use lamps rather than overhead lighting.
- Choose soft, calming colors for curtains, bedspreads, rugs, and furniture.
- Consider adding heavy curtains or blackout blinds so you can have complete darkness at night.

- Balance your taste with the effect of the overall stimulation. For example, if you or your child wants certain pictures, decorations, or posters on the walls, you might want to keep other parts of the room plain (such as using a plain bedspread or a plain rug on the floor).

Small Changes = Big Difference

A few months later, Amanda had a huge smile on her face. She couldn't believe that making what seemed like small changes could have such a big impact. Simon seemed like a different kid.

Amanda and her family had done a big decluttering of the playroom, turning it back into a second bedroom so Simon and his brother could each have his own space. The boys chose the toys that were most important to them, and Amanda gave away many of the rest and put others in storage for toy rotations. They removed the flashing lights from the boys' bedrooms, replacing them with softer lamps. Much of the bright decor was gone too. The boys had chosen their favorite decorations, and they put the rest away. Toys were put in labeled crates and designated areas in the wardrobe so the boys could clearly see where everything went. The boys' rooms were visually and physically calmer.

"Not only has Simon's behavior significantly improved and calmed own, but the added bonus is that the boys are now more responsible for cleaning up their rooms!" Amanda reported.

Small changes can make a big difference.

Simplifying, One Day at a Time

If simplifying sounds like an overwhelming task, consider taking small steps. Get a large box, and every day for a month, choose one item to donate (whether it's a toy, an item of clothing, or a decoration). At the end of the month, donate the items in the box. Sometimes these small steps can give you momentum to keep making progress toward simplifying.

CHAPTER 13

SHEPHERDING:

NAVIGATING MEDIA AND THE ONLINE WORLD

> A true shepherd leads the way. He
> does not merely point the way.
> LEONARD RAVENHILL

Lying on the cold floor of my bathroom, I could just see my eighteen-month-old son dancing in front of the television as the sun was slowly setting.

Pregnant with my second child, I'd had nausea all day, but on top of that, I also seemed to have contracted food poisoning.

The vomiting had started in the afternoon. The first time, it scared my toddler, who became worried about me and quickly got very upset. Like all mothers, I was more concerned about how he was feeling than about myself, so I faked a smile. With my head spinning, I told him that Mommy was okay and asked if he wanted to watch some television. He was excited about the idea, and I turned on the TV to distract him while I recovered.

But I didn't recover. Over the course of four hours, I vomited five times. I spent almost all that time lying on the bathroom floor. My son didn't notice much because he was distracted by the show he was watching.

I was counting down the minutes until my husband arrived home from an interstate business trip so he could look after my son and put him to bed.

Lying on the bathroom floor, even as I knew these were extenuating circumstances, I still felt the familiar pang of guilt that my toddler had been watching television far too long.

Parenting in Our World

The conversation about screens and children is a hot-button topic for parents. Parents often feel judged—by other parents, by previous generations, or even by themselves—for the way they navigate media and the online world for their children. You may have even felt some resistance when you saw the title of this chapter, wondering if it would bring up feelings of guilt or regret.

This chapter is not intended to trigger any shame—we are all in this struggle together! My goal is to provide a framework to help you think through how to shepherd your child when it comes to technology and share some best practices and boundaries. But I want you to understand that these are simply that—best practices—and need to be considered in the context of real life. There are real-life circumstances that cause you to make different choices at times, including when there's sickness in the family, when you're facing a traumatic situation, or when you're raising a child with learning or attentional differences. It's my belief that parents who are educated about the dangers of technology can make the best decisions for their children in their unique circumstances.

As you read this chapter, it's important to keep in mind your family's specific situation and to do so with grace—for yourself and those around you.

Screens and Child Development

Children don't process screens the same way adults do. Their brains are developing, and they're still establishing their understanding of the world. This means that the stimulation, information, and exposure they receive through screens impacts them differently than adults.

Here are some of the reasons screens have such a significant impact on children.

1. **Children struggle to tell the difference between what's imagined and what's real.** Developmentally, children under the age of five to seven struggle to discern reality from imagination. This is why younger children fear monsters under their bed (a fear that morphs into a fear about "bad guys" around age seven). It's why younger children believe in superheroes, fairies, and Santa Claus. But this also means that young children are particularly vulnerable to media with villains or scary characters. Children with a highly sensitive temperament are especially affected by scary content even in age-appropriate shows.

2. **Children relate the information from screens to their real life.** Whatever the conflict is in a story, young children tend to worry that the same thing will happen to them. Many movies for children involve the death of a parent and a child becoming orphaned. Although this adds drama to the storyline, it often leaves children scared about their own parents dying. This is particularly true for children with a highly sensitive temperament or for children with a high level of empathy. For this reason, you may want to wait until your child is seven to ten years old before letting them watch movies with content that may scare them.

3. **Children do not yet have a proper concept of the largeness of the world.** Children under the age of eight to ten often struggle to grasp the breadth and largeness of the world. They process information and stories through the filter of their real-life environment. So if a child is exposed to information about war in another country, they may become anxious even if we tell them that the war is "far away." They can't quite conceive how far away these events are happening, and they may even worry that they're just down the road.

4. **Children expect that others are being honest with them.** One of the most beautiful parts of childhood is their tender hearts and their belief that the people around them are telling them the truth. They assume they can trust everything someone tells them, and they haven't yet reached the stage of development when they begin to question these things. This becomes problematic if they're exposed to online content at an early age and don't understand that companies are marketing to them and seeking to hook their attention.

5. **Children's brains are developing.** Excessive exposure to screens can be overstimulating for younger children and can even slow development. One study shows that one-year-olds who were exposed to more than four hours of screen time a day showed significant delays in communication and problem solving at two to four years of age. Even when shows are "age appropriate," excessive screen time over a prolonged period can be damaging to a child's brain development.[1]

In order to protect childhood, we need to create boundaries around the *amount* of screen time our child consumes as well as the *type* of content they're watching. As parents, we don't need to rush to expose our child to news media, exciting movies, or deep concepts, particularly before the age of seven to eight years old.

It doesn't build resilience in a child to be exposed to real-world events or scary topics through media. This only increases anxiety. Resilience is built through navigating their real-life events and leaning on the support networks around them.

As children get older and become developmentally ready, you can gradually introduce them to news stories and world events and talk about what you learn together.

Screens Are Stimulating

This may seem fundamental, but watching a screen—whether it's a television, a tablet, or a smartphone—is stimulating for the brain.

Sometimes, when we watch our child's behavior in the short term, we forget this. It can seem like the only time of day our child is calm (outside of when they are sleeping) is when they're in front of a screen. It's tempting to view screen time as a break because our child is finally quiet, not screaming, and not running around.

Even though they seem settled when they're watching something, it's important to remember that any screen time is stimulating for them. The more time they have in front of a device, the more stimulated they will be. If they watch screens excessively, they will quickly become overstimulated.

Exposure to Information and the World

Screens and media bring with them two particular challenges: the amount of information and the type of information.

THE AMOUNT OF INFORMATION

As adults, our brains aren't designed to process the level of information we're exposed to each day. It's no wonder we're stressed when we see the news and social media, because we have a limited processing capacity, and the world is functioning at a much higher rate. This is even more the case for children, who have a lower processing capacity than adults. One of the goals for placing boundaries around screen time is to ensure that the amount of information they are exposed to each day is appropriate for their age and developmental level.

THE TYPE OF INFORMATION

As technology has advanced, so has our children's access to the world. This means they can easily be exposed to adult issues such as world crises, violence, or sexually explicit content. They are also facing pressure to grow up faster. For example, seven- to eight-year-old girls watch online platforms and want to be like the older girls they see there, and they're starting to make clothing choices and demonstrate behaviors previously not seen until girls were around thirteen years old.

If we don't place boundaries on the type of media children are watching, they will likely be exposed to topics they're not developmentally ready for. We need boundaries to help protect our children's childhood.

As parents, we need to be a safe place for our children to process whatever information they are exposed to. But if we place healthy boundaries around the types of media they are exposed to, they will have fewer issues to process at a younger age.

This doesn't mean we shouldn't talk to our children about real-life issues. Throughout their lives, we need to have age-appropriate conversations about relationships, sex, decision-making, friendships, drugs, alcohol, and what's happening in the world. But there's a big difference between having these parent-child conversations and letting our child consistently take in content that frames their worldview about these topics.

Real-life conversations with safe people build a child's resilience. Exposure to endless problems online, however, erodes their resilience.

Tackling Challenging Conversations with Your Child

In general, we want children and adolescents to have the conversations about hard topics (such as sex, drugs, relationships, health, world events, violence, war, and politics) first with their parents rather than their peers. This allows parents to share their values and perspectives with their child in a safe environment before the child is exposed to other people's opinions. This can be tricky when you're trying to balance protecting them and speaking honestly with them before they're exposed to something outside your home.

> Doing it "badly" is so much better than not doing it at all.

Even though these conversations may be uncomfortable to have, not having the conversations leaves your child alone to work out these topics. So dive in! Doing it "badly" is so much better than not doing it at all.

Here are some things to keep in mind when talking about difficult topics with your child or adolescent:

1. When your child asks you a question, say, "I'm so glad you asked me that!" rather than responding in a way that might make them feel like they are in trouble for asking or makes them feel embarrassed to ask.
2. When responding to their question, tell the truth in a clear, factual way. If they ask where babies come from, don't tell them a story about the stork! Every time they ask and you answer, you are building trust.
3. If they bring up a big topic, ask them what questions they have about it, and answer only those questions. Sometimes we assume our child understands the scope of the topic they're bringing up, but in reality, they may have only one or two questions they want answered.
4. If they are growing older (around ten years or older) and haven't brought up a topic you feel they need to know about, introduce the topic and information in a gentle way. You can talk about the topic in lots of smaller conversations rather than in one big conversation.
5. If you find out they've been exposed to a topic before you've talked to them about it, tell them you wanted to talk with them about it, but you didn't know they were thinking about it yet, and ask if they have any questions.
6. Share your values and perspectives on the topic and why you've come to those conclusions. This is more effective than just saying "Because I said so" or "Because it's the right way," as it creates more openness and curiosity in your children. This doesn't guarantee your child will take on your values as they grow, but it does mean that they won't rebel against what feels like an arbitrary set of rules.

No one feels like they have these conversations perfectly. We often feel thrown off when our young child asks something we're unprepared for, we're hard on ourselves when we fumble through a conversation with our tween, or we question whether we've shared our values enough or too much with our teen. The most important thing is that we're in the game, giving it a try. This is far better than leaving our child or adolescent alone with hard topics.

Guidelines for the Amount of Screen Time

Here are the current general guidelines for daily screen time for healthy development:

> Preferably no screen time for infants under eighteen months old
> One hour daily for children eighteen months to five years
> Two hours daily for children five to ten years old
> Two to three hours daily for children older than ten years old
> After ten years old, the recommendations focus more on making sure screen time doesn't interfere with sleep, family or social relationships, school, or work.

Every family is different, and every season of your family's life is different, so you may decide on different screen time guidelines. But it's helpful to be aware of the general guidelines so you can make wise decisions for your family.

Guidelines for the Type of Screen Time

Not all screen time is the same—different types of media impact children in different ways. There are low-stimulation and high-stimulation TV shows and movies. There are video games and computer activities that require a child's involvement. There's social media and the online world that require discernment and decision making.

As a general rule, the goal is for children to slowly progress through these different types of media in that order. This helps them to be ready developmentally for the amount of stimulation each type of media offers. Here is a framework to consider:

1. low-stimulation TV shows (eighteen months plus)
2. low-stimulation movies without scary characters or plot (four years plus)
3. higher-stimulation TV shows (five years plus)
4. lower-stimulation video games and computer/tablet activities (seven years plus)
5. higher-stimulation movies (eight years plus)
6. higher-stimulation video games, computer/tablet activities, and YouTube (twelve years plus)
7. social media and the online world (sixteen years plus)

If you're raising multiple children, it's common to find that younger children are exposed to various media earlier than you would prefer because their older siblings are watching more stimulating content. If you anticipate that this will happen, you can offset this by telling a younger child some of the storyline or parts that might be scary or upsetting before they watch. You might want to also give them a "bathroom break" when those scenes come on the screen. You could also do an activity afterward that might help calm the overstimulation (such as going for a walk, taking a bath, or reading a book together).

Not all screen time is the same.

There are multiple factors that stimulate a child's brain. It's important to consider the *speed of interaction* for your child's age. Television and movies are entertaining. Video games are more interactive, increasing the rate and number of stimuli a child is processing. Social media and the online world significantly increase the speed and number of stimuli a child needs to process.

This is why watching a low-stimulation TV show is far less overwhelming for a three-year old's brain than pressing buttons on an iPad. Playing a lower-stimulation video game is far less intense for an eight-year-old than scrolling through YouTube or TikTok. Not all screen time is the same.

This framework also naturally limits the exposure to age-inappropriate content, as they're not being introduced to higher-stimulation media and the online world until late childhood and early adolescence. Having a framework like this helps protect their childhood.

Consider carefully what *types* of screen time your child is engaging with. A four-year-old watching a *Winnie the Pooh* television show and a four-year-old scrolling on YouTube may both have the same amount of screen time, but it will affect them differently (even if the content on YouTube is age appropriate). One is lower stimulation and not as interactive. The other is highly stimulating and interactive. The result is that the child will reach a threshold of overstimulation more quickly, resulting in exhaustion and a crabbier mood. Higher-stimulation media also desensitizes their brain to the boredom of ordinary life, meaning they will have a lower tolerance for everyday activities and over time will continually crave more stimulating entertainment.

Principles for Creating Screen-Time Boundaries

It's okay if your boundaries are different from those of the families around you. What's important is that you have boundaries and you stick to them. Unlimited screen time or access is unhealthy for any child.

1. **Create a routine.** Decide ahead of time what the screen-time routine will look like for your family. This will give your children a clear sense of the expectations and reduce the questions and complaints you hear from your kids.

2. **Decide on your "best practice" rhythm.** Best practice is what you would like screen time to look like when life is functioning well. This means that when there are extenuating circumstances (such as a work deadline or sickness in the family), children may get more screen time than they do in their usual routine.

3. **Keep devices out of bedrooms.** Whenever possible, keep devices and televisions in the family's shared spaces. When devices are in bedrooms, children have more access to them. Studies show that having technology in the bedroom disrupts sleep (even if it's not on).[2] Keeping devices in the shared space also lowers the risk of children accessing inappropriate content.

4. **Try to finish screen time two to three hours before bedtime.** The blue light from screens has been shown to interfere with our ability to fall asleep.[3] When there's space between screen time and bedtime, children (and adults!) are likely to fall asleep more quickly.

5. **Create check-ins for your family.** Take time to regularly consider how much time your family is spending with screens and how it's working for you. We all have times when we realize our technology has gotten out of balance, so don't be afraid to make adjustments.

6. **Curate what shows and media your kids can choose from.** This may include setting up a list for them on a cable subscription or being present when they're choosing what to watch. It's also good to check reviews for age-appropriateness. This is particularly helpful for younger children and highly sensitive children, as the age ranges are often based only on the inclusion of explicit issues. Highly sensitive children may be negatively affected by media that's in their age range, so check the comments and reviews before watching. Watching the trailer can also give you a sense of how scary the show will be and if it's a good fit for your child.

Smartphones

"Why can't I have a phone? Sam has a phone, and he's three years younger than me!"

We were walking in the door after school, and my kids were decompressing after their day. That's when my eleven-year-old brought up this conversation for the hundredth time.

"Why do you need a phone?" I asked.

"Because everyone else has one . . ."

Navigating parenthood in this world is challenging. On the one hand, you want to protect your child, and on the other hand, you understand that the world has changed and you question whether you're being old-fashioned. I was expecting my children to start wanting a phone around nine or ten, but what I didn't expect was that other children at their school would have a smartphone at six years old.

The introduction of media creates what feels like a no-win situation because it's not just about your own views of technology. The community surrounding your child influences whether or not they have access. Smartphones have created another huge set of decisions for parents in determining what's best for their child.

While it may seem obvious, it may be helpful to break down why a smartphone is different from an "old school" phone. Today, having a phone doesn't just mean children can call someone or get messages from their friends. A smartphone gives them access to the online world, as well as countless notifications and distractions.

Although every child is different, here's a general rule to follow for smartphones: Wait as long as you can, and try to get as close to fourteen years old as possible, when their brain is not as vulnerable.

In a study of more than 27,000 people, researchers found that the earlier a child got a smartphone, the worse their mental health was as an adult.[4]

Even as adults, we know that it changes our brains to have our phones near us all the time. We know about the research on attention and how this technology distracts us and hinders our ability to concentrate. At the risk of sounding like a broken record, I must mention that children are even more significantly impacted since their brains are still in development.

Children in previous generations had play-based childhoods. Although the shift was gradual, experts say that this changed around 2010, when childhood became screen-based for many children. Social psychologist Jonathan Haidt calls this the "Great Rewiring," as children started seeing their friends in person less frequently and spent more time online.[5]

If we can keep our children off smartphones for as long as possible, we are protecting them from exposure to an addictive, distracting influence during a particularly vulnerable time in their development. Without this constant distraction, the path is clearer for them to learn and grow academically, as well as interact with others socially and through play in real life. We are giving our child the gift of greater emotional health, now and in the future.

"I'm sorry, buddy, but the answer is no," I told my son. "I know you feel like I'm the strictest mom in the world, but getting a phone too early can have a negative impact in all those ways we've talked about. We will get you a phone closer to fourteen years old."

My son left the conversation resigned and disappointed (and I know it won't be the last time we talk about it!). But I am willing to exchange his temporary disappointment for his long-term flourishing.

Social Media

Children are accessing social media at a younger and younger age. This is something we need to be prepared for as parents so we can have a plan instead of just reacting when situations come up.

Social media is by far the most damaging type of media and should not be assumed to be harmless or neutral, no matter how entertaining the content is.

There are many concerns with social media when it comes to the development of children's and adolescents' brains:

- **Speed of information:** The sheer number of stimuli can be too much for a child or adolescent, leading to neurological overwhelm.
- **Comparison:** They are exposed to curated content with unrealistic images. Even adults are negatively affected by this content, forgetting that it's set up to look perfect. But children and adolescents often don't have this filter or perspective.

- **Social pull:** Before social media, if we didn't get invited to a party, we might not have even realized we were left out. Now this is thrown directly in our children's faces. Real-life relationships are challenging enough for tweens and teens, and the online world has only added more pressure.
- **Algorithms:** This can be a benefit if we're looking at funny animal videos, but if we're struggling mentally and consuming topics that aren't helpful, the algorithm continues to suggest even more of this content.
- **Oversexualized content:** With the increase of adolescent influencers online, what's considered "normal" in terms of movement, attire, and behavior has become sexualized at a young age.
- **Online bullying:** Social media is an avenue for bullying, with no accountability.
- **Predator risk:** Anonymity increases the risk of an adult building an inappropriate relationship with a child online.

It's no wonder this generation is struggling with mental and emotional health.

When it comes to social media, here's a good general rule: wait as long as you possibly can, upwards of sixteen years old, to begin.

The research is clear that if an individual can wait until sixteen plus to begin social media, their risk of developing anxiety, depression, self-harm, and eating disorders (particularly for girls) dramatically decreases.[6]

Whatever your child is exposed to, you need to process it with them. That means that before you decide they can have access to social media, you need to discuss all the issues with them in detail, sharing your own family value system in the process.

Here are some of the issues to discuss with your child when it comes to social media:

- People who look perfect online have spent time and money to create a perfect image—this isn't real life.

- People can screenshot your photos or copy your videos, so be mindful of what you share.
- Nothing is ever truly deleted on the internet—keep your private life offline.
- You never know who is seeing your content—assume everything is public.
- If you wouldn't say it to someone's face, don't say it online.
- Don't share personal details such as your birth date, home address, the school you attend, or places you're going ahead of time as a way to protect your privacy and security.
- People can be really mean on the internet—it's okay to take a break sometimes.
- If people are bullying others, tell a trusted adult.
- People aren't always who they appear to be online. Don't trust who someone says they are (without running it by parents) if you don't know them in real life.
- Your future employer (or future spouse!) will likely see your content at some point.
- We all (including parents and adults) need to take a break from social media sometimes. If you start to feel anxious or negatively impacted by the content you're seeing, this is normal and doesn't mean something is wrong with you.

Family Rules for Technology

Once you introduce smartphones and social media, you may want to include some guidelines for your family to follow. Here are a few examples you might consider.

1. Technology is a privilege, not a right.
2. Real-life relationships, homework, and chores come before technology.
3. No technology during dinner, after 8 p.m., or in bedrooms.

4. We want to create more than we consume.
5. Parents have total access to children's devices.
6. Trust with technology is an evolving process.
7. We show up in person and invest in real-life relationships.

This is in no way suggesting that waiting this long is easy or that it won't cause conflict between you and your child or adolescent. But it's worth the challenging conversations. We don't have to let our children fall into technology by default simply because that's what their peers are doing.

When you get pushback, remember that love doesn't mean giving your children whatever they want; it's giving them what they truly need. Just as we make sure they wear seatbelts and don't allow them to drink alcohol until a certain age, the boundaries we create around the online world provide safety for our child, now and in the future.

Practical Tips for Smartphones and Social Media

1. **Consider getting a family "dumb" phone.** This is a phone that only allows for calls and texts. It gives your child a way to talk to their friends or call you without the added complexity of online access.

2. **Make a plan with the parents of your child's closest friends.** Talk to the parents of your child's friends and decide together to delay giving your children access to a smartphone and social media. When your child isn't the only one left out of their peer group, they are much more likely to be on board with the boundary. Doing the right thing by yourself is challenging, but it's easier when you do it together.

3. **Have open conversations with your child.** Have ongoing, open conversations with your child about your decisions around these topics and why you've made the decisions you've made.

4. **Offer a reward to your child for staying off social media until they're a certain age.** This may be taking a special trip together or giving them something less expensive that they really want.

5. **Don't give a smartphone as a gift to your child.** When you decide your child is developmentally ready for a smartphone, don't give it to them for their birthday or Christmas. They need to understand that it's actually *your* smartphone that you're letting them use (and you can take it away from them if necessary).

6. **Consider your own smartphone habits.** Meet as a family and determine your boundaries around technology. This may include putting phones away at dinnertime, turning them off after 8 p.m., or keeping all phones in the kitchen and not in the bedroom.

7. **Consider downloading a control app.** A control app allows you to set your child's daily amount of phone time, in addition to limiting access to specific apps. Once your child has reached the limit, the app shuts the phone down.

8. **Set boundaries for social media.** You may decide they have to let you follow them so you can see the content they post (as long as you promise not to embarrass them!). Or you may require full access to their account. This may need to change as your child develops, because we want to respect our growing child's need for privacy and autonomy while also making sure they're safe.

9. **Have important conversations with them before they start using social media.** Here are some of the topics you'll want to talk about: how the online content world isn't real, how people tend to be meaner online than they would be in person, how nothing posted online ever really goes away, how people aren't always who they appear to be online, how you should never post your location while you're there, how you shouldn't share personal details such as your birth date or home address, and how we all need to take a break from social media at times.

CHAPTER 14

SABBATH:

CULTIVATING REST AND LIFE-GIVING ROUTINES

> Dear God, speak gently in my silence.
> When the loud outer noises of my
> surroundings and the loud inner noises of
> my fears keep pulling me away from you,
> help me to trust that you are still there.
>
> HENRI NOUWEN

An ancient African story tells of a European explorer who hired a group of local porters to support his venture into the unmapped lands of Africa.

They made great progress during the first three days, hacking through the thick vegetation, fording rivers, and scaling hills. The explorer was encouraged by the progress and woke early on the fourth day, expecting to cover even more territory.

But when he was ready to leave, he noticed that the local porters weren't moving. When he asked them about it, they said that they intended to rest that day.

When the explorer asked why, they said, "We have been moving very quickly, so we have left our souls behind. Now we have to wait for them to catch up with us again."

The Need for Rest

To rest means to cease movement or work in order to recover strength. We stop our working, our hurrying, and our progress to pause, breathe, and recalibrate our lives.

We were made to have times of rest. Research shows that the benefits of rest include a stronger immune system, decreased risk for serious health problems, reduction in stress, increased concentration and productivity, more emotional bandwidth, and renewed energy and motivation.[1] We also need rest for our spiritual health. God created us to live in rhythms of work and rest so we have time to reconnect with ourselves, our faith, and the things that are most important to us. The truth is, it's impossible to live an emotionally healthy life without integrating times of rest.

Yet despite our deep, intrinsic need for rest, many of us don't experience it.

If you're a parent, you may be rolling your eyes right now. You don't need someone to explain what rest is or why it's good for you—it's likely the very thing you've been craving since your beautiful child was born.

As a parent who is deeply interested in emotional health, I've always been curious about practices for cultivating rest. Yet when I hear people's suggestions, most of them make me exasperated or even angry.

I might hear someone on a podcast talk about getting up early and having an hour of silence or meditation before starting their day or see someone online share their "life-changing" sleep habits or perfected morning routine.

Although these practices sound amazing and like something I would love to have in my life, they're not even close to my reality.

My son was two years old when my daughter was born. He followed a fairly typical progression as an infant when it came to sleep (lots of long, wakeful nights at first, but he began to sleep through the night after a few months). My daughter was a different story. She had the most beautiful temperament—smiley and cuddly—but she just wanted to be awake . . . like, all the time. It was as if she thought she was going to miss out on an exciting party if she slept any longer than a short nap. For many different reasons (and believe me, we tried *so* many different things), my daughter did not consistently sleep through the night until she was four years old.

What this meant was that for the first six years of my parenting journey, I didn't regularly get a full night of sleep. Once everyone was sleeping through the night and I began to feel more like a human again, I attempted to get up early before everyone else for some time to myself. Yet no matter what time I got up, a few minutes later, I would inevitably see a little face with a mop of tousled hair asking me if it was time to get up.

This chapter isn't intended to make you feel worse about the lack of rest you're experiencing as you tend to your child's needs. Rather, I hope to share practices you can implement in your family's real life in order to cultivate rest—for both you and your children.

The Importance of Sleep

Most of us know how important sleep is. When we get enough sleep, we see improvements in our health, mood, and brain performance. Research shows that when children get adequate sleep, they show improvements in their attention, mood, problem-solving skills, and overall mental and physical health.[2] Parents need sleep for emotional and mental health; children need sleep for healthy development.

Yet many of us struggle to get adequate sleep, especially once we become parents. Research has found that new parents lose an average of 109 minutes of sleep every night during the first year they have a baby.[3] That's almost two hours of sleep every night. It is no wonder we're all exhausted!

If you (or your child) have the trait of high sensitivity, you likely have a higher need for sleep than your peers. This is because you're more vulnerable to overstimulation—your brain needs more sleep to recover from deep thinking and processing. So whenever you see "average recommended sleep time," keep in mind that those with high sensitivity will be on the higher side of the range and may even need more than the recommended amount.

In family life, the problem isn't that we need to be convinced of the importance of sleep, but rather that even when we want to sleep, we often have someone we love very much waking us up. There are no strategies or life hacks to get around this. This is just part of raising children.

The two key things to remember regarding sleep and parenting are *awareness* and *grace*.

In my bleary-eyed days of sleep deprivation, I underestimated just how exhausted I had become. That's because life keeps on going. When you're a parent, losing sleep at night doesn't mean you get to sleep in or take the day off, because you have children who are awake and ready to party for the day. You may also have to go to work outside the home or keep other commitments. So you just keep going, pushing yourself to get up again and again.

Yet what comes with sleep deprivation isn't just a grumpy mood or heightened emotions, but also a stronger inner critic, which keeps setting the standards higher and keeps pointing out all the ways you're failing to measure up. When we're sleep deprived, we become the darker versions of ourselves—not only toward our children or others, but also toward ourselves.

Without enough sleep, we lose perspective. We lose emotional bandwidth. We lose the awareness of just how exhausted we've become. You can only push yourself so far before you need to allow yourself to sleep and recover. It's amazing how much a good night of sleep can make problems seem smaller and the world feel new again.

Practical Sleep Tips for Children

No matter how old your child is, it's important to set them up for success when it comes to good sleep.

1. Have a consistent bedtime for your child. This teaches their body and circadian rhythm to be prepared to fall asleep.

2. Create a calming bedtime routine for your child. This will help their mind and body slow down, and cue them for sleep.
3. Stop exposure to screens or blue light for one to three hours before bedtime. Exposure to screens can disrupt circadian rhythms, making it challenging for your child to sleep after watching a screen.
4. Highly sensitive children need more sleep, so plan for an earlier bedtime or naps during the day.
5. Highly sensitive children need time before bed to decompress and process their day. Most children struggle to transition directly from lots of activity to sleep, but this is especially true for highly sensitive children. Allow your child some quiet time alone with an audiobook or calming music to help them relax.

Practical Sleep Tips for Parents

We think a lot about sleep for our kids, but we often put our own sleep needs on the back burner. However, sleep is a critical part of our health as adults too.

1. Increase your awareness of your body's needs. Most of the time, if we recognize how exhausted we are, we can work out ways to remedy the situation. Yet in the busyness of family life, this is often the last thing we think about. If you notice that you're more reactive than usual or that the world feels especially heavy, it might be a cue that you need some more sleep.
2. If possible, take turns dealing with your child's needs in the night. You might take the first half of the night while your spouse takes the second, or you might be "on" one night and they're "on" the next.
3. Set aside a "catch-up day." If you're consistently experiencing sleep deprivation, include a catch-up day in your week. This may be on the weekend, when you have an opportunity to sleep in or take an afternoon nap. You might get up early with

the kids on Saturday morning so your spouse can sleep, and then they can get up early on Sunday morning so you can sleep. If you're solo parenting, you might try napping at the same time as your kids on the weekend or organizing a safe activity for them to do ahead of time while you doze on the couch.
4. Try to find other pockets of time for yourself. One of the main reasons parents don't go to bed when they're exhausted is because it's often the only time they get to themselves. Try looking for other pockets of alone time throughout your day so you don't try to cram in those things at night. If you aren't able to find windows of time during the day, you might designate a few nights a week as early nights to leave responsibilities for the day and take the rest for time to yourself. If you plan this ahead of time, you'll be less likely to be pulled in by another episode of a show or endless memes on your phone.

The Freedom of Sabbath

In our busy world, there will rarely be times when rest just happens—for us or our children. Even though most of us have a weekend, considered to be two full days off work for many of us, this time is even busier than the weekdays. Our days off are filled with sports games, children's parties, community and church gatherings, shopping, running errands, and catching up on household chores. When our rest days aren't in any way restful, it's no wonder we always feel exhausted.

Rest isn't something that just happens; it's something we need to intentionally plan for.

This is where the Sabbath comes in. Sometimes we're the kind of tired that requires more than a good night's sleep to fix.

Sabbath is a tradition with Jewish-Christian roots in which one day a week is set apart for rest. The purpose of Sabbath is to cease all work (this includes both paid and unpaid work, such as taking care of the home) and cultivate a day of rest, celebration, and connection with loved ones.

The practice of Sabbath comes from the Genesis story of creation, in which God made the world in six days and rested on the seventh day, giving us a model for living in a rhythm of work and rest. Sabbath also has ties to the Israelites' slavery in Egypt, when they worked without rest or relief. When God freed them from slavery through the Exodus, he instructed them to practice a weekly Sabbath as a foundation for their new way of life. Many biblical scholars believe that this practice was given because although the Israelites had been physically freed from slavery, they still hadn't learned a new way of *being*. They hadn't yet embraced the freedom of knowing their value apart from a pressure to keep endlessly producing. Sabbath was a practice to regularly remind them of what was most important.

Even if you don't come from a tradition that observes the Sabbath, this practice can still be life-giving to you and your family. It provides a framework for being intentional about rest and connection so we don't get so caught up in work and daily life that we forget what's most important.

As with any other practice, Sabbath begins as a decision.

> As with any other practice, Sabbath begins as a decision.

A decision to trust that despite our lack of productivity, life will go on.

A decision to prioritize what's most important, even when it doesn't feel like what's most urgent.

A decision to rest in a world that's shouting at us to keep moving.

A decision to pause, even when we're afraid of being left behind.

Practical Ways to Implement Sabbath

Intentionally preparing for rest may seem counterintuitive, but if we don't, it won't happen—other things will fill the vacuum of our time. Carving out spaces of rest is the only way to ensure that we're living out what we value most. Your practice of Sabbath doesn't have to be on a specific day of the week; it can be a specific period of time you set apart to rest from work.

If the idea of practicing a Sabbath seems daunting, here are some ideas to help you get started.

1. **Choose a time.** If you've never practiced Sabbath, it might feel overwhelming to set aside an entire day each week. Begin by choosing one period of time, such as several hours or half a day, as a starting point. Then, as this practice becomes more natural for you and you experience the benefits, you may decide to implement it more regularly.

2. **Plan to remove all paid and unpaid work.** This time period needs to be protected from calendar commitments as well as from household chores. In order to experience the fullness of the time off, you want to guard against the feeling that you *need* to complete chores.

3. **Find activities that your family finds restful and enjoyable.** Sabbath is a day to slow down and go on a walk, play at the park or the beach, read books, or watch a movie together as a family. It may also be the day you attend your church or the gathering of your faith community.

4. **Swap time off.** Particularly if you have young children, you and your spouse might want to swap time off during Sabbath. You might look after the kids for a few hours, and then your spouse can take them to the park. This gives both of you some time to yourself as well as time together as a family. If you are solo parenting, consider swapping childcare with a friend or asking a relative to spend time with your kids so you can rest.

5. **Have the mindset of Sabbath.** Practicing Sabbath probably won't be as restful as you'd like while you're in an intense season of caring for your children. But experiencing even small chunks of time when you release yourself from the expectation of productivity can be life-giving. It may allow you to sleep while your children nap, or read a book while they play in the backyard. As a parent,

you'll always have a to-do list. Sometimes the hardest part of practicing Sabbath is not the loud children who are demanding your attention but your own internal voice telling you that you really *should* be doing something else.

6. **Practice Sabbath regularly.** The practice of Sabbath will be most life-giving to you and your family if you are able to practice it consistently. This will also help your children learn what to expect during this time, and they will slowly lean into the routine too.

Resting from Technology

"Mom just needs five minutes!"

I was hiding in our bedroom while dinner was in the oven. After the typical evening routine and hearing "Mom!" called every few minutes, I was looking for a moment to myself. I'd locked myself in my bedroom and was scrolling social media, looking for something funny to take my mind off everything.

That week, on top of all the usual responsibilities, our online business had run a product promotion, meaning our whole team was on technology nonstop to make sure everything was working well and customers were supported. Typically, I have firm boundaries about not working outside set hours, but this particular moment in our work-world required us to be more available and online more frequently.

I was exhausted from a busy work week, but despite being on my phone a lot more than usual, I found myself subconsciously craving even more time on it. But more time online didn't deliver the rest I craved; in fact, it only made me more weary and restless.

It's no secret that the increased use of technology over the past decade has negatively impacted our relationships and mental health.

The conversation about technology is usually about its impact on children. But technology hinders our relationships as adults too. Surveys show that middle schoolers and adolescents desire a deeper connection with their parents but feel their parents' technology use sometimes blocks that.[4] Technology is clearly impeding family connections—the relationships we desire most.

Now before you start feeling guilty about your or your child's technology use, it's important to remember that the technology over the past decade has been *intentionally designed* to be addictive.

Dopamine is a neurotransmitter that's related to reward pathways in the brain. It's primarily responsible for feelings of pleasure, satisfaction, and motivation. The brain releases a small amount of dopamine every time we interact with our phones. This means that every time we see a new post on social media, get more likes, or receive a text message or email, our brain sends out a surge of pleasure. What happens with continual use, over time, is that the brain's reward system gradually becomes desensitized.

This is the same process that occurs with drug addiction. The first time an individual takes a drug, there's a huge dopamine release, but over time, the same amount of the drug results in the release of less dopamine. This causes the individual to need more and more of the drug just to return to their baseline again. One of the biggest problems with technology is that it's slowly desensitizing our brain's reward system, making our ordinary life feel increasingly boring.

It's common to feel that technology is more enjoyable than real life. This isn't something most of us would feel comfortable saying out loud, but it's what we sometimes feel in our ordinary daily lives.

Sitting on the floor playing Legos with a four-year-old seems boring compared to watching our favorite show.

Having a chat with our child about something they're interested in (but maybe we're not) seems boring compared to sending funny memes to our friends.

The truth is, the more we lean into our technology use without intentional breaks, the more boring and uninteresting our real life begins to feel.

This is why a regular technology Sabbath practice can be life-giving—for the whole family.

A technology Sabbath is when you put away all technology—phones, computers, tablets, and TV—for a specific period of time. Ideally, this would be for at least twenty-four hours. This time frame is based on the principle of dopamine fasting. If you remove yourself from activities that constantly activate a dopamine release, you will reset the sensitivity of your brain's reward system.

By implementing a regular technology Sabbath, you can not only have time with your loved ones that's unencumbered by distractions but also reset your brain so it's more sensitive to the joys of your real life.

Practical Ways to Implement a Technology Sabbath

Depending on the role technology plays in your life, the idea of a technology Sabbath might sound anywhere from refreshing to impossible. If you aren't sure how to get started or how to get your family on board, here are some suggestions.

1. **Choose a period of time.** Begin with a twenty-four-hour period, and prepare your family ahead of time. During this window, all technology is turned off and put away.

2. **Be prepared for how uncomfortable it will feel.** In particular, the first few hours away from technology may make you feel lost or even anxious as you notice how much you're inclined to check your phone. Without the distraction of technology, you may also become aware of just how exhausted you are or confront negative emotions that you haven't had the space to process yet.

3. **Prepare activities for this time.** In order to combat the potential "down" everyone experiences when they put technology away, plan ahead to do some life-engaging activities that your family loves.

4. **Notice how you feel at the end of the technology Sabbath.** Take a moment to reflect, both on your own and with your family. You may not notice the difference right away, but a day or two later you may realize that you're reaching for your phone less or that you have more desire to spend "ordinary" time with your family.

The Power of Quiet Time

"Would you please stop shushing me?!"

Colin and I were out on a date night at a nice farm-to-table restaurant. We were talking about the things that were going on in our lives, and the topics were getting more and more personal. I was becoming agitated because my husband has an "outside voice."

Colin is an extrovert and has a career as a professional speaker, so it's understandable that he's a loud talker. But he only has two modes: loud and even louder. As the general noise of the restaurant grew louder, the topics of conversation between us became more and more personal. I'm a pretty private person by nature, and I was shushing him every few minutes. Not only did I not want strangers at the nice restaurant to know all our personal business, but the noise of the conversation was beginning to feel overwhelming.

This situation may have been more intense because we were in a public setting, but it's not unusual for me to wish I could shush the noise around me. As parents, we almost never have the luxury of quiet. Life is loud; relationships are loud; children are loud. They are playful, rambunctious, and very, very noisy. The idea of having moments of quiet in family life often seems unrealistic and unattainable.

But quiet isn't just a luxury; it's something our bodies and minds and souls need.

Times of silence and quiet are de-stimulating for our nervous system. When our children are little, we intuitively scoop them up and take them somewhere quiet when they're overwhelmed. Yet we sometimes forget how important this is as our children get older (and how important it is for us, too!).

> Quietness is a practice that helps us return to ourselves.

Quietness is a practice that helps us recover from the noise of life and return to ourselves. It's why we're drawn to nature or places such as an empty church or chapel. We know at a core level that silence is restorative to our soul.

A quiet time is a dedicated space when everyone in the family rests or engages in quiet, independent play. This practice gives us regular respite from the noise of the world.

Once your child no longer needs a nap, you can introduce a daily quiet time. You may get some resistance to this idea at first, but practicing it regularly will make it an expected part of your family life.

The length of time will vary depending on the age and temperament of your child. For children around three years old, you might begin with twenty minutes; for five- to six-year-olds, you might try forty minutes; for children seven years and older, you could aim for sixty minutes of quiet time.

Quiet times will look different for each family, but in general, it means that every family member spends time in their room or in a designated place in the house. Each person can engage in a quiet activity, such as reading books, coloring, playing with Legos, or doing creative hobbies such as art, writing, sewing, or STEM projects. Your child might like playing in silence, or they might prefer listening to calming music or an audiobook (try using headphones or earbuds so it doesn't add noise for the rest of the family).

Set a timer so your child knows what to expect, and when the timer goes off, everyone can come out of their room or designated spot. When you begin this practice, your child may come out of quiet time before the timer goes off. If this happens, just be consistent about redirecting them back to quiet time. Or you may consider starting with a shorter time frame and increasing it as they get accustomed to the idea.

You can use the practice of quiet time both as a regular part of your daily routine and as a tool when your child is overwhelmed. For example, if you notice—through their increasing levels of frustration, grumpy mood, or higher emotions—that your child is becoming consistently overstimulated, you may decide that everyone is going to have a twenty-minute quiet time before transitioning to another activity.

If you have younger children, you might consider putting together a "quiet-time box" that is brought out only at quiet time. It can include simple activities such as coloring books or Legos that are special since they can only be played with during quiet time. If you have older children, you might talk with them about their favorite creative hobbies or activities and create a designated family time when everyone does quiet activities separately.

The Benefits of Solitude

Solitude isn't just about having a break or finding some time alone. Social scientists who study the effect of noise pollution on the nervous system define solitude as being free from input.[5]

This means that true solitude isn't just escaping to another room while your children are playing or taking a shower while your family is yelling outside your bathroom. It's also not scrolling on your phone in bed or on the couch. We often use things to try to fill our craving for solitude. Yet true solitude is found when we spend time alone, free from input.

True solitude has many benefits.

First, it calms our outer world and our nervous system. Our nervous system needs both demand and rest to develop strength. In our fast-paced world, we typically experience only demand. True solitude gives our nervous system a break.

Secondly, solitude helps us reconnect with ourselves. Parenting requires us to sacrifice so many of our wants and needs for those of others that it's easy to forget who we are. Time in solitude reminds us who we are and bolsters our confidence, self-esteem, and intuition.

Big and Little Ways to Find Solitude

We all have a need for time alone. This may be something you've always known, or you might have discovered it when you entered parenting. Even my extroverted friends joke that they've become introverts since becoming parents because they so desperately crave time to themselves.

Although each family is different, this tends to be particularly true for mothers, since they are often the default parent and children gravitate toward them when they need something. My children will walk straight past my husband to find me at the other end of the house so I can open something for them or brush their hair. It's infuriating and hilarious at the same time.

The need for solitude is especially important for individuals with a highly sensitive temperament. Their nervous system is far more attuned to their environment, so they have a higher need for breaks from this input.

Your temperament, your family situation, and your season of life all contribute to how much solitude you need, but you *do* need it!

There are big and small ways you can give yourself the gift of solitude. Not all of them will work for you, nor will they work in all seasons of parenting. But these options can help you be intentional about finding some solitude, even if it's just a little bit.

1. **Make a list of practices that help you calm inner and outer noise.** Some ideas include taking a hot bath, reading a book, praying, drinking a cup of tea or coffee, sitting by the fire, and journaling.

2. **Get up before your children.** If you can, wake up twenty minutes to an hour earlier than your children and do activities that feed your soul. (If your kids are little, skip this one for now!)

3. **Use time in the margins of your day.** If you know you'll be waiting for your child in the car during activities or in the school pickup line, plan to use this time as a solitude retreat. Bring something to help you focus, such as your journal, a prayer guide, or a book you enjoy.

4. **Ask your spouse or a family member to take the kids out of the house for an hour.** Instead of using this time to do household chores, use the quietness for some time alone, free from input.

5. **Swap an afternoon of babysitting with a friend.** Be sure to use your time off to do activities that fill your soul rather than trying to be more "productive."

6. **Take time off just for you.** If you work outside the home, take the day off when your child is in school or with a babysitter. Use this time for yourself.

7. **Schedule a personal retreat away.** If finances and childcare allow, book an overnight stay somewhere. Plan some enjoyable activities you love as well as some time to reflect and journal in solitude.

Making Room for Rest in Your Ordinary Life

Take some time when you're not feeling rushed to sit down with your calendar. Look at each of these categories and schedule a day and time to do them in the next month. (You don't need to feel guilty if they don't all work out, but none of them will happen if you're not intentional about it!)

REST

Activity:
Day/Time:

SLEEP

Activity:
Day/Time:

SABBATH

Activity:
Day/Time:

QUIET TIME

Activity:
Day/Time:

SOLITUDE

Activity:
Day/Time:

EPILOGUE

CONDUCTING YOUR FAMILY'S SYMPHONY

In the peak of the summer heat, my family slowly climbed the steep gravel driveway. The air was hot and thick, adding invisible resistance to our climb. When we reached the top, we came upon a grand home covered in ivy. We stood, gazing at the building for a while, until we turned to walk to the side of the house, where a small door stood open. As we stepped through, we were met with our first view of the gardens.

The spacious grounds were full of lush green grass, with tall oaks shading the pathway and leading to an expansive view across the valley of trees, all swaying in the warm wind. My children ran around the grounds as we imagined what it would have been like to live in such a noble house, all of us jokingly agreeing that what our family really needed was to own a large estate. As we walked, we encountered manicured plants, wild vegetation, Christmas holly, and beautiful flowers in full bloom. Although everything had been intentionally planned and planted, there was a sense of natural ease to the environment.

We were visiting Dumbarton Oaks in Washington, DC, named by *National Geographic* as one of the top ten gardens in the world.[1] It has been intentionally curated by a team of professional horticulturalists to ensure that it thrives in every season. As we walked, I was reminded that whether it's the small bed of zinnias in my backyard or sprawling gardens at an estate, these gardens thrive because their environment has been cultivated for them to flourish.

As we raise children, we live in a tension between nature and nurture. Your child was born with their own unique DNA, and specific strengths and vulnerabilities. There's nothing you can do to influence or change their makeup. But you can take responsibility for the environment they grow up in and create space for them to thrive.

H. Jackson Brown Jr. says, "Remember that children, marriages, and flower gardens reflect the kind of care they get."[2] Although there are exceptions and extenuating circumstances (especially in our adult relationships), the overall principle is true: when we invest our heart in something or someone, they expand to reflect this care.

As parents and caregivers, we have the opportunity to invest in the hearts of the children in our lives. Our children need our investment of love, time, attention, and encouragement to thrive in the future. When we, as parents, grandparents, teachers, or professionals, take responsibility for their nurture, we protect their environment and invest in their little hearts.

The lights dim, and a hush comes over the crowd.

The whole venue is quiet, the audience waiting for the sound they've invested their time and money to hear.

As the curtain rises, thunderous applause fills the air. The orchestra conductor walks onstage, bows to the crowd, and climbs to the raised podium to face the musicians. At the swing of the baton, the music begins.

The conductor's hearing is expertly attuned to hear every note the orchestra plays and make decisions about what needs to be adjusted. This maestro has the rare ability to listen to what other people aren't paying attention to.

As parents, we are the conductors of our family environment.

We are the ones who cultivate the factors our children are most influenced by.

We are the ones who give direction and leadership and determine what comes into our home.

The environment of our world isn't going to become slower, less complicated, or less pressurized. If the past is any indicator, our world will only grow more intense and more complex. The droning foghorn of stress will only get louder.

As we become aware of the noise of our environment and the impact it's having on our souls, we have the opportunity—and the responsibility—to make decisions to adjust.

When the noise is at an acceptable level and your family is thriving, celebrate that things are going well.

When you notice that your family or your children aren't thriving, pay attention to ways the noise in the environment may be impacting them.

The conductor is able to close their eyes and listen for what others may not notice.

The conductor indicates adjustments, turning up the volume in some areas and turning it down in others until the symphony sounds the way it was intended: beautiful and balanced, giving life and joy to all who listen.

As much as we might wish we could somehow make all the overstimulation and stress from our lives disappear completely, this isn't realistic. You will feel stressed and overstimulated in the future. Your child will be overstimulated and stressed in the future. Yet it's my hope that you will now be able to recognize these signs more quickly and use a variety of tools to help them regulate and calm their emotions.

As you approach family life through the lens of this philosophy and these practices, you will notice your connection with your child deepening over time as you understand them more and learn how to support them in their emotions. This will also help you feel more confident in your own parenting (with less second-guessing!). The overall feeling in your home will become calmer as well. When you know how to regulate and lower the stress of the environment, joy is able to reenter the room.

As your child matures, they will face all kinds of difficult real-life situations. We parents love our children so much that we often want to protect them from the darkness of the world. Yet as much as we might wish we could take away these uncomfortable and often painful situations, that's not always possible. But we can provide a space of recovery away from the pressure and draw from a toolbox of practices (which we also implement in our own lives) so they're empowered in their own emotional coping skills. As they grow in these skills and practices, their resilience and emotional health will also improve.

This is how we make the next generation stronger. Not by removing the hard things but by equipping our children with the tools they will need to overcome the giants they face. These tools might not look like much at first, but neither did the rock and sling used by a shepherd boy to conquer Goliath. It's time to try a different approach—one that helps our children thrive. Here's to cultivating the resilience and emotional health of this next generation together!

May you have the courage to embrace how you and your child have been uniquely made.

May you find the wisdom to discern the noise that is eroding your family's peace.

May you remember the joy from play, the wonder of slowness, and the softening power of rest.

May you know encouragement and endurance as you raise your children in strength, hope, and love.

Turning Down the Noise: A Manifesto

In my commitment to turning down the noise for my family and myself, I will

- know myself and my child
- find ways to calm myself
- protect their childhood
- cultivate play
- slow down
- notice the beauty
- simplify the environment
- shepherd my child's heart
- make space for rest

You are the conductor of your family's symphony. Give yourself permission to make the decisions you need to in order to create a beautiful family life.

ACKNOWLEDGMENTS

I'm immensely grateful for the encouragement and support of others who helped bring these words into the world. This book would not have been possible without them.

To the whole team at Tyndale: To Cassidy, Kaylee, Dean, Julie, and the whole team for your expertise in bringing this message into the world. To Stephanie, for your patience, encouragement, and prowess to improve what was on the page. To Jillian, for your belief in me and my writing, for taking a chance on me, and for bringing your expertise to fortify every part of this project. I'm deeply grateful.

To many friends who have been a safe place, both for this book and in life—I love you all.

To my family: To Colin, for being my steadiness through this huge project and meeting my overwhelm with compassion and humor. Marrying you was the greatest decision of my life. To Jonah, my brilliant thinker and wise sage; and Georgia, my sunshine girl, bringing the craziness and laughter always. Getting to be your mom is the greatest honor and love of my life. Thank you for supporting me with this project and all it has required, and for teaching me as much as I hope I've taught you.

To God, for being the deep sustaining foundation of my life and the voice that continues to call through all the seasons.

To every reader who has invested their time and attention in these words: I am praying and believing this promise over your family: "And great shall be the peace and undisturbed composure of your children" (Isaiah 54:13).

NOTES

INTRODUCTION
1. Nicole Racine et al., "Global Prevalence of Depressive and Anxiety Symptoms in Children and Adolescents during COVID-19," *JAMA Pediatrics* 175, no. 11 (November 2021): 1–10, https://www.ncbi.nlm.nih.gov/pmc/articles/PMC8353576/.
2. "Quotes," on Alexander den Heijer's official website, accessed May 31, 2024, https://www.alexanderdenheijer.com/quotes.

CHAPTER 1: HOW LOUD IS YOUR WORLD?
1. Sam Woods, "'Off-Key, Off-Tempo': A Former Milwaukee Symphony Conductor Battles the Foghorns," WUWM, October 13, 2023, https://www.wuwm.com/2023-10-13/off-key-off-tempo-a-former-milwaukee-symphony-conductor-battles-the-foghorns.
2. "Noise vs. Nature: How We're Upsetting America's Soundscapes," NBC News, February 17, 2015, https://www.nbcnews.com/science/environment/noise-vs-nature-how-were-upsetting-americas-soundscapes-n307216.
3. "Noise Pollution Is a Major Problem, Both for Human Health and the Environment," European Environment Agency, March 20, 2020, https://www.eea.europa.eu/articles/noise-pollution-is-a-major.
4. "Gordon Hempton: Silence and the Presence of Everything," *On Being with Krista Tippett* (podcast), May 10, 2012, https://onbeing.org/programs/gordon-hempton-silence-and-the-presence-of-everything.
5. Gordon Hempton, "One Square Inch: A Sanctuary for Silence at Olympic National Park," accessed May 31, 2024, https://onesquareinch.org/.
6. Elizabeth P. Derryberry et al., "Singing in a Silent Spring: Birds Respond to a Half-Century Soundscape Reversion during the COVID-19 Shutdown," *Science* 370, issue 6516 (September 24, 2020): 575–579, https://www.science.org/doi/10.1126/science.abd5777.

7. Daniel J. Levitin, "Why the Modern World Is Bad for Your Brain," *The Guardian*, January 18, 2015, https://www.theguardian.com/science/2015/jan/18/modern-world-bad-for-brain-daniel-j-levitin-organized-mind-information-overload.
8. Marta Lenart-Bugla et al., "The Association between Allostatic Load and Brain: A Systematic Review," *Psychoneuroendocrinology* 145 (November 2022), https://pubmed.ncbi.nlm.nih.gov/36113380/.
9. Kate Gawlik and Bernadette Mazurek Melnyk, "Pandemic Parenting: Examining the Epidemic of Working Parental Burnout and Strategies to Help," Ohio State University Office of the Chief Wellness Officer and College of Nursing, May 2022, https://wellness.osu.edu/sites/default/files/documents/2022/05/OCWO_ParentalBurnout_3674200_Report_FINAL.pdf.
10. Emily Laurence, "Stay-at-Home Moms and Depression: What to Know and How to Get Help," Forbes Health, August 14, 2023, https://www.forbes.com/health/womens-health/stay-at-home-moms-depression/.
11. Nikolai A. Shevchuk, "Adapted Cold Shower as a Potential Treatment for Depression," *Medical Hypotheses* 70, no. 5 (2008): 995–1001, https://www.sciencedirect.com/science/article/abs/pii/S030698770700566X.
12. Jerrold Petrofsky et al., "Moist Heat or Dry Heat for Delayed Onset Muscle Soreness," *Journal of Clinical Medicine Research* 5, no. 6 (December 2013): 416–425, https://www.ncbi.nlm.nih.gov/pmc/articles/PMC3808259/#R05.

CHAPTER 2: THE INDIVIDUAL'S WORLD

1. Bianca P. Acevedo et al., "The Highly Sensitive Brain: An fMRI Study of Sensory Processing Sensitivity and Response to Others' Emotions," *Brain and Behavior* 4, no. 4 (July 2014): 580–594, https://doi.org/10.1002/brb3.242.
2. Elaine N. Aron, *The Highly Sensitive Person: How to Thrive When the World Overwhelms You* (Naples, FL: Birth Lane Press, 1966), 98.
3. Bożena Gulla and Krystyna Golonka, "Exploring Protective Factors in Wellbeing: How Sensory Processing Sensitivity and Attention Awareness Interact with Resilience," *Frontiers in Psychology* 12 (November 15, 2021), https://www.ncbi.nlm.nih.gov/pmc/articles/PMC8634940/.
4. Andre Sólo, "Do These Genes Help Make You a Highly Sensitive Person?," *Psychology Today*, December 20, 2018, https://www.psychologytoday.com/us/blog/highly-sensitive-refuge/201812/do-these-genes-help-make-you-highly-sensitive-person.
5. Acevedo et al., "The Highly Sensitive Brain."
6. Acevedo et al., "The Highly Sensitive Brain."
7. Acevedo et al., "The Highly Sensitive Brain."
8. Acevedo et al., "The Highly Sensitive Brain."
9. Jadzia Jagiellowicz et al., "The Trait of Sensory Processing Sensitivity and Neural Responses to Changes in Visual Scenes," *Social Cognitive and Affective Neuroscience* 6, no. 1 (January 2011): 38–47, https://doi.org/10.1093/scan/nsq001.

10. Bianca Acevedo et al., "The Functional Highly Sensitive Brain: A Review of the Brain Circuits Underlying Sensory Processing Sensitivity and Seemingly Related Disorders," *Philosophical Transactions of the Royal Society of London, Series B* 373, no. 1744 (February 26, 2018): 20170161, https://doi.org/10.1098/rstb.2017.0161.

CHAPTER 3: THE CHILD'S WORLD

1. Merve Cikili Uytun, "Development Period of Prefrontal Cortex," chap. 1 in *Prefrontal Cortex*, ed. Ana Starcevic and Branislav Filipovic (London, UK: IntechOpen, 2018), 6, https://www.researchgate.net/publication/328081981_Development_Period_of_Prefrontal_Cortex.
2. Satoshi Tsujimoto, "The Prefrontal Cortex: Functional Neural Development during Early Childhood," *Neuroscientist* 14, no. 4 (August 2008): 345–358, https://pubmed.ncbi.nlm.nih.gov/18467667/.
3. Uytun, "Development Period of Prefrontal Cortex," 12.
4. Mariam Arain et al., "Maturation of the Adolescent Brain," *Neuropsychiatric Disease and Treatment* 9, (2013): 449–461, https://www.ncbi.nlm.nih.gov/pmc/articles/PMC3621648/.
5. Vincent J. Felitti et al, "Relationship of Childhood Abuse and Household Dysfunction to Many of the Leading Causes of Death in Adults," *American Journal of Preventative Medicine* 14, issue 4 (May 1998): 245–258, https://www.ajpmonline.org/article/S0749-3797(98)00017-8/fulltext.
6. Harris Cooper and Jeffrey C. Valentine, "Using Research to Answer Practical Questions about Homework," *Educational Psychologist* 36, no. 3 (September 2001): 143–153, https://doi.org/10.1207/S15326985EP3603_1.
7. Kate Rix, "How Much Recess Should Kids Get?" *US News and World Report*, October 14, 2022, https://www.usnews.com/education/k12/articles/how-much-recess-should-kids-get.
8. Tom Loveless, "Homework in America," Brookings, March 18, 2014, https://www.brookings.edu/articles/homework-in-america/.
9. Cooper and Valentine, "Using Research to Answer Practical Questions."
10. Martin Whitely et al., "Annual Research Review: Attention Deficit Hyperactivity Disorder Late Birthdate Effect Common in Both High and Low Prescribing International Jurisdictions: A Systematic Review," *Journal of Child Psychology and Psychiatry* 60, no. 4 (April 2019). 380–391, https://doi.org/10.1111/jcpp.12991.

CHAPTER 4: THE PARENT'S WORLD

1. James W. Pennebaker, "Putting Stress into Words: Health, Linguistic, and Therapeutic Implications," *Behaviour Research and Therapy* 31, no. 6 (July 1993): 539–548, https://doi.org/10.1016/0005-7967(93)90105-4.
2. Pennebaker, "Putting Stress into Words."

3. "Hell Week," Navy SEALs website, accessed June 7, 2024, https://navyseals.com/nsw/hell-week-0/.
4. Stephanie Pappas, "Are Naps Good for You?" *Scientific American*, August 5, 2023, https://www.scientificamerican.com/article/are-naps-good-for-you/.
5. Dian Land, "Study Shows Compassion Meditation Changes the Brain," University of Wisconsin–Madison, March 25, 2008, https://news.wisc.edu/study-shows-compassion-meditation-changes-the-brain/; "The Extraordinary Effect of Mindfulness on Depression," transcript of interview with Daniel Goleman, Big Think website, accessed June 7, 2024, https://bigthink.com/neuropsych/the-extraordinary-effect-of-mindfulness-on-depression/; Amanda Ruggeri, "Can Slow Breathing Guard against Alzheimer's?" BBC, July 24, 2023, https://www.bbc.com/future/article/20230724-can-slow-breathing-guard-against-alzheimers.
6. David Rock, *Your Brain at Work* (New York: Harper Business, 2020), 21.
7. Rock, *Your Brain at Work*, 9.
8. Andrew Newberg et al., "Cerebral Blood Flow during Meditative Prayer: Preliminary Findings and Methodological Issues," *Perceptual and Motor Skills* 97, no. 2 (October 2003): 625–630, https://pubmed.ncbi.nlm.nih.gov/14620252/.
9. Andrew Newberg and Mark Robert Waldman, *How God Changes Your Brain: Breakthrough Findings from a Leading Neuroscientist* (New York: Ballantine, 2010), 7.
10. Anne Lamott, *Crooked Little Heart* (New York: Anchor Books, 1997), 185.
11. Carl Jung, *Aion* (Princeton University Press, 1979), 70–71.

CHAPTER 5: THE STATE OF THE WORLD

1. Max Roser, "Technology over the Long Run: Zoom Out to See How Dramatically the World Can Change within a Lifetime," Our World in Data, February 22, 2023, https://ourworldindata.org/technology-long-run.
2. Jim Rendon, *Upside: The New Science of Post-Traumatic Growth* (New York: Touchstone, 2015), 16.
3. Daniel A. Cox, "The Childhood Loneliness of Generation Z," Survey Center on American Life, April 4, 2022, https://www.americansurveycenter.org/the-lonely-childhood-of-generation-z/.
4. "America's Trust in Its Institutions Has Collapsed," *The Economist*, April 17, 2024, https://www.economist.com/united-states/2024/04/17/americas-trust-in-its-institutions-has-collapsed; Jonathan Gruber, "A Sobering Snapshot of Distrust in America," Einhorn Collaborative, June 22, 2021, https://einhorncollaborative.org/a-sobering-snapshot-of-distrust-in-america/.
5. Elizabeth J. Carter and Kevin A. Pelphrey, "Friend or Foe? Brain Systems Involved in the Perception of Dynamic Signals of Menacing and Friendly Social Approaches," *Social Neuroscience* 3, no. 2 (2008): 151–163, https://pubmed.ncbi.nlm.nih.gov/18633856/.
6. Paul J. Zak, "The Trust Molecule," *Wall Street Journal*, April 27, 2012, https://www.wsj.com/articles/SB10001424052702304811304577365782995320366.

7. Michael Hopkin, "Trust in a Bottle," *Nature*, June 1, 2005, https://www.nature.com/articles/news050531-4.
8. Rachel Minkin and Juliana Menasce Horowitz, "Parenting in America Today," Pew Research Center, January 24, 2023, https://www.pewresearch.org/social-trends/2023/01/24/parenting-in-america-today/.
9. Naomi I. Eisenberger et al., "Neural Pathways Link Social Support to Attenuated Neuroendocrine Stress Responses," *NeuroImage* 35, no. 4 (May 1, 2007): 1601–1612, https://www.ncbi.nlm.nih.gov/pmc/articles/PMC2710966/.
10. Thomas R. Verny, "Intuition: What It Is and How It Works," *Psychology Today*, August 22, 2023, https://www.psychologytoday.com/us/blog/explorations-of-the-mind/202308/intuition-what-it-is-and-how-it-works.

CHAPTER 6: SELF-REGULATION: CULTIVATING EMOTIONAL MATURITY

1. Jaime R. Herndon, "What Is Self-Regulation?" VeryWell Health, January 20, 2024, https://www.verywellhealth.com/self-regulation-5225245.
2. Harvard Second Generation Study, Harvard Medical School, accessed June 12, 2024, https://www.adultdevelopmentstudy.org/; Robert Waldinger and Marc Schulz, "What the Longest Study on Human Happiness Found Is the Key to a Good Life," *The Atlantic*, January 19, 2023, https://www.theatlantic.com/ideas/archive/2023/01/harvard-happiness-study-relationships/672753/.
3. Liz Mineo, "Work Out Daily? OK, but How Socially Fit Are You?," *Harvard Gazette*, February 10, 2023, https://news.harvard.edu/gazette/story/2023/02/work-out-daily-ok-but-how-socially-fit-are-you.
4. Naomi I. Eisenberger et al., "Neural Pathways Link Social Support to Attenuated Neuroendocrine Stress Responses," *NeuroImage* 35, no. 4 (May 1, 2007): 1601–1612, https://www.ncbi.nlm.nih.gov/pmc/articles/PMC2710966/.
5. Lois M. Collins, "Research Shows It's Relationships, Not Genetics That Lengthen Your Life," *Deseret News*, May 7, 2022, https://www.deseret.com/2022/5/7/23060482/harvard-longevity-study-happiness-relationships-physical-mental-health-byu-waldinger-super-ager.
6. Nathan Yau, "Who We Spend Time With as We Get Older," FlowingData, accessed June 12, 2024, https://flowingdata.com/2022/04/22/changing-who-we-spend-time-with-as-we-get-older/.
7. Martha Rosenberg, "Author Brené Brown Discusses Embracing Our Ordinariness," HuffPost, February 21, 2011, https://www.huffpost.com/entry/embracing-our-ordinariness_b_802808.
8. Yau, "Who We Spend Time with as We Get Older."
9. Gillian M. Sandstrom and Elizabeth W. Dunn, "Social Interactions and Well-Being: The Surprising Power of Weak Ties," *Personality and Social Psychology Bulletin* 40, no. 7 (July 2014):, 910–922, https://pubmed.ncbi.nlm.nih.gov/24769739/.
10. Matthew Lieberman, "The Brain's Braking System (and How to "Use Your Words" to Tap into It)," Academia, 2009, https://www.academia.edu/2790115/The_brain_s_braking_system_and_how_to_use_your_words_to_tap_into_it_.

11. Lieberman, "The Brain's Braking System."
12. Brett J. Peters, Nickola C. Overall, and Jeremy P. Jamieson, "Physiological and Cognitive Consequences of Suppressing and Expressing Emotion in Dyadic Interactions," *International Journal of Psychophysiology* 94, no. 1 (October 2014): 100–107, https://doi.org/10.1016/j.ijpsycho.2014.07.015.
13. "Psychologists Find the Meaning of Aggression: 'Monty Python' Scene Helps Research," ScienceDaily, March 24, 2011, https://www.sciencedaily.com/releases/2011/03/110323105202.htm.
14. Benjamin P. Chapman et al., "Emotion Suppression and Mortality Risk Over a 12-Year Follow-Up," *Journal of Psychosomatic Research* 75, no. 4 (October 2013): 381–385, https://doi.org/10.1016/j.jpsychores.2013.07.014.
15. Viktor E. Frankl, *Man's Search for Meaning* (Boston, MA: Beacon Press, 2014), 62.
16. Lieberman, "The Brain's Braking System."
17. Amy J. C. Cuddy, Caroline A. Wilmuth, and Dana R. Carney, "The Benefit of Power Posing Before a High-Stakes Social Evaluation," Harvard Business School Working Paper, No. 13-027, September 2012, https://dash.harvard.edu/handle/1/9547823; Julia Hanna, "Power Posing: Fake It until You Make It," Harvard Business School, September 20, 2010, https://hbswk.hbs.edu/item/power-posing-fake-it-until-you-make-it.
18. Sunder Kala Negi, Yaisna Rajkumari, and Minakshi Rana, "A Deep Dive into Metacognition: Insightful Tool for Moral Reasoning and Emotional Maturity," *Neuroscience Informatics* 2, issue 4 (December 2022): 100096, https://doi.org/10.1016/j.neuri.2022.100096.
19. John D. Teasdale et al., "Metacognitive Awareness and Prevention of Relapse in Depression: Empirical Evidence," *Journal of Consulting and Clinical Psychology* 70, no. 2 (April 2002): 275–287, https://doi.org/10.1037/0022-006X.70.2.275.
20. Jim Rendon, *Upside: The New Science of Post-Traumatic Growth* (New York: Touchstone, 2015), 76–77, 114–117.

CHAPTER 7: CO-REGULATION: BEING YOUR CHILD'S SAFE PLACE
1. Edwin H. Friedman, *Generation to Generation: Family Process in Church and Synagogue* (New York: Guilford Press, 2011), 27, 208–210.
2. Friedman, *Generation to Generation*.
3. Erica Cirino, "What Are the Benefits of Hugging?," Healthline, April 11, 2018, https://www.healthline.com/health/hugging-benefits.
4. Wanda Thibodeaux, "This Might Be the Simplest Scientific Way to Get Rid of Stress You've Ever Heard Of," *Inc.*, September 17, 2018, https://www.inc.com/wanda-thibodeaux/this-might-be-simplest-scientific-way-to-get-rid-of-stress-youve-ever-heard-of.html; Kristen Corey, "From Shushing to Singing: Reminding New Mothers of Their Power to Soothe," *U.S. News & World Report*, June 27, 2017, https://health.usnews.com/health-care/for-better/articles/2017-06-27/from-shushing-to-singing-reminding-new-mothers-of-their-power-to-soothe.

Notes

CHAPTER 8: CONNECTION: BUILDING HEALTHY ATTACHMENT
1. "The Story of a Mom That Raised the Inventor of the Light Bulb," Children LearningReading.com, accessed July 1, 2024, https://www.childrenlearning reading.org/blog/thomas-edison-story.html.
2. "Story of a Mom That Raised the Inventor."
3. "Life of Thomas Alva Edison," from the collection "Inventing Entertainment: The Early Motion Pictures and Sound Recordings of the Edison Companies," Library of Congress website, accessed June 14, 2024, https://www.loc.gov/collections/edison-company-motion-pictures-and-sound-recordings/articles-and-essays/biography/life-of-thomas-alva-edison/.
4. Linda L. Carpenter et al., "Effect of Childhood Physical Abuse on Cortisol Stress Response," *Psychopharmacology* 214, no. 1 (March 2011): 367–375, https://www.ncbi.nlm.nih.gov/pmc/articles/PMC3580170/.
5. Children's Attachment: Attachment in Children and Young People Who Are Adopted from Care, in Care or at High Risk of Going into Care," National Institute for Health and Care Excellence (NICE) Guidelines, no. 26, November 2015, https://www.ncbi.nlm.nih.gov/books/NBK356196/.
6. "'Good Enough' Parenting Is Good Enough, Study Finds," *ScienceDaily*, May 8, 2019, https://www.sciencedaily.com/releases/2019/05/190508134511.htm.
7. Bruce Perry, *The Boy Who Was Raised as a Dog: And Other Stories from a Child Psychologist's Notebook* (New York: Basic Books, 2006), 230.
8. Gordon Neufeld and Gabor Maté, *Hold On to Your Kids: Why Parents Need to Matter More than Peers* (New York: Ballantine, 2006), 103.

CHAPTER 9: COPING SKILLS: GIVING CHILDREN EMOTIONAL TOOLS
1. Fred Rogers, "What Do You Do with the Mad That You Feel?," Mr. Rogers' Neighborhood website, 1997, https://www.misterrogers.org/videos/what-to-you-do-with-the-mad-that-you-feel/.

CHAPTER 10 SPACE: MAKING ROOM FOR CREATIVE PLAY
1. Stuart Brown, *Play: How It Shapes the Brain, Opens the Imagination, and Invigorates the Soul* (New York: Avery, 2010), 60. Italics in the original.
2. Ingrid Fetell Lee, *Joyful: The Surprising Power of Ordinary Things to Create Extraordinary Happiness* (New York: Little, Brown Spark, 2018), 135.
3. Brown, *Play*, 126.
4. Stuart L. Brown, "Consequences of Play Deprivation," Scholarpedia 9, no. 5 (2014): 30449, https://doi.org/10.4249/scholarpedia.30449.
5. John Kounios and Mark Beeman, "The Aha! Moment: The Cognitive Neuroscience of Insight," *Current Directions in Psychological Science* 18, no. 4 (August 2009): 210–216, https://www.researchgate.net/publication/233507940.
6. Clare Thorp, "How Boredom Can Spark Creativity," BBC, May 22, 2020, https://www.bbc.com/culture/article/20200522-how-boredom-can-spark-creativity.
7. Attributed to Anne Lamott.

8. Edwin H. Friedman, *Generation to Generation: Family Process in Church and Synagogue* (New York: Guilford Press, 2011), 50–51, 209.

CHAPTER 11: SLOWING: REDUCING THE PACE OF FAMILY LIFE
1. Kosuke Koyama, *Three Mile an Hour God* (Maryknoll, NY: Orbis Books, 1980), 7.

CHAPTER 12: SIMPLIFYING: DE-STIMULATING YOUR HOME
1. "Ten-Year-Olds Have £7,000 Worth of Toys but Play with Just £330," *Telegraph*, October 20, 2010, https://www.telegraph.co.uk/finance/newsbysector/retailand consumer/8074156/Ten-year-olds-have-7000-worth-of-toys-but-play-with-just-330.html.
2. Barry Schwartz, "More Isn't Always Better," *Harvard Business Review*, June 2006, https://hbr.org/2006/06/more-isnt-always-better.
3. Joshua Becker, "21 Surprising Statistics That Reveal How Much Stuff We Actually Own," accessed June 26, 2024, Becoming Minimalist, https://www.becomingminimalist.com/clutter-stats/.
4. "Almost 1 in 4 Americans Say Their Garage Is Too Cluttered to Fit Their Car," PR Newswire, June 9, 2015, https://www.prnewswire.com/news-releases/almost-1-in-4-americans-say-their-garage-is-too-cluttered-to-fit-their-car-300096246.html.
5. Jack Feuer, "The Clutter Culture," UCLA Newsroom, July 1, 2012, https://newsroom.ucla.edu/magazine/center-everyday-lives-families-suburban-america.

CHAPTER 13: SHEPHERDING: NAVIGATING MEDIA AND THE ONLINE WORLD
1. Ippei Takahashi et al, "Screen Time at Age 1 Year and Communication and Problem-Solving Developmental Delay at 2 and 4 Years," *JAMA Pediatrics* 177, no. 10 (August 21, 2023):1039–1046, https://doi.org/10.1001/jamapediatrics.2023.3057.
2. Eric Suni and Abhinav Singh, "Technology in the Bedroom," Sleep Foundation, January 5, 2024, https://www.sleepfoundation.org/bedroom-environment/technology-in-the-bedroom.
3. Suni and Singh, "Technology in the Bedroom."
4. Jon Haidt and Zach Rausch, "Kids Who Get Smartphones Earlier Become Adults with Worse Mental Health," After Babel, May 15, 2023, https://www.afterbabel.com/p/sapien-smartphone-report.
5. Jonathan Haidt, *The Anxious Generation: How the Great Rewiring of Childhood Is Causing an Epidemic of Mental Illness* (New York: Penguin, 2024), 7.
6. Jonathan Haidt, "End the Phone-Based Childhood Now," *Atlantic*, March 13, 2024, https://www.theatlantic.com/technology/archive/2024/03/teen-childhood-smartphone-use-mental-health-effects/677722/.

CHAPTER 14: SABBATH: CULTIVATING REST AND LIFE-GIVING ROUTINES

1. "The Benefits of Resting and How to Unplug in a Busy World," *Forbes*, January 15, 2021, https://www.forbes.com/sites/womensmedia/2021/01/15/the-benefits-of-resting-and-how-to-unplug-in-a-busy-world/.
2. Eric Suni and Nilong Vyas, "Improve Your Child's School Performance with a Good Night's Sleep," Sleep Foundation, March 1, 2023, https://www.sleepfoundation.org/children-and-sleep/sleep-and-school-performance.
3. "Managing Adult Sleep with Baby on Board," Brevard Health Alliance, accessed June 27, 2024, https://www.brevardhealth.org/blog/managing-adult-sleep-with-baby-on-board/.
4. Jingjing Jiang, "How Teens and Parents Navigate Screen Time and Device Distractions," Pew Research Center, August 22, 2018, https://www.pewresearch.org/internet/2018/08/22/how-teens-and-parents-navigate-screen-time-and-device-distractions/.
5. Cal Newport, *Digital Minimalism: Choosing a Focused Life in a Noisy World* (New York: Portfolio, 2019), 93.

EPILOGUE: CONDUCTING YOUR FAMILY'S SYMPHONY

1. "Top 10 Gardens," *National Geographic*, January 21, 2010, https://www.nationalgeographic.com/travel/article/gardens.
2. H. Jackson Brown Jr., *Life's Little Instruction Book* (Nashville: Thomas Nelson, 1997).

ABOUT THE AUTHOR

SARAH BOYD is an author, child and adolescent development expert, and entrepreneur. She is the founder of the educational company Resilient Little Hearts, which empowers parents, teachers, and professionals to cultivate resilience and emotional health in children.

Sarah holds a master's degree in educational psychology and a diploma in the neuroscience of leadership.

Sarah is married to Colin, and together they have two beautiful children.